Practicing Romance

Practicing Romance

NARRATIVE FORM AND
CULTURAL ENGAGEMENT IN
HAWTHORNE'S FICTION

Richard H. Millington

PRINCETON UNIVERSITY PRESS

PRINCETON, NEW JERSEY

Copyright © 1992 by Princeton University Press
Published by Princeton University Press, 41 William Street,
Princeton, New Jersey 08540
In the United Kingdom: Princeton University Press, Oxford

Library of Congress Cataloging-in-Publication Data

Millington, Richard H., 1953–
Practicing romance: narrative form and cultural engagement
in Hawthorne's fiction / Richard H. Millington
p.   cm.
Includes index.
ISBN 0-691-06876-3
1. Hawthorne, Nathaniel, 1804–1864—Political and social views.
2. Hawthorne, Nathaniel, 1804–1864—Technique.
3. Social problems in literature   4. Romanticism—United States
5. Narration (Rhetoric)   I. Title.
PS1892.S58M55   1991
813'.3—dc20   91-19554

This book has been composed in Linotron Sabon

Princeton University Press books are
printed on acid-free paper, and meet the guidelines for
permanence and durability of the Committee on
Production Guidelines for Book Longevity of the
Council on Library Resources

Printed in the United States of America

1   3   5   7   9   10   8   6   4   2

For my family

Kay, Bill, and Pam,
and
Stephanie and Callie

CONTENTS

ACKNOWLEDGMENTS

BECAUSE THIS IS a book about the life of writing within a community, I am pleased to acknowledge the debts I owe to my own community of friends and colleagues. Two of these are abstract but nevertheless significant. My work, like that of other recent readers of Hawthorne, is hard to imagine without the rich rethinking of Hawthorne's fiction that took place, mostly in the seventies, in books by Frederick Crews, Nina Baym, Richard Brodhead, Edgar Dryden, and Kenneth Dauber, among others. I am also grateful for what I can only describe as lucky timing: to be working on American literature during the current return to history, a development for which I can claim little personal credit but that has helped me resee the force of Hawthorne's work and made describing his fictive enterprise a much more interesting activity. I am deeply grateful to the people, more distinctly embodied, who have helped this book find its present form. Alan Trachtenberg presided over its first incarnation as a dissertation; Richard Brodhead was immensely helpful to me then and has continued his generosity through the intervening years. Wai-chee Dimock, Donald Weber, and Christopher Wilson provided insightful comments at different stages of composition, and I want to thank my fellow Americanists at Smith College—Francis Murphy, Dean Flower, and Susan Van Dyne—for their interest and support throughout this book's prolonged gestation. Much of what I have to say about Hawthorne grew out of the experience of teaching him, and my students helped me to see Hawthorne's educative enterprise as we practiced our own. Two anonymous readers for Princeton University Press helped me see my argument more clearly as I completed final revisions. My attempt to become better informed about antebellum culture was aided by Stephen Nissenbaum, who graciously allowed me to participate in his seminar on the literary marketplace, and by an opportunity, funded by the National Endowment for the Humanities, to explore the rich collection of family papers in the Sophia Smith Collection. I want also to thank Robert E. Brown, my editor at Princeton, for his interest in my work and for his tact in managing a manuscript evaluation that coincided rather dramatically with a tenure decision. Only I know how much this book has benefited from the wonderful alertness and excellent advice of Lauren Oppenheim, who edited the manuscript.

Not all contributions to a book follow the customary academic channels. I feel that two friends, Abbe Blum and Rena Fraden, have been companions, despite geographical distance, throughout its writing. My parents, Catherine and William Millington, have been supporting my literary endeavors since the days of the bedtime story; I am more grateful to them than I can say. My deepest debts are to my wife, Stephanie Rosenfeld, and my daughter Callie, whose first summer coincided with the manuscript's last. I thank both of them for their unfeigned lack of interest in the contents of these pages, and for helping me, each in her own way, to get them written.

Two chapters of this book have appeared in print elsewhere. A slightly different version of chapter 5 appeared in *Prospects* 15 (1990), and *The New England Quarterly* printed a briefer version of chapter 6 in its December 1990 issue. I am grateful to both journals for their permission to reprint here.

LIST OF ABBREVIATIONS

QUOTATIONS from the works of Hawthorne are followed by abbreviated titles and page numbers in parentheses, while in chapters dealing with a single work, quotations from that work are followed simply by page numbers. Abbreviations refer to the following titles and editions:

AN   *The American Notebooks. The Centenary Edition of the Works of Nathaniel Hawthorne.* Edited by William Charvat et al. Vol. 8. Columbus: Ohio University Press, 1972.

BR   *The Blithedale Romance and Fanshawe. Centenary Edition.* Vol. 3, 1964.

HSG   *The House of the Seven Gables. Centenary Edition.* Vol. 2, 1965.

Letters 1   *The Letters, 1813–1843. Centenary Edition.* Vol. 15, 1984.

Letters 2   *The Letters, 1843–1853. Centenary Edition.* Vol. 16, 1985.

MF   *The Marble Faun: Or, the Romance of Monte Beni. Centenary Edition.* Vol. 4, 1968.

MOM   *Mosses from an Old Manse. Centenary Edition.* Vol. 10, 1974.

SI   *The Snow-Image and Uncollected Tales. Centenary Edition.* Vol. 11, 1974.

SL   *The Scarlet Letter. Centenary Edition.* Vol. 1, 1962.

TTT   *Twice-told Tales. Centenary Edition.* Vol. 9, 1974.

Practicing Romance

INTRODUCTION

THIS BOOK PROPOSES that we see Hawthorne as a cultural analyst of extraordinary acuity, ambitious, most fully in his four romances, to reshape—in a sense, to cure—the community he addresses. This complicated form of engagement in the life of his culture is, most deeply, what Hawthorne means by "romance." My purpose is to offer the readings that will make this claim convincing: to show how the curative purpose of his fiction animates his narrative practice, to describe the connection with its reader that romance seeks to invent. In several senses, Hawthorne's work is shaped by the problem of constructing a career. While this is most obviously true in his scrambles to make his writing pay, I will be arguing that romance is his answer to more inward-looking versions of the question of how to have a career: By what authority does a writer presume to speak to and for his audience? How might the ambition that drives a writer's hunger for response be controlled? How is story telling to justify itself as a form of work and a way of life?

If we follow his suggestion that we need to "look through the whole range of his fictitious characters, good and evil, in order to detect any of his essential traits" (*SI* 4), we emerge with a figure of Hawthorne troubled by a persistent anxiety about the private impulses that inform his work and the social effects they might body forth. It is entirely characteristic of Hawthorne's habits of mind that his anxiousness expresses itself in two quite contradictory ways of representing the private psychology and cultural role of the writer. His tales imply, on the one hand, that the impulse to write—like the analogous forms of public ambition he so often depicts—is driven by aggression: it is a bid to win power at the expense of the reader, to extort an acknowledgment of one's own incontrovertible significance from others. On the other hand, his works frequently admit to a suspicion that the writer may be both powerless and self-deceived, isolated in a world of his own devising in which his sense of connection to an audience is the most empty of his fantasies. The first of these anxieties is expressed in the coercive, predatory, creative figures who populate his tales: characters—careerists, in a sense—whose desperate attempts at eminence despoil the lives around them. I infer from Hawthorne's persistent, even obsessive, way of making stories out of the repudiation of such figures a sense of affiliation with them that needs to be scrupulously managed. The counter to this vision, the fear that writing may be a form of idle self-enclosure, is most strikingly acknowledged in the prefatory writings, with their litanies of self-doubt and their repeated descriptions of the writer's near erasure by his (entirely deserved) failure to locate a responsive audience.[1]

In Hawthorne's case one can rarely fix with much confidence the place where strategic self-dramatization ends and self-revelation begins. Still, there are some striking signs of the kind of anxiousness I am inferring in the notoriously equivocal facts of Hawthorne's life. However much one downplays the years of seclusion and alienation that he describes as beginning his career, so single-minded a sequestration—even the need to veil ambition in such a myth of ineffectuality—is the act of a man both extraordinarily ambitious and extremely diffident about presenting himself to the public, a combination that intense uneasiness about the meaning of one's ambition might well produce. Hawthorne did, in frustration or self-disgust, burn some of his earliest stories when they failed of publication. There are, moreover, several reasons to conclude that Hawthorne found the acts of self-presentation and reception involved in writing and reading genuinely unsettling. A strong conviction of the unreliability of linguistic representation, especially attempts to represent intimate emotion to others, runs through his love letters; and a remarkably intense vision of the dangerous permeability of one self to the power and influence of another emerges from a famous letter half-warning and half-begging Sophia not to try the services of a mesmerist. Whatever one thinks about the psychological origins of these worries, their particular intensity belongs in part to his time. The descriptions of reading, whether celebratory or censorious, found in antebellum magazines, book reviews, and letters imagine a consciousness—especially if it is attached to a person young and female—laid open to the transformative effect, for good or ill, of the book and its writer. And the conception that underlies this notion of reading, of a self incompletely in control of its boundaries and liable to unforeseen intensities of response, can be glimpsed in the shadows around the idea of "influence" so central to the contemporary vision of women's cultural power and in the peculiar force that attaches to the word "interesting" in everyday usage, where it expresses not the mild approval we expect but signifies a condition of intense relation, of reciprocal absorption.[2] Finally, it is easy to find, in his prolonged struggles to justify a marriage and support a family by the force of his pen, the literal origins of his scenarios of ineffectuality and self-erasure. A mute, inglorious Hawthorne, silenced either by self-distrust or the vagaries of the marketplace, is scarcely unimaginable.[3]

Taken together, the curious consistency of Hawthorne's dramatizations of his writerly career; the persistent questioning, either directly or by implication, of the impulses that generate his work and the legitimacy of his ambitions for it; and the accord between those doubts and the worries about representation that he expresses privately in his letters argue that the interlocked problem of ambition and authority plays a central role, at once inhibitory and provocative, in generating his fiction. To a latter-day reader, whose model of reading is likely to have more to do with consumption than transformation or danger, the reanimation of Hawthorne's anxieties about authorship may take an act of imaginative recovery. We might call to our assistance the meditation on the motives for story telling and the relation between writer and reader offered by Peter Brooks in his extraordinarily rich study of narrative, *Reading for the Plot*.

> There can be a range of reasons for telling a story, from the self-interested to the altruistic. Seduction appears as a predominant motive, be it specifically erotic and oriented toward the capture of the other, or more nearly narcissistic, even exhibitionistic, asking for admiration and attention. Yet perhaps aggression is nearly as common, and, of course, often inextricably linked to the erotic: a forcing of attention, a violation of the listener. The nature of the transference established between speaker and listener can be positive and productive of satisfaction, but it can also involve dependency and abjection, the incapacity to free oneself from the interlocutor—or from the shadowy figures for whom the interlocutor is surrogate.[4]

This is, as we will see, the vision of the relation between writer and reader that, as a fear, haunts and troubles Hawthorne's work, and, as a subject of analysis, shows him the way to a narrative practice that will defend both author and audience against the lure of domination.

In his anxiety about the shapes that his ambition might assume and his struggle to locate a legitimate form of cultural authority—in his attempt, that is, to establish a career—Hawthorne is engaging a problem that is not only privately but culturally central. A number of important, differently focused, works of cultural history identify Hawthorne's difficulty—to define an outlet for ambition and a vision of personal authority both safely democratic and personally compelling—as at the center of male experience in antebellum America. They thus help us to understand why Hawthorne might have felt the problem of authority with such force, and why his tales of the "careerist" take the distinct shape they do. Taken together, these historical accounts suggest that Hawthorne began to write at a time when the life structure we now call the professional career was only beginning to take shape, leaving the path of male ambition particularly undefined and uncertain; when the need to measure up to the heroic stature of the Revolutionary generation was felt with great intensity, both consciously and unconsciously; when the image of the transcendent individual was particularly alluring and suspicions of his danger to the community nevertheless especially strong; and when attempts to assuage the anxieties occasioned by this complex knot of circumstances seemed likely to take forms projective, paranoid, or punitive.[5] All of these patterns of

mind, as I will be demonstrating in chapter 2, find their way into Hawthorne's tales of the male career; and, as in the case of his worries about
the psychology of writing and reading, I see the effect upon his work as,
at last, more enlivening than inhibiting. For it is the diagnosis and cure of
the dangers of ambition that defines a legitimate object for Hawthorne's
ambitions and a valid cultural role for his fiction.

I see Hawthorne's work, then, as an attempt to find in authorship a
valid form of cultural authority. Romance is best understood as the complex answer he makes to the questions his anxiety posed for him, the act
of cultural engagement that disciplines ambition and cures marginality.
His meditation on his own unfolding career—and this is why, it seems to
me, he so often introduces his fiction with an account of the state of his
career—thus becomes his route from isolation into representativeness,
opening out into the themes and strategies that give his fiction its contemporary cultural force and present interest: the distrust of the authoritarian, whether psychological or communal; the analysis of the self-isolating
psychology of ambition and the victimizations it sponsors; the resistance
to the tendency of people and communities to flee complexity and, consequently, to narrow the experiences and emotions they can accommodate;
and, finally and most richly, to an interest in the connection between
inner experience and shape of the community one inhabits.

In following the story of Hawthorne's way of engaging his community
as it unfolds, not smoothly or suddenly, but as a series of experiments in
fictive strategy, I have been especially alert to three elements of his work:
the psychology of character, particularly as it is understood as a kind of
cultural symptom or expression; the cultural reach of the stories he tells;
and the narrative tactics he invents to shape the experience of reading.
Characters in Hawthorne's fiction, most notably his ambitious men, endure lives narrowed by anxiety or driven by a longing for eminence, a
condition they address by trying to find for themselves a fixed, absolute,
or unassailable form of authority, whether moral, religious, scientific, or
sexual. His builds his work, in important ways, upon a careful diagnosis
of minds fully entrapped by the predicament that preoccupies his own.
Even the conscientiousness that governs his insistent interrogation of the
impulse to write emerges as an object for analysis in his exploration of the
psychology of guilt. I think that Hawthorne is so intensely and exhaus-
tively interested in the operation of conscience precisely because of the
access it offers to the relation between the inner life and the community
that enfolds it. Speaking in a voice both intimate and communal, conscience is the institution of mind that represents the entanglement of psychological and cultural authority—and its dangerous excesses—most
clearly. The authoritarian conscience is thus the favorite target of the
counterauthority Hawthorne sets out to create in his work.

The rich description of middle class life in antebellum America that has in recent years emerged from the work of social and cultural historians—and, more generally, the return to history that is making this such an interesting time to be an Americanist—has made it newly possible and newly necessary to specify the contemporary force of Hawthorne's fiction. Because I will often be arguing that Hawthorne's work establishes its value to the reader by diagnosing, subverting, or recasting authoritative cultural values or cherished habits of feeling, I have tried to specify the orthodoxy being resisted. On the other hand, I have tried also to show the significant ways he shares or seeks to reanimate some of the convictions and emotions that hold middle-class culture in configuration—in turning, for instance, to private intimacy as at once the model for his relation to the reader and the way to renovate a communal life despoiled by anxiety or cruelty. In general, my readings suggest that what might be called the political force of Hawthorne's fiction—its capacity to free or transform its reader's way of seeing—derives from its making accessible to analysis, and thus transformation, the most elusive manifestations of our affiliation to the community: in his exploration of the culturally given processes of self-construction, in his analysis of the etiology of private emotion, in his effort to make legible the usually unexamined or unacknowledged consensuses that govern communal life.[6]

Hawthorne's practice of romance must finally be defined by the way it behaves upon the page. For what most distinguishes Hawthorne's fiction is the way his analysis of American character and his understanding of antebellum culture find expression in narrative form. The textual strategies that distinguish his work and offer the best access to its purposes derive from an extraordinary awareness of the way discourse carries and deploys cultural authority and of forms of language that might animate positions counter to it. A perception that acts of story-telling resist or carry coercion—that the tactics of narrative authority can replicate or parody the operations of cultural authority—enables Hawthorne to translate his diagnoses of the ills of character and culture into a narrative practice that makes interpretation curative. His works teach a canniness about literary authority designed to induce in his reader a more self-conscious, freer relation to authority at large.[7] And the connection with his reader that this invitation to uncoerced interpretation brings about at once suggests a version of social connection alternative to the unhappy ones his fiction depicts and offers Hawthorne a compelling way out of the self-enclosure he fears.

Because Hawthorne's fiction, especially the four romances, render cultural authority dramatically, as an interplay or contest of communal voices—because, that is, his analysis of cultural structure is typically expressed ironically, as imitation—his own stake in his work must be inferred with extreme alertness and tested by the closest kind of reading. I pause upon this point because of the tendency of some "rehistoricizing" accounts of his work to narrow Hawthorne as badly as the moralizing or psychologizing criticism of old. The readings I have in mind displace Hawthorne too easily from the position of analyst. Because they do not read him closely enough, they reduce him to a site through which ideology plays or deprive him of the intellectual acuity and ideological maneuverability that we think we possess. I have tried not to hunt over-eagerly for signs of ideological contradiction or cultural blindness. My method has simply been to see how far the figure of Hawthorne the cultural analyst might take me; the reader will discover that it has taken me far indeed, through the whole trajectory of his finished work. If I have composed a figure of Hawthorne remarkably alert to the condition of his community and uncannily in control of the strategies of narrative, this is not, I hope, because what Jane Eyre calls the Organ of Veneration is, in my case, unhappily enlarged, but because this version of Hawthorne accounts most plausibly for the way his fiction behaves. My point here is not that Hawthorne as a man was above or beyond ideology or free from contradictory emotion; this is simply untrue, as his angry comments on women novelists and the agonizing story of his daughter's life reveal.[8] I propose, rather, that what precisely distinguishes him as a writer is the capacity to locate in the discomfort of his experience the subjects of his fiction and, in a sense therapeutic as well as aesthetic, to bring that unhappiness up for treatment. Perhaps, like most of us, he was able to write more coherently than he lived.

Let me forecast for the reader the shape of my account of Hawthorne's fiction and anticipate the pivot upon which both his career and my argument turn. In part 1 I will identify the elements of his earlier work that respond to the complex understanding of the writer's cultural situation I have been describing: his scrutiny of the psyche's manifold capacity to poison its own experience; his alertness to the cultural representativeness of private emotion; his perception that a rich analogy between the deployment of authority within a culture and within a narrative might make reading an exercise in analyzing and revising our relation to the authoritative in general; his development of a steadily more capacious and forgiving theory of the writer's cultural role. Together these characteristic features of Hawthorne's fiction compose a process that I have called the invention of romance. While this development is not neatly linear, it is, as I see it, cumulative; the full emergence of a narrative practice that transforms Hawthorne's anxieties about authority into a legitimate form of authorship frees him to write the four romances.

The move from story to novel—from the invention of romance to its fully mature practice—realizes a possibility nascent in the elements of narrative I have been describing. The tales examine culturally characteristic individual acts or habits of mind that endanger the community; they are thus always revealing in their implicit account of culture but psychological in their scope and purpose, aiming to revise the inner life of their readers. In *The Scarlet Letter* and the works that follow, characters and their states of mind are located within "thickly described," historically specific cultural systems; the romances examine the conditions of our affiliation to our culture and set out to revise our relation to the community. This is to propose that romance as a form is fully defined by the discovery of what we now call "ideology" as its characteristic subject. The romances conceive of the culture they describe as a field in which human lives find their meaning, and they propose to intervene in the process by which culture makes us ourselves.

My chapters on each of the romances set out to render these abstractions concrete. But let me remain in abstraction long enough to specify the way of thinking about culture that finds expression in my work and, in my view, animates Hawthorne's. My understanding of what ideology is and how it operates—and the meaning that the term will have in these essays—has been shaped by Clifford Geertz's indispensable essay, "Ideology as a Cultural System." Geertz argues that our capacity to think about cultural expression has been held back by two insufficiently sophisticated theories: that ideology is a mask for the operation of the interests of particular political or social groups; and that ideological expressions, from myths to political rhetoric, are reducible to symptoms of particular kinds of anxiety or "strain" within a culture. Geertz arrives at his more capacious and useful definition by observing that "the extreme generality, diffuseness, and variability of man's innate response capacities" means that culture rather than genetic templates is the primary organizer of patterns of human behavior and that we create ourselves through our capacity to construct symbolic fields in which to act. "The tool-making, laughing, or lying animal, man is also the incomplete—or, more accurately, self-completing—animal. The agent of his own realization, he creates out of his general capacity for the construction of symbolic models the specific capacities that define him." "Ideology," then, means all the strategies and structures of meaning making that belong to a particular culture. "It is . . . the attempt of ideologies to render otherwise incomprehensible social situations meaningful, to so construe them as to make it possible to act purposefully within them, that accounts both for the ideologies' highly figurative nature and for the intensity with which, once accepted, they are held. . . . Whatever else ideologies may be—projections of unacknowledged fears, disguises for ulterior motives, phatic expressions of group solidarity—they are, most distinctively, maps of problematic social reality and matrices for the creation of collective conscience."[9] Implicit in my reading of Hawthorne's four romances is a demonstration that a similar conception of the imaginative life of a culture animates his work; and implicit in my account of his narrative practice is the suggestion that Hawthorne saw in the way ideology is carried by discourse—by stories, figures, voices—a way for fiction, a similarly but strategically composed form of expression, to transform it. Hawthorne, we might say, became a formidable theorist of the novel by becoming a lucid interpreter of culture.

I take it to be a sign of the way Hawthorne's meditation upon the problem of authority generates his fiction that from the very beginning of his career he insists upon presenting his tales and sketches in relation to a dramatization of the writer's cultural situation. With "Passages from a Relinquished Work" (*MOM* 405–21), the first of these prefatory vignettes, Hawthorne embarks upon his own career by offering an account of the writer's problematic relation to authority. He designed "Passages" as part of the elaborate frame for a set of tales he hoped to publish as "The Story-Teller," a collection that he planned as his first substantial act of self-presentation.[10] Hawthorne invents a young fiction maker who introduces his stories by introducing himself, tracing, as he purveys his tales, the shape of his career: from a rebellious self-exiling, to triumphant popular success, to the transformation of a successful storyteller, by a guilty conscience, into a bitter moralist. Like his creator, this youthful storyteller refuses to adopt an established profession, optimistically declaring his "purpose of keeping aloof from the regular business of life" (407). A double logic governs the tale: a depiction of an artistic career and a psychology of maturation unfold as versions of one another.

The orphaned narrator has from infancy been under the guardianship of a Parson Thumpcushion, and his "gay and happy temperament" can no longer abide the education inflicted by his guardian's "stern old Pilgrim spirit"(407). In an act of rebellion calculated to enrage the puritanical Thumpcushion ("who would rather have laid me in my father's grave than seen me either a novelist or an actor" [408]), he resolves to become a wandering storyteller. The boy enacts a fantasy of self-fathering, leaving his birthplace on a foggy morning that renders the village as insubstantial as the Platonic cave, "more like a memory than a reality" (410); he confirms the delicious freedom he discovers by giving himself a "fictitious name" (411). He then enters a happily infantile world, which seems to be governed by the psychic logic of the oral stage, but this idyll is interrupted by the itinerant's encounter with his opposite, a wandering would-be preacher named Eliakim Abbott. This pilgrim is as shy and tremulous of voice as the storyteller is boisterous; while rebellion drives the storyteller's travels, Eliakim gives himself over to a principle of authority,

awaiting "an inward conviction . . . an outward sign" (414). The two—
"strikingly contrasted, yet curiously assimilated"—keep together "till
[their] union appears permanent" (415), in analogy, I think, to the acqui-
sition of conscience, the development of the moral self. The pair arrives in
a village—the narrator to test his act at the local theater, Eliakim to "address sinners on the welfare of their immortal souls" (418). The storyteller achieves a brilliant success, which offers him not only applause but
a privileged entrée into a playful community where entertainment is un-
troubled by instruction and utter freedom of action obtains—a characteristic exemplified by the ability of one of the actors to change gender at
will.

Precisely at this moment of triumph, a letter from Parson Thumpcushion is delivered, evoking in the storyteller an image of "the puritanic figure" of his guardian as a "type of austere duty," and transforming his
new companions into a group portrait of life's vanities (421). But more
disturbing to the youth than this image of rebuke is the vision that follows
it, the Parson as Good Father, "softening his authority with love," apolo-
gizing for his disciplinary excesses—suggesting that the really insidious
power belongs not to the overtly coercive Parson but to his more modern
and lovingly reproachful avatar. The storyteller, in an act of fidelity to his
original rebellion, burns the letter unopened. But, now "indisposed" toward the enjoyment of his triumph, he leaves town in the company of
Eliakim, who—true to his consciencelike role—"groaned in spirit, and
labored, with tears, to convince me of the guilt and madness of my life"
(421). The result of the Parson's letter, even unread, is to transform the
improvisatory storyteller into a different kind of artist, a "bitter moral-
izer" who offers this theologically tinged reinterpretation of his triumph:
"I took this scene for an example, how much of fame is humbug; how
much the meed of what our better nature blushes at; how much bestowed
on mistaken principles; how small and poor the remnant" (420). Though
the narrator delivers the patriarchal pronouncements to the flames, authority—and the conscience that speaks its language—demand their due.
The premature triumph of a wholly playful art is repudiated, the carefree
improviser yields to the figure of the alienated, self-conscious moralist.
The Parson's influence, though failing to turn the storyteller pious, renders him ambivalent about the value of fiction making, moralistic in a
merely propitiatory way, disconsolately mature.

In "Passages from a Relinquished Work" Hawthorne confronts the
unformed storyteller with the inevitability of his affiliation to the community that has produced him. And though the mere recoiling that is the
storyteller's response to this bitter knowledge is hardly the form that
Hawthorne's engagement with his community will take, the story does
suggest that the place of ambivalence, the interesting borderland between

the pleasurable and the punitive, the authoritarian and the subversive may be, at last, the writer's home territory. I think, finally, that it is through Hawthorne's complicated engagement with the problem of cultural authority that we are most significantly his heirs. Hawthorne, we might say, saw emerging with remarkable acuity the world we fully inhabit: a world of characters made predatory or defensive by anxiety, of careers conducted to appease the expectations of an authority at once exigent and elusive, of wistful attempts to call community into being.[11] His effort to invent, through the shared work of romance, a different kind of story about human connection still teaches, still frees.

PART ONE

The Invention of Romance

Chapter One

READING AS DISRUPTION

> When I contemplate the accumulation of guilt and
> remorse which, like a garbage-can, I carry through life,
> and which is fed not only by the lightest actions but
> by the most harmless pleasures, I feel Man to be of all
> living things the most biologically incompetent and ill-
> organized. Why has he acquired a seventy-years' life
> span only to poison it incurably by the mere being of
> himself? Why has he thrown Conscience, like a dead rat,
> to putrefy in the well?
> —W. B. Yeats

BECAUSE THE RELATIONSHIP most important to understanding Hawthorne's fiction is that between him and his reader, I will begin my account of his invention of romance by examining the experience that reading his tales induces. For several reasons, I have chosen "Roger Malvin's
Burial" as my exemplar. It is one of his earliest tales, and thus confirms
the generativeness of the question of authority within Hawthorne's career. It focuses on the psychology of guilt, and the tale's encounter with
the authority of conscience offers a particularly rich example both of
Hawthorne's understanding of the dynamics of mind and of the cultural
reach of his thematic concerns. Most importantly, the tale offers a striking instance of the act of formal invention that makes possible Hawthorne's invention of an antiauthoritarian narrative practice: his discovery of a fruitful analogy between the operation of the authoritarian,
whether psychological or cultural, and the narrative structures of fiction.
In "Roger Malvin's Burial," Hawthorne sets out to transform the reader's
relation to cultural and psychological authority by inviting us to transform our relation to authority within his text.

Many of Hawthorne's explorations of psychology are governed by
what might be called the logic of the case history. From the meaning-
laden extreme case we infer the conflicts and psychic strategies inarticu-
lately at work beneath the surfaces of everyday life; the neurotic unveils
the normal. Thus in "Roger Malvin's Burial" Hawthorne explores the
origin and operation of guilt by depicting a conscience gone murderously
awry. The tale begins the reexamination of the moral authority of con-

science—carried out with particular intensity in the work of Dickinson, Twain, Howells, and James—that is one of the crucial cultural tasks of nineteenth-century American fiction.

The extremity of "Roger Malvin's Burial" is suggested by a brief summary of its plot. Reuben Bourne and Roger Malvin, the father of the woman Reuben loves, barely escape from a disastrous Indian battle. Both men are wounded, but Malvin, sure that he will die before they reach settled territory, and fearful that his infirmity would cause the death of the younger man as well, prevails upon Reuben to leave him to die in the forest, invoking what is almost "a father's authority" (MOM 339) and his hopes for his daughter's future. Reuben, reluctant to leave, but activated as well by the "hidden strength of many another motive" (343), promises to return to the desolate spot to bury his defunct father-in-law. Bourne finds his way back home, and is nursed back to health by Malvin's daughter Dorcas, whom he eventually marries. But Bourne cannot bring himself to tell his wife that he left her father alive, and thus the fulfillment of his promise is impossible. Bourne lives out his years in remorseful self-absorption until he sets out with Dorcas and his beloved son Cyrus to find a new home in the wilderness. Compelled by what is clearly an unconscious impulse, Bourne leads his family to the spot where Malvin died. He and Cyrus go out to shoot their dinner; Reuben fires at a movement in a thicket, killing his son. Yet instead of the redoubled remorse one would expect, Bourne feels a sense of release and redemption, his sin apparently expiated by the shedding of "blood dearer to him than his own" (360).

The reader's task is to discover what bizarre logic determines this turn of events. The most persuasive interpretation of the psychological action of the story remains that offered by Frederick Crews in *The Sins of the Fathers*—a happy moment in the history of Hawthorne criticism, for in Crews's account Hawthorne fully emerged as psychologist of great acuity and originality, rather than as a predictable moralist or an illustrator of nineteenth-century faculty psychology. Crews observes both that Bourne comes to identify Cyrus completely with his younger, better self, and that Reuben feels his breaking of the vow to bury Malvin not as betrayal but as murder. He argues that Bourne's killing of Cyrus must be seen as an act of symbolic self-sacrifice, the expiation extracted by Bourne's conscience not for his desertion of Malvin or failure to disclose his act to Dorcas, but for his unconscious desire for Malvin's death; hence Bourne's feeling of release from guilt when Cyrus dies. "In killing Cyrus," Crews writes, Bourne "is destroying the 'guilty' side of himself, and hence avenging Roger Malvin's death in an appallingly primitive way. The blood of a 'father' rests on the 'son,' who disburdens himself of it by becoming a father and slaying his son. This is the terrible logic of Hawthorne's tale."[1]

By exposing the "logic of compulsion" that controls Bourne's behavior, this reading suggests the nearly absolute power available to conscience in Hawthorne's psychology. What we need to add to Crews's reading is a fuller account of the way Hawthorne's depiction of conscience unfolds as an anatomy of the potential tyranny of our own conditions of mind and a lesson in how that culturally inflected tyranny might be resisted. When Crews explains the virulence of Bourne's conscience by inferring the existence of an unconscious wish for Malvin's death ("By a certain association of ideas, he at times imagined himself a murderer," Hawthorne's narrator remarks [349]), we notice that for Hawthorne, as for Freud, the conscience communicates directly with the repository of repressed wishes. Conscience thus punishes not merely deeds or even thoughts, but impulses necessarily unavailable to the conscious self, and thus outside the bounds of the ethical.[2] From the curious point of view of the conscience, then, the sacrifice of Cyrus is a punishment commensurate with Bourne's hidden wish. Implicit in Hawthorne's depiction of the tyranny of conscience is a vision of the mind divided against itself; the conscious self is—however scrupulous—not only troubled by impulses it can only partially recognize, but at the mercy of a punishing agency that has a more comprehensive view of the mind than the ego possesses.

To accompany this depiction of conscience at work, the story provides an account of the origin of its power. Hawthorne links the existence of an independent, authoritative inner voice to the demands of civilized life. The extremity of the situation that Malvin and Bourne confront—the threat posed to the life of the younger man by the lingering death of the elder—makes readable the ambivalence inscribed upon the relation between fathers, or father figures, and their offspring in everyday life. Both men obey a principle for defusing the conflict between generations: each must sacrifice desire, even the desire to live—even, the story suggests, unconscious desire—for the preservation of the other. From the absolutism of this demand, which expresses itself as guilt, we infer the extreme danger posed to settled life by untrammeled desire. But in its impossibility lurks the capacity of guilt to entrap as well as to preserve. For it becomes clear that the most constructive desires of youth—to love and marry, to found a family—are felt, despite the conscious approval of the elders, to occur at their expense, and are thus experienced as guilty. Conscience possesses a dangerous doubleness: in enforcing the principle of self-sacrifice, it seems to put aggression at the service of love; but Bourne's expiatory murder of his son reveals how readily aggression—the power-seeker within—infiltrates the ethical.

The dialogue between Bourne and the fatherly Malvin that begins the story poignantly reveals the dilemma at the center of moral obligation. For in fulfilling his patriarchal duty to sacrifice his private wish to the younger man's safety, Malvin must find a way to free Bourne from the very claims of conscience under which he himself labors. Malvin beguiles Bourne's conscience by creating a fiction accordant with the demands of duty: he tells the story of his abandonment of a wounded comrade, which led not to a death but to a rescue. He thus suggests to the younger man what he knows to be untrue: that the purpose of his flight is not self-preservation but the salvation of another. On his own behalf, Malvin eases the pain of his solitary death with visions of familial continuity. He tells Bourne that his daughter "will marry you after she has mourned a little while for her father; and Heaven grant you long and happy days, and may your children's children stand round your death bed" (344). In Malvin's sacrifice of the personal to the familial, we see conscience in its benign aspect, allied not with punishment but with love. Yet Malvin's attempt to free Bourne from the excessive filial obligation that his conscience seeks to enforce finally fails; Malvin's story telling allows Bourne to follow his urge to love and marry, but—as the murderous conclusion of the story reveals—Bourne's conscience remains essentially unconvinced by the very deception it has demanded. So insistent is conscience's prohibition against self-interest that Bourne's leaving cannot fail to be *felt* as guilty, no matter how justifiable it is on rational grounds. This is the brutal irony encoded in the absolutism of conscience: for all his fidelity to the dictates of self-sacrifice, Malvin only succeeds in bequeathing the fierce principle of sacrifice itself. In the biblical story of Abraham and Isaac, the patriarchal voice that demands the act of sacrifice possesses the inclination to forgive its own demand; in Hawthorne's revision of that tale, the inner voice of conscience has replaced the voice of God, but with this crucial difference: the capacity for forgiveness has disappeared, and been replaced by an appetite for punishment.

How is it that Bourne's abandonment of Malvin comes to define itself as guilty? When Bourne returns to his village he fails to acknowledge his flight, allowing Dorcas to think that he awaited the death of her father and dug his grave. It is this act of "concealment," the narrator states, that "imparted to a justifiable act much of the secret effect of guilt" (349). It is as though by behaving guiltily, by disguising his action, Bourne invites his conscience to intensify its punishment of him. One of the story's most curious moments suggests that, for Hawthorne, conscience is made virulent by the fact of concealment itself. After hurrying ashamedly away from Malvin, Bourne abruptly returns: "he crept back, impelled by a wild and painful curiosity, and, sheltered by the earthy roots of an uptorn tree, gazed earnestly at the desolate man" (345). Bourne's voyeurism—his act of self-concealment—constitutes a kind of primal scene governed not by erotic but by aggressive emotion. He sees portrayed the submerged aspect of his desire to live: the death of the older man. By his morbid return,

Bourne himself converts a morally complicated act—his leaving—into an apparently guilty one. But to conclude from this incident that Bourne gets the guilt he deserves would be to underestimate the insidiousness that Hawthorne attributes to conscience, for Bourne's action is not freely chosen but "impelled." We might see conscience here as getting Reuben's story into one of the conventional punitive shapes it favors; his return to the scene of the (absent) crime marks him as guilty only in a formal sense, but a formality is all it takes. Conscience seems empowered to induce, given a sufficient degree of moral ambiguity, the very behavior it intends to punish.

In the years that follow Bourne's return, conscience—encouraged by and encouraging his self-absorption—comes progressively to take control of Reuben's life. When Bourne recovers from his wound he finds his memory of the way back to the scene of Malvin's abandonment elided, as though some part of the self sought protection from the duty to return and from the emotions associated with that forest scene. Yet this attempt to suppress his sense of guilt is ineffectual: "There was . . . a continual impulse, a voice audible only to himself, commanding him to go forth and redeem his vow; and he had a strange impression that, were he to make the trial, he would be led straight to Malvin's bones" (350). Conscience comes quite literally to usurp the direction of Bourne's life when he sets out with his family for their new home; it leads him away from his anticipated course and straight to the scene of Malvin's death. Hawthorne depicts Bourne "musing on the strange influence" that leads him astray: "Unable to penetrate to the secret place of his soul where his motives lay hidden, he believed that a supernatural voice had called him onward, and that a supernatural power had obstructed his retreat. He trusted that it was Heaven's intent to afford him an opportunity of expiating his sin" (356). What I find interesting here is Bourne's interpretation of the compulsion he senses within him. Bourne locates the agency behind the "voice" not, with Hawthorne, in the imperatives of his own unconscious—"the secret place of his soul where his motives lay hidden"—but in a benevolent heavenly authority. Bourne thinks, and persists in thinking even after the death of his son, that he is engaged in an appropriate, divinely sanctioned act of expiation and redemption. Despite Bourne's mystification of the voice within him, we realize that he is simply obeying the dictates of his own conscience, and the validity of his act of expiation is grounded not in any rationally explicable moral system but in the enclosed logic of his own psychology.

"Roger Malvin's Burial" allows us to see that conscience can become an autonomous principle of aggression within the self, which measures the ego according to its own irrational imperative. It overturns conscious desires and generates cruel patterns of expiation. Conscience within the tale is a kind of inner storyteller, inventing and impelling the narratives that alone will satisfy its desire to punish. In this diseased form, conscience is no longer the inner site of moral choice, nor is its voice—guilt—an advocate in an interior ethical debate. Its object, rather, is the extinction of choice, the pure pleasure of authority. Thus Reuben Bourne's killing of his son is not a moral or immoral act but a "premoral" one, and the analysis of mind implicit in the tale invites us to complicate our understanding of conscience, seeing it as a psychological as well as an ethical institution of mind.

But what, given this understanding of Hawthorne's representation of conscience, are we to make of the forcefully redemptive language that brings the tale to its close?

> She heard him not. With one wild shriek, that seemed to force its way from the sufferer's inmost soul, she sank insensible by the side of her dead boy. At that moment, the withered topmost bough of the oak loosened itself, in the stilly air, and fell in soft, light fragments upon the rock, upon the leaves, upon Reuben, upon his wife and child, and upon Roger Malvin's bones. Then Reuben's heart was stricken, and the tears gushed out like water from a rock. The vow that the wounded youth had made the blighted man had come to redeem. His sin was expiated, the curse was gone from him; and in the hour when he had shed blood dearer to him than his own, a prayer, the first for years, went up to Heaven from the lips of Reuben Bourne. (360)

Who speaks this passage? To whom does this patently authoritative language belong? When measured against the death of Cyrus and the magnitude of Bourne's ostensible "sin," the passage seems overwrought and repugnant, the organ of literary closure going all out in celebration of the murder of a child. Its powerful, Bible-tinged rhetoric does, however, match the psychological force that drives Bourne's compulsive quest for redemption. I suggest that the passage speaks in the voice of conscience itself; it expresses not the author's last word on the moral significance of Bourne's experience, but rather *enacts* the usurpation by the superego not only of Bourne's behavior but of the narrative itself. Conscience has seized the narration from the detached, analytic voice of the rest of the tale; it has appropriated the placement, the cadences, the imagery of narrative authority, and the power that our hunger for interpretive closure cedes to the endings of stories. Conscience cannily claims those elements of fiction that potentially replicate its own strategies of coercion, and uses them to enforce upon us its expiatory reading of Cyrus's murder—the very reading that the tale's analysis of mind has been engaged in overturning.

An interpretation of this tale that is not repellent on humane grounds, that does not complacently accept Cyrus's murder as a fair price for Reuben's "redemption"—and Hawthorne criticism will supply examples of such compliant reading—depends upon our refusal to acquiesce in the potential tyranny of the story's forceful final paragraph. The purpose implicit in this risky narrative strategy is to induce in the reader an act of interpretive resistance—made possible by the analytic purchase the story has given us—analogous to the act of self-scrutiny and forgiveness that alone might have saved Reuben Bourne from his entrapment in the expiatory story his conscience sponsors. We resist, as we read, a narrative replication of the authority of conscience within the psyche. The closing paragraph of "Roger Malvin's Burial" thus creates for the reader what might be called a moment of interpretive demand and confers upon him an attendant interpretive independence.

The narrative tactic I have been describing, which depends upon the perception of an analogy between literary structure and the exercise of authority in the world at large, is crucial to the interpretation of Hawthorne's fiction, and at the center of his reimagining of literary authority. Such moments of interpretive demand, so widespread in Hawthorne's fiction as to constitute one of its essential formal features, take a variety of forms. Moments of closure characteristically parody themselves, frustrating the reader's desire for the authoritative: think, for example, of the pseudoidealistic gobbledygook that ends "The Artist of the Beautiful" (itself a demonstration of the bankruptcy of the notion that art is above or beyond everyday experience); of the utter neutrality of the last sentence of "Rappaccini's Daughter"; or of the advertisements in "Wakefield" for a grandiose moral that may or may not actually arrive. Alternatively, in stories like "Young Goodman Brown" and "My Kinsman Major Molineux," the ontological status of particular events is itself left disconcertingly unspecified or strangely mixed, its determination becoming one of the tasks of the interpreter. The sudden disappearance of a once-voluble narrator at moments of interpretive decision or the tendency to provide authorial commentary in a way that exposes its "interestedness" or inadequacy as interpretation—both characteristic tactics of the novels—suggests a desire not to enforce absolutes but to elicit from the reader demanding acts of rethinking. Authoritative narrative pronouncements in Hawthorne's fiction are *almost* always (there is no absolute rule, even here) imitations of the authoritative or illustrations of particular ideological positions. Throughout his fiction, as in "Roger Malvin's Burial," Hawthorne is engaged in the invention of an antiauthoritarian authorship.

Despite the subversiveness of Hawthorne's narrative strategy, ethical authority reasserts itself as we interpret "Roger Malvin's Burial." Yet our understanding of our own moral psychology is unmoored, complicated, revised, and renewed. There is, I have suggested, an inhumane and thus "guilty" reading available in this tale, one that takes the bait and rationalizes Bourne's expiation-by-murder. But guilt is redefined as unexamined submission to a powerfully self-justifying but immoral authority. Similarly, the reader's denial of the authority of the story's close is the crucial act in what I would claim is an authoritative interpretation of this fiction. The story aims not at the extinction of ethical authority but at its rescue; if "Roger Malvin's Burial" does its work—and if we, as readers, do ours—our relation to the mind's structures of authority will have become more conscious, more critical, more free.

In its narrative strategy, then, Hawthorne's analysis of the excesses of conscience is simultaneously an attempt to invent a legitimate, freeing form of literary authority. Precisely because conscience in "Roger Malvin's Burial" exemplifies a diseased form of authority, the tale constitutes a kind of test of the power of fiction. If his writing is to disrupt the habit of acquiescence, Hawthorne must find a way to free his reader from the confines of the authoritarian without simply substituting the fiat of the writer—as he does, I have argued, in disrupting our acquiescence in the coercions of conscience. But to see the full scope of Hawthorne's attack upon the authoritarian, to recognize this fiction as culturally as well as psychologically ambitious, we need to attend to the stories about conscience that "Roger Malvin's Burial" competes with, and measure his depiction of conscience against the orthodox moral psychology celebrated by middle-class culture.

I will be juxtaposing with "Roger Malvin's Burial" two passages: one from T. C. Upham's *Elements of Mental Philosophy* (1839), and one from *Uncle Tom's Cabin* (1852). Each of these passages demonstrates how the authority of conscience underwrites moral authority in the culture at large; each exemplifies the kind of story the narrative strategy of "Roger Malvin's Burial" teaches us to challenge. There are a number of reasons to accept Upham as a representative of orthodox thinking in Hawthorne's America: his *Elements*, which ran to many editions, was the standard textbook of psychology in America until William James wrote his *Principles*; he was a notable proponent of the comfortable Scottish "Common Sense" philosophy that dominated American academic and critical circles; and, intriguingly, he was a professor of philosophy at Bowdoin during Hawthorne's last year there, thus playing the role of cultural authority in the most literal way. Here is Upham's description of the "Nature of voluntary moral derangement."

> A man is not in the first instance *turpissimus* or a villain, because his conscience makes resistance, and will not let him be so. But if the energies of the will are exercised in opposition to the conscience, if on a systematic plan and by a permanent effort the remonstrances of conscience are unheeded and its

action repressed, its energies will be found to diminish, and its very existence put at hazard. . . . We say in such cases the conscience is virtually annihilated. And by this remark we mean, that it is inert, inefficient, dormant, paralyzed. We do not mean, that it is dead. The conscience never dies. Its apparent death is impregnated with the elements of a real and terrible resurrection. It seems to gather vivification and strength in the period of its inactivity; and at the appointed time of its reappearance inflicts a stern and fearful retribution, not only for the crimes which are committed against others; but for the iniquity, which has been perpetrated against itself.[3]

Upham's high-temperature celebration of the "fearful retribution" inflicted upon the self by the ignored and insulted conscience has the same "plot" as "Roger Malvin's Burial": conscience gets its man. For Upham, conscience is as powerful as it is for Hawthorne, but its resurgence is not pathological but reassuring. The "real and terrible resurrection" of conscience (note the religious force of his language) affirms that the operation of the inner world, like that of the outer, is governed by a just Authority. Indeed, the belief that conscience was intuitive and man morally inclined by "nature" rather than instruction was an essential tenet of the sentimental philosophy that Upham represents.[4] Upham's story of the restoration of conscience, its narrow but inevitable escape from its struggle with the will, seeks to establish both the naturalness—and hence the legitimacy—of moral authority and its ultimate reliability. The danger to Upham is that the will may succeed in "repressing" the moral impulse. For Hawthorne the logic of repression is reversed: conscience is capable not only of overcoming one's conscious will but of subverting one's instincts for self-preservation and one's capacity to love. Hawthorne strips guilt of its customary, unquestioned connection to a divinely sanctioned or rationally explicable morality and exposes it as a psychological mechanism, a potentially abusive inner tyrant whose triumphs must at times be resisted.

No claims need be made for the cultural authority of *Uncle Tom's Cabin*. Late in the book, Harriet Beecher Stowe offers a depiction of the revenge of conscience at least as intense and celebratory as Upham's. Simon Legree is brought the curl of little Eva's golden hair that Tom carries with him as a talisman; the lock of hair sends him into a panic, which Stowe explains with an excursion into Legree's past. "Hard and reprobate as the godless man seemed now," she begins, "there had been a time when he had been rocked on the bosom of a mother." The moral training, a product of "unwearied love" and "patient prayer" given her son by this holy woman, is repudiated by Legree, who goes to sea, following in the reprobate steps of his "hard-tempered sire, on whom the gentle woman had wasted a world of unvalued love." Legree returns home for a visit, and his mother struggles, with near success, "to win him from a life of sin, to his soul's eternal good": "That was Legree's day of grace; then good angels called him; then he was almost persuaded, and mercy held him by the hand. His heart inly relented,—there was a conflict,—but sin got the victory, and he set all the force of his rough nature against the conviction of his conscience." Like the subject of Upham's analysis, Legree exercises "the energies of the will . . . in opposition to the conscience." He spurns and curses his mother, and flees to his ship. One night, in mid-carouse, he receives a letter containing a lock of his mother's golden hair, news of her death, and the message that "dying, she blest and forgave him." This apparently happy news produces quite another effect on Legree: "There is a dread, unhallowed necromancy of evil, that turns things sweetest and holiest to phantoms of horror and affright. That pale, loving mother,—her dying prayers, her forgiving love,—wrought in that demoniac heart of sin only as a damning sentence, bringing with it a fearful looking for a judgment and fiery indignation." Legree burns the lock and the letter, and attempts to ward off guilt by intensifying his revels "but often, in the deep night, whose solemn stillness arraigns the bad soul in forced communion with herself, he had seen that pale mother rising by his bedside, and felt the soft twining of that hair around his fingers, till the cold sweat would roll down his face, and he would spring from the bed in horror."[5]

For Stowe, as for Upham, conscience will extract its revenge on the willful libertine; the "pale mother" will rise. For each of these moral psychologists, the resurgent conscience testifies that an inner order mirrors the moral coherence of the cosmos; the "fiery indignation" that Legree fears and deserves will be delivered figuratively, as mental torment, in this life and literally in the next. Both Stowe and Upham see the psychological torment extracted by conscience as an expression of the divinely sanctioned moral order of an explicable universe. Moreover, the rhapsodic tone of these two hymns to conscience argues that both writers identify their moral authority with the authority of conscience; its claims to power underwrite their own. The two use their identification with conscience in different ways—Upham on behalf of his authority as the mind's explicator, Stowe on behalf of the righteous dispossessed. But in each case a cherished story about the meaning of guilt is retold. Academic psychology and sentimental psychology, science and the evangelical imagination, are in accord, each reinforcing—and depending upon—the authority of conscience.[6]

Anyone who has read around in some of the documents historians consider as defining the middle-class sensibility in antebellum America will be struck by how often such passages of intense identification with conscience appear. We encounter this heroicization of conscience, for in-

stance, in Susan Warner's account of the development of Christian character in *The Wide, Wide World*, in Catharine Beecher's writings on domestic economy, and in Horace Mann's anxious exhortations on the
moral education of children.[7] Along with passages like the ones I have
cited, recent work by historians on the development of a distinct American middle class suggests that a kind of alliance with conscience lay at the
center of middle-class identity. The production of conscience in her children became the primary task of the middle-class mother, for this internalized expression of parental authority was seen as the guarantor of the
disciplinary virtues that might underwrite a stable middle-class life. Mary
P. Ryan writes that "all the gentle admonitions and sly manipulations of
maternal socialization conspired to equip children with sensitive con-
sciences. This faculty would operate as a kind of portable parent that
could stay with the child long after he left his mother's side and journeyed
beyond the private sphere out into the streets and into the public world."[8]

We are now in a position to see that Hawthorne sets out in "Roger
Malvin's Burial" to loosen this ideological knot, to drive a wedge between the psychological and the rational, between guilt and morality,
between morality and established authority. To mount such an attack on
the authority of conscience is not only to open the rigid, guilt-seeking
moral psychology of his culture to some uncomfortable but enfranchising
complication but to disrupt the habit of mind that complacently lends
authority to what is customary.[9] In his treatment of conscience, Hawthorne at once explores the nature of psychic authority and engages the
authority of the middle-class culture he addresses. Conscience is his subject; as a maker of entrapping inner fictions that mistake joylessness or
cruelty for virtue, it is his adversary; and to the degree that it comes to
dominate his culture as the implicit hero of its moral tales, conscience is
Hawthorne's audience. In "Roger Malvin's Burial" Hawthorne sets out
to win, even from conscience itself, allegiance to a different kind of story,
a story that values not expiation but freedom of mind. And in the curative
work implicit in the tale's conception and execution he locates the
grounds of his own claim to cultural authority.

Chapter Two

HAWTHORNE'S CAREERISTS

... this thing of darkness I
Acknowledge mine.
—Prospero on Caliban, *The Tempest*

IN "ROGER MALVIN'S BURIAL," the exposure of entrapping cultural pieties and a disruptive narrative strategy allow Hawthorne to establish a valid, anticoercive form of cultural authority. I want now to turn to a second way the tales are shaped by and set out to solve the twin problem of ambition and authority: they make it thematic, transforming a source of anxiety into a subject for analysis. While any reader of Hawthorne's letters will be struck by the amount of time he spent confronting the economic question of *whether* he could make a career of writing, just as striking, it seems to me, is the extent to which the issues implicit in having a career find their way into the examinations of male character that produce many of Hawthorne's most interesting tales: What are the origins of ambition? How does the hunger for power disguise or mystify itself? What is the nature of one's designs upon the community? Without arguing that Hawthorne's stories are in a sterile or narrow way "about art" or pretending to have exhausted what is interesting about them, we should notice that, to a significant extent, Hawthorne makes his early career by interrogating the meaning of having one.

The male protagonists of the tales I have in mind—"The Minister's Black Veil," "Wakefield," "The Birthmark," "Young Goodman Brown," "Ethan Brand"—are all engaged in what might be called a metaphysical careerism; in each case they set out to demonstrate their authority as determiners of meaning, a form of activity that persistently invites us to entertain their analogy to the writer. Reality in the world of Hawthorne's tales is distinctively unmoored; his characters inhabit an epistemological marketplace where interpretations of experience compete with one another for authority, where the self may mingle with projections of its own fears and desires. Because experience offers no unambiguous or transcendent version of significance, we take the moral measure of these characters by how they respond to the lack of an authoritative confirmation of their self-worth. In the tales I am describing, Hawthorne is especially concerned to analyze and repudiate characters who live by extorting from others a confirmation of their power or meaning rather than by risking the self-disclosure and uncertainty that participation in communal life entails. These seekers of power customarily begin their careers with an act of isolation or fixation that dramatizes the refusal of the world to supply the absolute significance they desire. Often what they fix upon is a projection of an aspect of self—a desire, a lack—that they cannot directly acknowledge.[1] The ambition to fulfill such a wish or repair such an absence generates, in each case, the professional life of the protagonist, which takes the form of a struggle to have the world on his own terms or on no terms at all. And in each case a woman—usually possessed of the capacity to love, that is, to live by the risky interchange these men repudiate—is cast in the dual role of victim of and audience to the careerist's bid for eminence.

For both Rappaccini and Aylmer, for example, the scientific career veils, thinly, an attempt to deny the uniqueness of divine creativity by outdoing it, thus creating an unimpeachable claim to authority. Rappaccini composes a dark parody of the biblical creation story, while Aylmer punishes Georgiana for bearing the emblem of his own human limitation. In each case, the experimenters achieve power by fixing on the sexuality of their female subjects, as though that capacity itself were, like the world these characters set out to regulate, the locus of some intolerable, essential uncontrol. Similarly, Ethan Brand seeks to arrogate to himself an ultimate significance by fantasizing and possessing a negative absolute, the "unpardonable sin." And Wakefield, in a strategy almost beautiful in its economy, fixes upon his own insignificance and attempts to repair it by disappearing—by replacing a null presence with a meaningful, mysterious absence. In the case of Wakefield, the most modern of these characters, Hawthorne suggestively connects the hunger for eminence to the changing shape of nineteenth-century life: to the newly felt urban anonymity that makes celebrity seem necessary, and to the newspapers that make it seem possible. In every instance, meaning is not sought through connection with others (all of these characters reject love or membership in a community) but inflicted upon them in an attempt to establish the potency of the careerist. Each of these "professions" is exposed as an anxiety-driven form of coercion.

I have been describing the punitive strategies through which Hawthorne's ambitious males live out their fantasies of authority; my deeper purpose is to think about Hawthorne's stake in the exposure and repudiation of these excesses of ambition, the way this prominent strain in his writing illuminates his conception of literary authority. Behind this persistent interrogation of power seeking, it seems to me, is a tactic we might call, in analogy to the psychological process by which we locate in the external world qualities we cannot bear to discover within, "projection."

Hawthorne evades the debilitating ambition of the careerists he de-scribes—and thus makes possible a differently constructed career of his own—by analyzing and repudiating the hunger for power at its core. The insistence with which Hawthorne returns to the careerist-protagonist throughout his career, his apparent need to tell and retell this particular kind of story, suggests that the work these tales do is "disciplinary" in two senses: he criticizes the way ambition operates in the culture at large, and, in so doing, he continues to scrutinize the power-seeker within.[2]

Just as Hawthorne's attack upon (and attempt to reform) the authori-tarian conscience in "Roger Malvin's Burial" examined values crucial to his antebellum audience, so his interrogation of the problem of ambition and authority places him in central ideological territory. The uncertainty about the grounds of meaning and value that Hawthorne's ambitious males find so hard to tolerate in the tales is a rendition, it seems to me, of the slippery cultural terrain that Hawthorne and his contemporaries in-habited. As Burton Bledstein, the premier historian of the development of the professions in America, has observed, the 1830s and 1840s comprise an especially improvisatory time in the social and economic history of this country. While an elaborate, city-based market economy was developing with great speed and often mystifying, anxiety-producing effects, the sta-ble educational and professional institutions that buffer, for middle-class people, the uncertainties of a such a competitive economy were only beginning to take shape. As the high-flying schemes, money troubles, business failures, and changes of profession that fill the letters reveal, Hawthorne and his notably ambitious friends (especially those engaged in literature and politics) seem to have felt the full material force of this uncertainty. Much of the financial success that Hawthorne encountered in later life was, in fact, due to the maturing of such structures—particu-larly the emergence of a more stable and aggressive publishing industry.[3]

At a deeper ideological level, the work of the historians who have thought most compellingly about male character in antebellum America lets us see that Hawthorne's prolonged emphasis on the dangers of ambi-tion at once participates in and criticizes the ways of seeking personal and cultural authority most characteristic of his generation. George Forgie argues, using the career of Lincoln as an example, that ambition in post-Revolutionary America was shaped by an unacknowledged sense that the heroic authority of the Revolutionary fathers was irrecoverable, by a sus-picion of the comparative imaginative squalor of one's own possibilities, and by a consequent yearning to reclaim heroic stature by vanquishing an anticipated or imagined tyrant. Hawthorne strikingly anticipates Forgie's analysis in his fictive demonstrations that excessive ambition originates in anxieties about personal authority that stem from an unacknowledged and culturally located sense of inadequacy. Michael Rogin finds a similar logic at work in "antebellum political crusades—against Indians, Catholics, Masons, the 'monster Hydra bank,' the abolitionist menace, and the slave-power conspiracy." "Each movement," he writes, "fixed upon a single 'alien power' (in Marx's words) as the source of hidden domination. Each aimed, on the model of the revolutionary fathers, to return to emotional sources of power and generate heroic authority."[4] There is a sense in which Hawthorne's attacks on his coercive male characters share in the strategy Forgie and Rogin describe—achieving a belated authority by disciplining a resurgent tyranny. But their work helps us see that, with their emphasis on the cruelly punitive forms taken by this projective habit of mind and their rigorous unmasking of the power-seeking psychology that drives it, Hawthorne's tales of ambition work to diagnose and unfix this ideological structure. His tales of the protocareerist set out to establish human connection, not personal eminence, as the locus of a life's value; to suggest that old visions of authority do not fit a shifting, unpredictable social and economic life; and to teach us to live, despite our anxiousness, without the heroic afflatus.[5]

In order to understand the operation of this doubly "disciplinary" strategy, we need to see it at work in detail. I have chosen "The Minister's Black Veil" because the Reverend Hooper's attempt to enhance his authority is itself so writerly: by making himself an emblem, he commits an act of figuration. "The Minister's Black Veil" asks its readers to become analysts of ambition by interpreting the motivation behind Hooper's emblem making. This is Hooper's own highflown interpretation of the meaning of his black veil: "What, but the mystery which it obscurely typifies, has made this piece of crape so awful? When the friend shows his inmost heart to his friend; the lover to his best beloved; when man does not vainly shrink from the eye of his Creator, loathsomely treasuring up the secret of his sin; then deem me a monster, for the symbol beneath which I have lived, and die! I look around me, and, lo! on every visage a Black Veil!" (TTT 52). Hooper's veiling is finally less a theological matter than a philosophical one; his text is "now we see through a glass darkly, but then face to face," but he fixes on the earthly clause of Paul's sentence. What bothers Hooper, and what the veil signifies, is subjectivity itself, our inability to know fully—or be revealed to—another, even to ourselves.

In the grips of this awareness of the degree of solipsism that necessarily attends consciousness, Hooper ironically commits a solipsistic act: he imposes his reading of reality on the community. Convinced of the impossibility of utter communion, he attacks the possibility of communication, and thus of communality itself. A suspicious contradiction inheres in Hooper's expression of his knowledge, however; his veiling is itself an act of communication and seeks a response from those who are forced to interpret it. The logic of Hooper's act is best understood by a certain old woman who sees it as a power play, a shell game; she notices that Hooper "has changed himself into something awful, only by hiding his face" (38). The effect of Hooper's coercive emblem making is, tellingly, to make all other kinds of communication impossible. The church elders who come to remonstrate with him find themselves unable to speak in his presence; his fiancée, Elizabeth, who understands the meaning of the veil, refuses to marry him unless he removes it; and his symbol making keeps him "in that saddest of all prisons, his own heart" (50). Hooper exposes as fiction the premise that we can be known to each other, which is the ground upon which speech, love, art, community all rest; yet what he fails to understand is that this fiction when shared—and when it remains un-named—makes possible a provisional but significant speech, love, and art in the community that accepts it. In insisting on the truth of his vision, Hooper undermines the community's ability to create and hold meaning, and as a consequence the town must isolate him. His social role is limited to those funereal occasions when it is useful to be reminded of the empti-ness of earthly things and the private depravity of the soul. Hooper's act of representation—his art—is dangerous because he seeks significance through isolation of the self and at the expense of others, and because his success is measured by the power over others that it provides. Confident of its own truth, it attacks the shared, fictive vision that grounds commu-nal life.[6]

The narrator of "The Minister's Black Veil" notes that Hooper's sarto-rial orientalism makes him a peculiarly effective clergyman: "Strangers came long distances to attend service at his church, with the mere idle purpose of gazing at his figure, because it was forbidden to behold his face" (49). Hooper's strategy has been to make himself a piece of art, a "figure" instead of a "face."[7] The minister's decision to live the life of a trope amounts to a refusal of full membership in his community, but it does offer one obvious payoff: he has an extremely successful career, achieving the peak of ministerial eminence when he is invited to preach the election sermon. Hawthorne's tale exposes the intolerance for com-plexity, the aggression, and the ambition that lurk within what seems to be an act of principled self-sacrifice. And the analogy between Hooper's coercive representational practices and those of the writer implicitly rec-ommends a fiction conceived not as the imposition of meaning but as its occasion: a narrative practice, like that we discovered in "Roger Malvin's Burial," that makes room for the reader's own achievement of interpre-tive authority.

Thus far, the strategy of "projection" for which I have been arguing seems to work in a straightforward way. In the course of criticizing an authoritarian, aggressively ambitious art, Hawthorne achieves a legiti-mate form of authority for himself. Yet if Hooper has made himself dan-gerous to the community merely by becoming an emblem, by making himself interpretable, might not representation in itself be dangerous in unpredictable ways? As an art object, moreover, Hooper has qualities peculiarly characteristic of Hawthorne's own work: he is intensely symbolic, epistemologically slippery, and hard to read. In a letter to his wife that reads like a gloss on "The Minister's Black Veil," Hawthorne reveals a suspicion that the very act of representing experience in language is inherently dangerous.

> Lights and shadows are continually flitting across my inward sky, and I know neither whence they come nor whither they go; nor do I inquire too closely into them. It is dangerous to look too minutely at such phenomena. It is apt to create a substance where at first there was a mere shadow. If at any time, dearest wife, there should seem—though to me there never does—but if there should ever seem to be an expression unintelligible from one of our souls to another, we will not strive to interpret it into earthly language, but wait for the soul to make itself understood; and were we to wait a thousand years, we need deem it no more time than we can spare. . . . It is not that I have any love for mystery; but because I abhor it—and because I have felt, a thousand times, that words may be a thick and darksome veil of mystery between the soul and the truth which it seeks. Wretched were we, indeed, if we had no better means of communicating ourselves, no fairer garb in which to array our essential selves, than these poor rags and tatters of Babel. Yet words are not without their use, even for purposes of explanation—but merely for explaining outward acts, and all sorts of external things, leaving the soul's life and action to explain itself in its own way.[8]

In warning against the inspection and representation of the "lights and shadows" that flit across the "inward sky," Hawthorne seems to repudiate his medium, language, and his characteristic subject, the inner life. He mistrusts words because they may become "a thick and darksome veil of mystery between the soul and the truth which it seeks"; like Hooper's black veil, they may assume "substance," a gratuitous mysteriousness, and become not communicative but opaque and self-enclosing. Hawthorne seems intent in this letter on protecting his private life from the very interests and methods of his work because his control over the power of language is so partial. The process of representation—looking minutely at psychological phenomena and their "interpretation" into earthly language—is doubly dangerous: the translation is likely to be inaccurate ("substance" instead of "shadow") and to assume a life of its own, foiling the attempt at understanding that it was designed to implement and communicating something dangerously other ("a thick and darksome veil of mystery"). Hawthorne's use of the verb "interpret" as part of the process of representation hints that the initial errors of representation can transmit themselves, even exfoliate, when they are part of a communication designed to be interpreted—like a work of fiction.

In the letter, Hawthorne counters the dangerous tendency of language to foil communication, finally to obstruct the self, by invoking a kind of utopian communion, some "better means" of representing—but still "arraying," not "revealing"—the essential self. What this nonlinguistic method of discourse is must remain a mystery to the profane, but it is certainly unavailable in the public, linguistic sphere of fiction writing. In his work Hawthorne cannot elude the tendency of representational language to escape from his control, to become dangerous—even dangerously true like Hooper's emblematic veil. Hawthorne's willingness to risk misinterpretation, which I have described at work in "Roger Malvin's Burial," can only increase the unreliability of the transaction between the writer and his audience. There may be in writing, then, an inevitable guiltiness, a danger for both the writer and the extremely permeable reader imagined in nineteenth-century accounts of literary response, in the capacity of fiction to seek power and to enclose the self in ways not available to the conscious awareness, or subject to the conscious control, of the writer.

The analogy between the work of the writer and Hooper's act of representation that surfaces, even in the midst of an effort to identify and avoid what is coercive about Hooper's ploy, suggests a second, more complex aspect to Hawthorne's attempt to establish a scrupulous form of cultural authority. While "The Minister's Black Veil" claims that Hooper's artistic project is crucially opposed in its aim and effect to the story that describes it, the story admits that their methods are crucially alike. If Hawthorne sets out to define what the artistic career should *not* be, he nevertheless names, in acknowledging the extent to which any act of representation may be incompletely in control of its ambitions, the dangers that cannot be resolved. Hawthorne claims authority in these tales obliquely, even defensively. He must find in his narrative practice a way to resolve the double ambivalence I have been describing: he suspects that what drives art's urge toward significance is aggression; and he senses that even the most scrupulous artist may be deceived about the psychic purpose of his work, and may overestimate his control over what he is representing. In combination with this strategy of projection, Hawthorne's acknowledgment—so unlike Hooper's absolutism—of the unavoidable dangers of performing his work and the resilient complexities of his engagement with his audience seems to provide a truce with the guilt necessarily attendant upon art sufficient to make possible the risk of writing.[9]

I have been arguing that one of the tasks repeatedly performed in Hawthorne's tales of ambition is the exploration of the meaning of his own: What drives the desire to come before an audience? How might that ambition, potentially coercive and self-isolating, become the basis of connection to one's community, the exercise of a form of authority not coercive but freeing? We can get a still fuller sense of the daunting complexity of Hawthorne's conception of the problem of literary and cultural authority in "Alice Doane's Appeal," where Hawthorne gives explicit consideration to the nature of his own ambitions by dramatizing the presentation of two of his stories to an audience. As we have seen, Hawthorne's tales of ambition repudiate characters who sacrifice the reality of others and the complexity of experience to their own dramas of need. This tale is interesting because the habit of mind analyzed and repudiated is a version—intensified to the point of illness—of the strategy of self-legitimation I have been describing: to guard oneself against guilty behavior by locating and punishing it in another. In this curious tale, Hawthorne examines the tendency of this very scrupulousness to turn into a kind of paralysis or issue in acts of incommensurate cruelty.

"Alice Doane's Appeal" is a story in three pieces. In the frame-narrative that begins and ends the tale, the narrator—Hawthorne playing himself—strolls with two comely young ladies to Salem's Gallows Hill, site of the infamous witch hangings. He ventures to read his companions a tale written years earlier, and saved by accident from the fire to which he consigned other early stories. The edited version of this gothic tale comprises the second, central part of the larger story. It depicts Leonard Doane's jealousy-driven murder of Walter Brome, the would-be seducer of his sister Alice and, it turns out, Leonard's long-lost twin. The whole bizarre encounter has been arranged by a wizard, the gothicist personified, who is trying to wring both fratricide and incest out of the plot materials supplied him. This tale ends with the trial, located on the very site of the witchcraft executions, of Alice before an audience of guilt-seeking fiends (masquerading as Salem's honored dead), but Walter Brome's ghost arrives to absolve Alice of all charges. The frame-tale's narrator is unsatisfied by the equivocal response of his audience to his horrific fantasy—though rapt enough during its telling, they laugh when he finishes—and he responds by trying his hand at history, evoking the actual procession of the alleged witches and their accusatory community up Gallows Hill. This last piece of the larger story achieves the ladies' sympathetic tears and, happy with both his artistic triumph and his success at reanimating the past, he leads them back to town.

"Alice Doane's Appeal," has generally been read as a botched piece of work, interesting for its failure to disguise its hot psychological material or for the way it telegraphs themes more subtly handled in later stories.[10] Is there a link that makes sense as intentional (rather than symptomatic) between the self-portraiture that frames the tale and the two stories—of wizardry and witchcraft, respectively—told within the frame? I see "Alice Doane's Appeal" not as a questionable attempt to salvage an abandoned piece of work but as an enactment of what Hawthorne has discovered about his art by returning to it, a thinking through of his relation to his fiction and its readers. For the psychology that transforms neighbors into witches and a virtuous sister into an adulteress might also have turned manuscripts into ashes.

Because this is a tale about a habit of mind, let me begin by working from the inside out, from its deepest, most primitive manifestation to its more everyday forms. Moments after he murders Walter Brome for claiming to have slept with Alice, Leonard Doane has an uncanny vision as he gazes at the corpse's face.

> It seemed to me that the irrecoverable years, since childhood, had rolled back, and a scene, that had long been confused and broken in my memory, arrayed itself with all its first distinctness. Methought I stood a weeping infant by my father's hearth; by the cold and blood-stained hearth where he lay dead. I heard the childish wail of Alice, and my own cry arose with hers, as we beheld the features of our parent, fierce with the strife and distorted with pain, in which his spirit had passed away. As I gazed, a cold wind whistled by, and waved my father's hair. Immediately, I stood again in the lonesome road, no more a sinless child, but a man of blood, whose tears were falling fast over the face of a dead enemy. (*SI* 273)

Doane's psyche replaces the present murder with a scene of childhood—his father's murder by Indians. This substitution of the vision of the murdered father for the rival he has killed gives us a glimpse of Doane's submerged inner life, revealing that he has all along identified himself with the killers of his father and that, like other children whose parents die when they are young, he blames himself for the death. Leonard's story has its origins, then, in the psyche's eagerness to ascribe guilt to itself, but inferring the origin of Leonard's sense of guilt is less important to our reading than understanding how guilt finds so punitive an expression.

After the murder, Leonard conveniently heads for an interview with the wizard that reveals the projective psychic logic that has governed the murder. Even Leonard explicitly understands his murder of Brome as an act of jealous rage, not as brotherly protectiveness: Brome "would have more than the love which had been gathered to me from the many graves of our household—and I be desolate!" (272). This jealousy depends in turn upon the conviction that Alice is in love with Brome precisely because of his similarity to Leonard; he reasons that "here was a man, whom Alice might love with all the strength of sisterly affection, added to the impure passion which alone engrosses all the heart," and notices that Alice "had betrayed an undefinable, but powerful interest" in Brome (272). He clearly projects his incestuous way of desiring onto Alice; moreover, as Frederick Crews points out in his reading of the story, what Leonard cannot tolerate in Brome is the latter's overt rendition of his own submerged desire. Thus Leonard admits that "his soul had been conscious of the germ of all the fierce and deep passions, and all the many varieties of wickedness" which he attributes, in "full maturity," to Brome, but from which Alice's good influence had saved him; and he shrinks with "sickness, and loathing, and horror" at his uncanny physical resemblance to Brome (271).[11] The narrator remarks that Leonard and Brome are "like joint possessors of an individual nature, which could not become wholly the property of one, unless by the extinction of the other" (272). Leonard, by murdering Brome, subscribes to this projective logic; he can reclaim guiltlessness only by extinguishing his desirous aspect, which he locates in his "counterpart," Brome. Leonard's inability to accept himself as a "man of blood" in a metaphorical sense—as a person troubled by desire, no longer a "sinless child"—makes him literally a man of blood, a murderer. What Leonard needs is the capacity to acknowledge and forgive himself feelings toward Alice that he would not enact, just as he needs to forgive himself the patricide he never committed. The absence of a way to such forgiveness, which would amount to an acknowledgment of the necessarily mixed character of love, dooms Leonard to extinguish his own desires by first locating them in others, and then punishing himself through their possessors.

There is, I think, a parallel to be drawn between the figure of Hawthorne that the story gives us and Leonard Doane; it emerges, though, not from the inadvertent eruption of shared obsessions that some readers have seen but from a series of analogies that is carefully established by the sharing of language between the different pieces of the larger story. Let us begin with the wizard, who, in his manipulation of Alice, Leonard, and Walter Brome, is the most apparent analogue to the teller of the story. ("In the course of the tale, the reader had been permitted to discover that all the incidents were results of the machinations of the wizard, who had cunningly devised that Walter Brome should tempt his unknown sister to guilt and shame, and himself perish by the hand of his twin-brother" [277]). The wizard should be understood simultaneously as the incarnation of the projective habit of mind that does indeed "devise" Leonard's actions and as the representative of a way of writing fiction that depends upon the psychology of projection. Hawthorne describes the wizard as "a small, gray, withered man, with fiendish ingenuity in devising evil and superhuman power to execute it, but senseless as an idiot to all better purposes" (270). Like the jealous, projecting mind, the wizard ingeniously invents evil where he would like to see it, but cannot see—or imagine—anything else. Thus when Leonard tells him the story of the murder, he is most helpful, "mysteriously filling up some void in the narrative," just as the projecting mind invents the "indubitable proofs" it needs to find.

The wizard is not simply a plotter; like the narrator of the frame, he has a particular audience in mind. In the gothic tale's last scene, Alice is brought to trial before what appears to be spiritual Salem—the hallowed ghosts of the deceased members of the community. These upstanding spirits turn out to be "fiends counterfeiting the likeness of departed saints," and their identities shift interestingly between essence and impersonation.

> The countenance of those venerable men, whose very features had been hallowed by lives of piety, were contorted now by intolerable pain or hellish passion, and now by an unearthly and derisive merriment. Had the pastors prayed, all saintlike as they seemed, it had been blasphemy. The chaste matrons, too, and the maidens with untasted lips, who had slept in their virgin graves apart from all other dust, now wore a look from which the two trembling mortals shrank, as if the unimaginable sin of twenty worlds were collected there. The faces of fond lovers, even of such as had pined into the tomb, because there their treasure was, were bent on one another with glances of hatred and smiles of bitter scorn, passions that are to devils, what love is to the blest. At times, the features of those, who had passed from a holy life to heaven, would vary to and from between their assumed aspect and the fiendish lineaments whence they had been transformed. (276)

These fiends, like the devil-worshipers in "Young Goodman Brown," are the people of Salem as reduced by the projecting habit of mind: not as they are, but in their desiring or aggressive aspect, as one's need to expel one's own forbidden impulses paints them. They also represent, in their eagerness to see the wizard's plot "consummated," the audience called into being by a projecting work of fiction.

For both "author" and "reader" of this debased gothic, the gratification its composition offers is this: it satisfies our hunger for scandal, for the guilt of others. The wizard's confirmation of Alice's supposed guilt offers Leonard—who, in adopting the projective way of seeing, cooperates in the authorship of his own story—the opportunity to confirm his own righteousness by projecting his desires onto her and Brome. His plotting offers its more jaded audience, who presumably have abandoned all notions of innocence, the negative but powerful solace that the virtue of others is illusory. The vacillation of these departed spirits between saint and fiend suggests that fiction has the power to create its audience in the image of the kind of gratification it offers, of the hungers it satisfies or elicits. The allegorical confirmation of the cultural effect of such art is, I think, the wood wax that sprouts from the wizard's "unhallowed bones"; this plant provides a "deceitful verdure," for "all the grass, and everything that should nourish man or beast, has been destroyed by this vile and ineradicable weed" (267). Still, we infer from this description of so unnurturing a fiction its possible opposite, which might engender the capacity for self-forgiveness that Leonard lacks: a way of telling stories that offers the mind a liberating awareness of itself.

The trial scene is followed by the narrator's homage to the victims of the Salem witch trials, which provides immediate testimony to the dangers of both the projective habit of mind and the fictions that it engenders.

> I strove to realize and faintly communicate, the deep, unutterable loathing and horror, the indignation, the affrighted wonder, that wrinkled on every brow, and filled the universal heart. See! the whole crowd turns pale and shrinks within itself, as the virtuous emerge from yonder street. Keeping pace with that devoted company, I described them one by one; here tottered a woman in her dotage, knowing neither the crime imputed to her, nor its punishment; there another, distracted by the universal madness, till feverish dreams were remembered as realities, and she almost believed her guilt. (278–79)

Michael D. Bell has noticed the connection between Leonard Doane's way of thinking and the communal psychology of the witchcraft episode: "The state of mind that led to the hanging of innocent victims in Salem in 1692 is of a piece with the 'diseased imagination' which permits Leonard to see around him only the tokens of his own repressed evil or libidinous urges."[12] (The same words—"loathing" and "horror"—are used to describe the crowd's reaction to the accused as to characterize Leonard's response to his uncanny resemblance to Brome.) And the narrator explicitly links the executions to fiction making when he remarks that he tells his story "on the hill where so many had been brought to death by wilder tales than this" (275).

Moreover, parallels of diction and detail in the frame narrative invite us to notice that the psychology of projection has been at work in the narrator's life as well. I give the central passage of autobiography in full:

> I had brought the manuscript in my pocket. It was one of a series written years ago, when my pen, now sluggish and perhaps feeble, because I have not much to hope or fear, was driven by stronger external motives, and a more passionate impulse within, that I am fated to feel again. Three or four of these tales had appeared in the Token, after a long time and various adventures, but had incumbered me with no troublesome notoriety, even in my birth place. One great heap had met a brighter destiny: they had fed the flames; thoughts meant to delight the world and endure for ages, had perished in a moment, and stirred not a single heart but mine. The story now to be introduced, and another, chanced to be in kinder custody at the time, and thus escaped destruction. (269)

Hawthorne presents himself as a victim of the same projective trend of mind that entraps Leonard Doane. For an unspoken reason, he, like Le-

onard, has revenged himself upon himself by burning his literary "counterpart," the version of himself written into his tales. Hawthorne hints
that this act of self-punishment has its origins in suspicions of the impulse
that drove his pen—he mentions his "dread of renewing my acquaintance
with fantasies that had lost their charm, in the ceaseless flux of mind"
(269).[13] But Hawthorne characteristically leaves us to infer the psychic
logic of the narrator's "persecution" of his stories by reading its analogy
with the tale's two other central actions: the murder that Leonard commits and the execution of the witches. The "incoherence" of "Alice
Doane's Appeal" disappears, then, when we discover that a similar psychology generates these three parallel moments. And certainly part of the
point of the narrator's exposure of his analogy to Leonard and the perse-
cutors is that projection is a psychic strategy as widespread and quotidian
as it is powerful and historic.

The relation between writing and projection implicit in this analogy is
a complicated one. Hawthorne is careful to draw our attention, by verbal
links, to the connections between the narrator's experience and what we
learn about projection in the story.[14] The feebleness the narrator feels is
echoed by the wizard's "feebleness to all better purposes." Leonard's
state of mind is described with a metaphor that refers us to the narrator's
burning of his tales: "the insane hatred that had kindled his heart into a
volume of hellish flame" (272; my italics). More curious is the following
parallel. The narrator depicts himself, in the aftermath of the burning of
his stories, as nearly impotent and utterly passive in relation to the movements of his own mind; his pen is "sluggish" and "feeble," he seems alienated from his emotions ("I have not much to hope or fear"), and he attributes agency—both external and internal—to something other than the
self ("I was driven by stronger external motives, and a more passionate
impulse within, than I am fated to feel again"). The psychic action depicted here—an act of revenge upon the self, made possible by projection,
followed by a loss of creative energy—recurs in the story the narrator
tells. Leonard describes the emotions that follow Brome's murder in this
way: "my spirit bounded as if a chain had fallen from it and left me free.
But the burst of exulting certainty soon fled, and was succeeded by a
torpor over my brain and dimness before my eyes, with the sensation of
one who struggles through a dream" (273). We understand Leonard's
"torpor" as the result of his execution of the part of himself that desires.
The narrator's "dread" of the "fantasies" encoded in his burned tales,
coupled with the analogical way of reading that the story teaches us, suggests that his creative torpor has a similar cause. The aspects of self that
he has repudiated in the burning of his tales are an essential source of the
power that once enabled his now enfeebled pen to stir hearts other than
his. Just as Leonard Doane needs to acknowledge the mixed nature of

love, so this Hawthornian narrator, if he is not to be silenced by guilt, needs to accept the morally mixed nature of the impulse that generates his writing. The analogy between the teller of this story and the characters that he invents suggests that the capacity for self-forgiveness is crucial if we are to avoid sacrificing the reality of others to obtain an illusory guilt-lessness; and if the writer is to avoid expressing and eliciting hunger for the guilt of others on the one hand, and condemning himself to silence on the other.

In light of this tale's suggestion that generosity begins with self-forgive-ness, Hawthorne's treatment of the encounter between the narrator and the two women who form his audience is worth attending to. Before be-ginning his tale, the narrator laments the blindness of his contemporaries to the meaning of their own history: "we are a people of the present and have no heartfelt interest in the olden time." This uninterest continues despite the recent appearance of a history of the witchcraft episode, "an honorable monument . . . of that better wisdom, which draws the moral while it tells the tale" (267). It is, we assume, this notion of the irrelevance of the past that the narrator attacks when he tells his two stories of projec-tion—a habit of mind that his episode of book burning testifies to be perennial. Yet his interest in the reaction of his auditors goes beyond the ethical, for it becomes clear that what is obliquely at stake in his tale telling is his own artistic potency. He is satisfied with the attention the two women pay him as he speaks the Alice Doane piece: "Their bright eyes were fixed on me; their lips apart" (275), a phrasing that invites other insinuations about the nature of his gratification. But when they follow the ending of the story with laughter, he is "piqued," and decides to try his narrative powers once more. His evocation of the witch execu-tions is immensely successful, for, as he pictures the scaffold, "my com-panions seized an arm on each side; their nerves were trembling; and sweeter victory still, I had reached the seldom trodden places of their hearts, and found the well-spring of their tears" (280). The explicit lan-guage of military triumph (along with allied hints of sexual penetration) suggests that, for the narrator, his success as a moralist is intimately linked to less laudable impulses. Hawthorne, in depicting the relation between the narrator and his audience, dramatizes the morally ambigu-ous nature of the gratification the author derives from telling his tales and from the fantasies that play in and around his work. It is precisely this awareness that the narrator could not accommodate when, fixed on the aggressive or erotic aspects of his creative impulse, he burned his tales. Hawthorne's joining of this workaday act of self-persecution to the mur-derous projections in the two stories that the narrator tells argues that the necessarily mixed nature of an artist's gratification is not a cause for si-lence, does not outweigh or deny the value of the sympathy he elicits from his listeners, or of the admonitory "monument" he has composed against the very inner tyranny that would silence him.

Our analysis of Hawthorne's tales of ambition reveals that he envisions the role of fiction as to assist in the retelling of the self. Expression for characters like Reuben Bourne, the Reverend Hooper, and Leonard Doane is reduced to a kind of symptomology, an unfolding of the mechanism of their obsessions. Where an art of coercion, like Hooper's emblem making, or an art of projection, like the wizard's in "Alice Doane's Appeal," can only propagate the anxiety and self-loathing that generate them, Hawthorne's analysis of this fixating psychology recovers for both writer and reader a sense of the mind as changeable, subject—like a twice- or thrice-told tale—to revision. And when Hawthorne adds himself to his gallery of ambition's casualties in "Alice Doane's Appeal," he includes himself among those who might learn from his tales, suggesting that the management of one's ambitions and the achievement of a significant form of relation to the community will call for self-forgiveness as well as self-scrutiny.

Hawthorne's hopes for his tales of ambition and his analysis of the cultural circumstances that have made them necessary are expressed, it seems to me, quite early in his career, in the one story in which a power-seeker comes to a good end. Much has been written about "My Kinsman, Major Molineux" as an exploration of the private psychology of maturation on the one hand and of the social psychology of revolution on the other, but it is most clearly a story about an attempt to establish a career. In leaving his rural village to find success in the city—as did thousands of young men in the urbanizing America for which Hawthorne writes— Robin lives out a brief history of cultural authority in America.[15] He leaves behind a conceptually stable (but economically fragile) rural home, presided over by his clergyman father, whose familial authority is underwritten by divine grace. Robin's more secular hopes for success in the city depend, in turn, upon the operation of another once-reliable system of authority: the influence of his aristocratic uncle, Major Molineux. The story works by subjecting Robin to the failure of the antique models of authority he holds in his mind. The urban night that Robin enters upon his arrival exposes him to a world of unmoored meanings, uncertain morals, and elusively dispersed authority. In short, the tale provides Robin both with the experience of entering the new America called into being by social and economic change and with the experience of reading a Hawthorne story—which turn out to be versions of one another.

Robin is forced by the carnivalesque spectacle of his uncle's fall from power to abandon the vision of heroic, aristocratic authority that brought him to the city. What saves Robin from the bitterness and escap-

ism that are his first responses to his difficult experience—and what identifies him as the kind of reader Hawthorne has in mind—is his capacity to
accommodate the complexity that the story thrusts upon him. After a
moment in which he feels "pity" for his uncle's suffering, an emotion
appropriate to the tragic matter of the fall of aristocrats, Robin laughs
and is joined in boisterous cachinnation by the assembled community.
This laughter is the outward expression of the inward difference made by
Robin's distressing but liberating realization that, like the innkeeper, the
prostitute, the politician, and the other denizens of the urban marketplace
(including the purveyor of fiction), he will be dependent for survival not
on the fulfillment of a fantasy of eminence but on the value of what he has
to sell. Forced to "rise in the world" without the help of his kinsman,
Robin must discover an authority of his own; his salutary, self-deflating
reading of the urban spectacle he witnesses marks his initiation into complexity and community.

Chapter Three

THE INVENTION OF ROMANCE

> We are forever telling stories about ourselves. In telling
> these self-stories to others we may, for most purposes, be
> said to be performing straightforward narrative actions.
> In saying that we also tell them to ourselves, however,
> we are enclosing one story within another. This is the
> story that there is a self to tell something to, a someone
> else serving as audience who is oneself or one's self.
> When the stories we tell others about ourselves concern
> these other selves of ours, when we say, for example, "I
> am not master of myself," we are again enclosing one
> story within another. On this view, the self is a telling.
> —Roy Schafer, "Narration in the Psychoanalytic
> Dialogue"

> An essay on the misery of being always under a mask.
> A veil may be needful, but never a mask.
> —Hawthorne, in the *American Notebooks*

"MAY THERE BE an ennui of the first idea? / What else, prodigious scholar, should there be?" writes Wallace Stevens in "Notes Toward a Supreme Fiction." Extraordinary as are the tales it produces, there is a problem with the disciplinary, self-scrutinizing strategy of self-legitimation that we might see as Hawthorne's "first idea" about literary authority. It eventually engenders, in its repeated repudiations, a kind of stasis, a rewriting of the same inner story. Hawthorne himself records a sense of needing to move beyond his customary forms—of having "done enough in this kind"—in "The Old Manse" (*MOM* 34). I will be suggesting that Hawthorne finds his way out of this confinement by recomposing the story of his writing, shifting his emphasis from the mastery of an ever-dangerous ambition to the possibilities of engagement with his reader and their community. Such a theory of narrative authority, emphasizing the idea of interchange with the reader that is always central to his narrative practice, emerges from the prefaces that introduce his novels and re-present his tales; it is intriguingly latent in the private letters most concerned with explaining his life to others. While the development of Hawthorne's claim to cultural authority is not in any simple way linear—indeed, his most powerful and generative tactic, the destabilization of narrative authority, is in place in his earliest tales—the prefaces are transitional or "middle" works, both retrospective and prospective, forecasting or marking the achievement of writerly maturity. In effect, Hawthorne finds his way to a more capacious conception of the cultural role of the writer by rereading his earlier work and meditating upon the meaning of the relation to the reader he finds enacted there. This reinterpretation of the potential meaning of the writer's career is codified in the story that he begins to tell in "The Old Manse" and brings insistently to the reader's attention in all the prefaces that follow. It is the story of the invention of romance and, by means of that invention, of the enfranchisement of the private self.

Because so much American literary scholarship has set out to discriminate the literary ideas and cultural pressures that produce the tradition of romance that culminates in the work of Hawthorne and Melville, I need to explain what I mean by Hawthorne's "invention" of romance. I do not mean that Hawthorne founded this particularly problematic genre, but that he portrays romance as a discovery, one that he takes particular pains to have his reader understand. We need, then, to examine Hawthorne's description of his artistic project idiosyncratically, not as though it were the key to an essentially American narrative practice.[1] Though he describes romance in the famous preface to *The House of the Seven Gables* as a kind of writing that permits an author to elude the "very minute fidelity, not merely to the possible, but to the probable and ordinary course of man's experience" demanded by the novel, he more often invokes, when introducing his fictions, a particular kind of setting and the question of his relation to the reader. Hawthorne's romance, I will be arguing, is represented less as a literary form than as the psychological and cultural place where his art happens, where writer and reader meet in a special sort of interchange. The prefaces are designed to establish this imaginative locale; they "pave the reader's way," Hawthorne remarks, "into the interior edifice of a book" (*SI* 3).

The story the prefaces tell about literary authority begins with the estrangement, even the unreality of the authorial self. Hawthorne claims, at the beginning of the 1851 preface to *Twice-told Tales*, to have been, "for a good many years, the obscurest man of letters in America" (*TTT* 3). The preface to *The Snow Image*, written several months later, reveals the nature of that obscurity. Hawthorne is addressing Horatio Bridge, the college friend whose secret willingness to back the first volume of *Twice-told Tales* made its publication possible.

> I sat down by the wayside of life, like a man under enchantment, and a shrubbery sprung up around me, and the bushes grew to be saplings, and the saplings became trees, until no exit appeared possible, through the entan-

gling depths of my obscurity. And there, perhaps, I should be sitting at this moment, with the moss on the imprisoning tree-trunks, and the yellow leaves of more than a score of autumns piled above me, if it had not been for you. For it was through your interposition,—and that, moreover, unknown to himself,—that your early friend was brought before the public. (*SI* 5)

Publication, Hawthorne suggests, has saved him from an isolation so complete that it amounts to a kind of unreality; "under enchantment," at a remove from active life, he was completely imprisoned within the bower of himself. Other prefatory pieces establish an alternative kind of estrangement. In both "The Old Manse" and "The Custom-House" Hawthorne makes himself an outcast by a ritualistic acceptance of "shame," in the former case "for having been so long a writer of idle stories" (*MOM* 4), and in the latter for the persecutory acts of his Puritan ancestors (*SL* 10). In either case of estrangement, the figure of the writer carries into the prefaces a sense of a dangerous distance between himself and the world, a burden of guilt for his self-enclosing withdrawal, for his choice of career, for his connection to acts of coercion.

Hawthorne records this moment of the self's lapse into unreality in his private letters as well as his public prefaces; the myth he composed to interpret the progress of his life, like that which describes the development of his art, begins in estrangement. He offered this self-portrait to Longfellow shortly after the publication of *Twice-told Tales*:

By some witchcraft or other—for I really cannot assign any reasonable why and wherefore—I have been carried apart from the main current of life, and find it impossible to get back again. Since we last met, . . . I have secluded myself from society; and yet I never meant any such thing, nor dreamed what sort of life I was going to lead. I have made a captive of myself and put me into a dungeon; and now I cannot find the key to let myself out—and if the door were open, I should be almost afraid to come out. . . . For the last ten years, I have not lived, but only dreamed about living. (*Letters 1*, 251)

Hawthorne makes explicit here the connection between estrangement—his withdrawal from society and consequent self-imprisonment—and the attenuation of the reality of the self: "I have not lived, but only dreamed about living." Hawthorne reflects on the same period of his life, his years of imprisonment in his "lonely chamber," in a letter to his wife-to-be:

Ownest, in the times that I have been speaking of, I used to think that I could imagine all passions, all feelings, all states of the heart and mind; but how little did I know what it is to be mingled with another's being! Thou only hast taught me that I have a heart—thou only hast thrown a light deep downward, and upward, into my soul. Thou only hast revealed me to myself; for without thy aid, my best knowledge of myself would have been merely to know my own shadow—to watch it flickering on the wall, and mistake its fantasies for my own real actions. Indeed, we are but shadows—we are not endowed with real life, and all that seems most real about us is but the thinnest substance of a dream—till the heart is touched. That touch creates us—then we begin to be—thereby we are beings of reality, and inheritors of eternity. (*Letters 1*, 495)

The reality of the self for Hawthorne, this passage makes clear, depends upon a complicated kind of interchange, a "mingling" with another. Self-discovery is an effect of being discovered—seen into—by someone else: "thou only hast thrown a light deep downward, and upward, into my soul. Thou only has revealed me to myself." An escape from the unreality of narcissistic self-enclosure—"my best knowledge of myself would have been merely to know my own shadow"—into the substantiality of a "being of reality" depends upon the "touch" of another. We know from Hawthorne's tales, moreover, the stakes of such an escape, for it is typically an act of protective self-enclosure that turns anxiety into compulsion within the psyches of his male protagonists.

Interchange with another, then, offers a way to recover—or, as Hawthorne's more radical language claims—to "create" the self. And it would seem that, in the story of the invention of romance that parallels his discovery of love, publication—an interchange with the reader—confers the kind of reality upon the artist that communion with Sophia provided the lover. Hence it is being "brought before the public" by *Twice-told Tales* that releases Hawthorne from his woody hermitage. This moment of enlivening connection with the reader is invoked universally in Hawthorne's prefatory writing. The *Twice-told Tales*, he notes in retrospect, were "attempts, and very imperfectly successful ones, to open an intercourse with the world" (*TTT* 6). He writes in "The Custom-House" that, "as thoughts are frozen and utterance benumbed, unless the speaker stand in some true relation with his audience—it may be pardonable to imagine that a friend, a kind and apprehensive, though not the closest friend, is listening to our talk" (*SL* 4). It is as the "friend," one of "the few who will understand him, better than most of his schoolmates and lifemates" (*SL* 3), that the reader is always, hopefully, called forth. Yet establishing "some true relation" with a reader—an unknown, silent, perhaps hostile figure—is considerably more problematic than carrying on the nearly ideal amorous communion that Hawthorne celebrates, and perhaps tries to call into being, in his love letters. Thus the interchanges that Hawthorne depicts with his readers are as notable for what they sometimes fail to deliver as for what they offer. He describes the effect of the nonexistent response accorded his stories when they first appeared ("he had no grounds for supposing that . . . they met with the good or evil fortune to be read by anybody") in the preface to *Twice-told Tales*: "To this total lack of sympathy, at the age when his mind would naturally have been most effervescent, the Public owe it (and it is certainly an effect not to be regretted on either part) that the Author can show nothing for the thought and industry of that portion of his life, save the forty sketches, or thereabouts, included in these volumes" (3–4). Encounters with readers, then, can be as chilling as they are enlivening.

The difficulty of the prefaces originates in the curious nature of the relationship with the reader that Hawthorne is engaged in inventing. They present a puzzling surface of assertion, reservation, contradiction, paradox, and self-criticism, all further veiled by the most elusively humorous tone. To be rescued from estrangement, to become real, even to oneself, one must be discovered by another. But what kind of interchange do the prefaces elicit? What sort of discovery does Hawthorne invite? In the *American Notebooks* Hawthorne makes a cryptic remark about the logistics of self-revelation: "An essay on the misery of being always under a mask. A veil may be needful, but never a mask" (23). What we need to discover in the prefaces is the needfulness of the veil, the reason self-presentation must always, for Hawthorne, be a strategic act.[2]

The beginning of an answer to this question—and of a description of the interchange with the reader, which Hawthorne envisions as romance—can be inferred from another of the prefaces' recurring moments. I have in mind Hawthorne's assurances that no transgression has been committed against the selfhood of either author or reader. As he notes in "The Custom-House"—right after the passage I have quoted on the necessity of "true relation" with the reader—he has kept "the inmost Me behind its veil" (*SL* 4). Self-revelation is presented both as a possible escape from the narcissism of self-enclosure and a potential violation of the rights of the reader. What is disturbing about self-presentation is apparent in this passage from "The Old Manse." Hawthorne, near the end of this autobiographical essay, defends himself against an imagined charge of egotism:

> My conscience, however, does not reproach me with betraying anything too sacredly individual to be revealed by a human spirit, to its brother or sister spirit. How narrow—how shallow and scanty too—is the stream of thought that has been flowing from my pen, compared with the broad tide of dim emotions, ideas, and associations, which swell around me from that portion of my existence! How litle have I told!—and, of that little, how almost nothing is even tinctured with any quality that makes it exclusively my own! Has the reader gone wandering, hand in hand with me, through the inner passages of my being, and have we groped together into all its chambers and examined their treasures or their rubbish? Not so. We have been standing on the green sward, but just within the cavern's mouth, where the common sunshine is free to penetrate, and where every footstep is therefore free to

come. I have appealed to no sentiment or sensibilities, save such as are diffused among us all. So far as I am a man of really individual attributes I veil my face. (*MOM* 32–33)

While Hawthorne repudiates the "mask," he also avoids a complete unmasking. What is the logic that makes the revelation of "sacredly individual" traits a guilty act, that makes a trip through the "inner passages" of another's being a dangerous one? If the only route to being for Hawthorne is a self-revealing interchange, why must that interchange be so carefully limited, so "narrow" and "shallow"?

Our answer lies, I think, in Hawthorne's evocation of a kind of psychic borderland where the interchange elicited by "The Old Manse" has taken place. Hawthorne and the reader have been occupying a place where the darkness of the psyche and the "common sunshine" of quotidian social life mingle—"on the green sward, but just within the cavern's mouth." This setting makes possible an interchange that the reader embraces or escapes freely, and without the assistance of a guide, a place "where every footstep is therefore free to come."[3] That freedom, purchased by Hawthorne's veiling, is necessary because a temptation lurks within the desire for self-presence as Hawthorne represents it. For the careerists in Hawthorne's tales, an authoritative identity is achieved through a perversion of interchange, an imposition of the self upon another in a way that steals away the other's reality. Hooper expresses his philosophical despair and Aylmer his sexual self-disgust by "placing" them in others—in effect, by enveloping others in the psychic drama playing in their "inner passages." They do not escape narcissism's unreality via interchange; they rather appropriate the available relationship—ministry, love—as the means of playing out their obsessions. Hawthorne and Hooper, then, veil to a different purpose—Hooper to enthrall his audience, Hawthorne to free his from an impulse to impose himself upon them.

For Hawthorne the interchange, with lover or with reader, that mutually confers reality on its sharers is a precarious one. It is too susceptible to infiltration by the desire for power, to the translation of free exchange into coercion. Hawthorne's sense of the extremity of the mind's susceptibility to such coercion is apparent in his reaction to his wife's flirtation with spiritualism.

I am unwilling that a power should be exercised on thee, of which we know neither the origin nor the consequence, and the phenomena of which seem rather calculated to bewilder us, than to teach us any truths about the present or future state of being. If I possessed such a power over thee, I should not dare to exercise it; nor can I consent to its being exercised by another. Supposing that this power arises from the transfusion of one spirit into another, it seems to me that the sacredness of an individual is violated by it;

there would be an intrusion into thy holy of holies—and the intruder would not be thy husband! Canst thou think, without a shrinking of thy soul, of any human being coming into any closer communion with thee than I may?—than either nature or my own sense of right would permit me? (*Letters 1*, 588)

Love here is as much a matter of restraint as of communion. Hawthorne's "sense of right" insists that he refuse the power that his intimacy with Sophia offers him lest her selfhood—"the sacredness of an individual"—be undermined. A similar principle of restraint, the "Old Manse" passage suggests, operates in his interchange with the reader. As Hawthorne puts it in "The Custom-House," it is only by keeping the autobiographical impulse within "limits," by veiling the "inmost Me," that an author avoids "violating either the reader's rights or his own" (*SL* 4). If self-presentation is not to turn into coercion on the one hand nor mere masking on the other, some mediating strategy of expression must be invented.

In an essay that sets out to sketch the outline of a psychoanalytic treatment of literary representation that escapes the confines of character analysis, Geoffrey Hartman speculates that a "communication-compulsion"—a desire to be represented—can be seen in the way that wishes achieve expression in dream symbols or in the formation of neurotic symptoms. Hartman sees these communications with the self as the beginnings of a cure, an attempt to limit the "demand" that the wishful psyche places upon others. He defines this demand as the attempt to "exact from the world a defining (accepting or accusatory) response to oneself." (Compare this "demand" to the representational strategies of Hawthorne's careerists.) Hartman suggests an analogy between these attempts at limiting demands by finding a way to communicate them and the work of the artist. "The idealism of art," he writes, "can likewise be seen as a therapeutic modification of this demand for a defining response: for achieving self presence despite or through the presence of others."[4] I am arguing that the animating purpose of Hawthorne's earlier writing, which he is allegorizing in this depiction of romance, is a sustained attempt to "limit demand," to enfranchise the self not at the expense of the reader but along with him. In the most revealing of his descriptions of the strategy of self-presentation that his works employ, Hawthorne again defends himself against the charge of egoism.

A person, who has been burrowing, to his utmost ability, into the depths of our common nature, for the purposes of psychological romance,—and who pursues his researches in that dusky region, as he needs must, as well by the tact of sympathy as by the light of observation,—will smile at incurring such an imputation in virtue of a little preliminary talk about his external habits, his abode, his casual associates, and other matters entirely upon the surface.

These things hide the man, instead of displaying him. You must make quite
another kind of inquest, and look through the whole range of his fictitious
characters, good and evil, in order to detect any of his essential traits. (*SI* 4)

The strategy of self-expression that Hawthorne chooses, then, is fiction.
Unlike the seemingly explicit bits of autobiographical information he
provides, which "hide the man," Hawthorne's veiling—his complex in-
vestiture in his fictional characters—provides the revelation of "essential
traits" that makes possible the reality-conferring interchange he needs.
The "reality" of the figure of Hawthorne, as it is written into his tales,
depends, then, upon the reader's act of interpretation, and upon his own
ability to limit his demand, to make his art a conceptual place where
interpretation is not coerced but freely chosen.

Implicit in the commitment to interchange that I have been attributing
to Hawthorne is a remarkable dependence upon the imagined reader of
his work. The effect of his art, he takes pains to admit, is peculiarly connected to the reader's angle of vision. Thus the editor of the burlesque
introduction to "Rappaccini's Daughter" remarks that "M. de l'Aubep-
ine's productions, if the reader chance to take them in precisely the proper
point of view, may amuse a leisure hour as well as those of a brighter
man; if otherwise, they can hardly fail to look excessively like nonsense"
(*MOM* 92). Hawthorne offers a similar warning in the preface to *Twice-
told Tales*: "The book, if you would see anything in it, requires to be read
in the clear, brown, twilight atmosphere in which it was written; if
opened in the sunshine, it is apt to look exceedingly like a volume of
blank pages" (5). Hawthorne is playing here, but his playfulness has a
point. The freedom from interpretive coercion that he allows his reader
puts his work extraordinarily at risk. The reader proceeds without guid-
ance, yet there is no margin for error; there are not many available lights
in which he might be read but only an elusive one—"precisely the proper
point of view." At stake, he hints, is not the meaning of the work but its
existence; seen awry, his work amounts to nothing: "nonsense" or blank-
ness. And when one's fiction becomes, as the prefaces imply, not simply
a structure of meaning but a strategy of being—when the self is invested
in the work and made real by being read—one risks not simply being
misseen but *un*seen, "exceedingly like a volume of blank pages." Hawthorne offers what I take to be a comic acknowledgment of the stakes of
this aesthetic of interchange when he remarks that his sense of himself has
oddly begun to conform to the image—of "a mild, shy, gentle, melan-
cholic, exceedingly sensitive, and not very forcible man"—that his readers have inferred from his fiction: "He is by no means certain, that some
of his subsequent productions have not been influenced and modified by
a natural desire to fill up so amiable an outline, and to act in consonance
with the character assigned to him" (*TTT* 7). The malleability of the self,

one begins to suspect, is at once the central hope and the chief anxiety of Hawthorne's work.[5]

There is, of course, an element of cagey, backhanded exhortation in Hawthorne's self-criticism; we feel challenged to provide the ideal reading, the precisely proper point of view. It nonetheless remains true that to write romance, for Hawthorne, is to risk invention by the reader. Yet if reading is to be the act of interchange that the prefaces invoke, the reader, too, takes risks, for in defining the figure of Hawthorne he is being defined himself. It is Hawthorne's sense of the risk of reading—of the susceptibility of the self to the demands of another—that accounts for the most curious aspect of his prefatory writing: its air of "relinquishment." By relinquishment I mean all the devices that seem designed to belittle the fictions that the prefaces introduce: the passages of criticism and self-depreciation, the generally bemused, offhand tone Hawthorne adopts. The following passage from the preface to *Twice-told Tales* is typical.

> At all events, there can be no harm in the Author's remarking that he rather wonders how the *Twice-told Tales* should have gained what vogue they did than that it was so little and so gradual. They have the pale tint of flowers that blossomed in too retired a shade—the coolness of a meditative habit, which diffuses itself through the feeling and observation of every sketch. Instead of passion, there is sentiment; and, even in what purport to be pictures of actual life, we have allegory, not always so warmly dressed in its habiliments of flesh and blood as to be taken into the reader's mind without a shiver. Whether from lack of power, or an unconquerable reserve, the Author's touches have often an effect of tameness; the merriest man can hardly contrive to laugh at his broadest humor; the tenderest woman, one would suppose, will hardly shed warm tears at his deepest pathos. (5)

Hawthorne accuses his work of attenuation of effect; his tales are trivial, passionless, colorless, insufficiently realistic, coldly allegorical, tame. He depicts himself as either irretrievably withdrawn or verging on impotence. Other prefaces supply additional charges: his writings are neither lively nor profound, and "often but half in earnest, and never, even when most so, expressing satisfactorily the thoughts which they profess to image" (*MOM* 34). He goes so far as to abandon his suspicions of self-enclosure, suggesting that "the talk of a secluded man with his own mind and heart" would be "more deeply and permanently valuable" than his attempt to "open an intercourse with the world" (*TTT* 6). And he discounts his own art by praising a realism he professes to be unable to write (*SL* 37), or by celebrating the value of treatises on ethics or "philosophic history" (*MOM* 34).

Why does Hawthorne raise these critical specters? These passages of relinquishment are designed, I suspect, to undermine the customary authority granted by the reader to the figure of author. Hawthorne's attacks upon himself put us in the curious position of either defending his fiction against these seemingly authoritative condemnations of it, or abandoning our sense that something far more interesting and powerful is going on in the tales than the prefaces admit. He invites us to take a doubly critical position, suspicious both of the tales and of his criticism of them.[6] We are, finally, induced to value the covert, and we compose out of Hawthorne's disaffection a hidden agenda: the tameness is designed to distribute a power the more subversive for its obliqueness; he aims at more complex effects than laughter or tears. We are denied the pleasures of interpretive confirmation, lest our act of reading comprise not an interchange but an acquiescence.

To add this understanding of the curiously offhand attacks upon himself that Hawthorne serves up in the prefaces to our unfolding account of the relation to the reader that romance inscribes is to recognize the achievement in the prefaces of a theory of literary authority—called "romance"—that compellingly resolves the anxieties about ambition and self-enclosure that endanger Hawthorne's career. The potential for coercion implicit in a writer's designs upon the reader is circumvented by leaving the reader unusually free to speculate, by refusing to limit the risk of being read into existence by another. Hawthorne is attempting to invent a mode of self-presentation that is not a guilty imposition of the "inmost Me," but an elaborate structure of mutual self-discovery. Hawthorne succeeds in achieving authority—what Hartman calls "self presence"—by achieving in his art the limitation of the tyrannical demand for significance that his fictive careerists extort from others. He risks a radical limitation of his own authority and, by doing so, offers us an escape from the anxious authoritarian we carry within us.

I began by suggesting that Hawthorne characteristically calls his particular version of romance into being by defining, in the oblique way I have been describing, his relation to the reader and by invoking a particular setting and atmosphere. These descriptive passages establish not a literal place but the conceptual and psychological borderland where Hawthorne's work takes place. An analogy connects these two aspects of Hawthorne's definition of romance. Just as it is only Hawthorne's veiling that makes his presence possible, so—to hear another implication in a passage we have already noted—it is only the "veiled" atmosphere of romance that releases the power of his writing: "the book, if you would see anything in it, requires to be read in the clear, brown, twilight atmosphere in which it was written; if opened in the sunshine, it is apt to look exceedingly like a volume of blank pages" (TTT 5).

The prefaces, Hawthorne notes, are designed "to pave the reader's way into the interior edifice of a book" (SI 3). It is in the nature of that "interior edifice"—where the "place" of romance is, what happens there—that we must look for Hawthorne's account of the effects of the engagement with the reader he envisions. Let us begin with some of the passages that establish our sense of the romance place. This is Hawthorne's description of the Old Manse, the quintessential "interior edifice": "The glimmering shadows, that lay half asleep between the door of the house and the public highway, were a kind of spiritual medium, seen through which, the edifice had not quite the aspect of belonging to the material world. . . . In its near retirement, and accessible seclusion, it was the very spot for the residence of a clergyman; a man not estranged from human life, yet enveloped, in the midst of it, with a veil woven of intermingled gloom and brightness" (*MOM* 3–4). The Old Manse, he suggests later, is located in "fairy-land," where "there is no measurement of time" (33). Hawthorne's most famous exercise in genre painting, the description of his study in "The Custom-House," describes the play of moonlight, mirror, and the fire's glow, which invests daytime things "with a quality of strangeness and remoteness": "the floor of our familiar room has become a neutral territory, somewhere between the real world and fairy-land, where the Actual and Imaginary may meet, and each imbue itself with the nature of the other" (*SL* 36).

The language of these passages suggests that romance is a place of mixing, of mediation. Opposites intermingle, comfortably modifying one another: "near retirement," "accessible seclusion." Conventions of order and measurement are suspended, and boundaries of all kinds—between light and dark, spiritual and material, strangeness and familiarity, "Actual" and "Imaginary"—are elided. This release from definition allows for all sorts of mingling; thus "The Old Manse" vacillates imperceptibly between house tour and psychic autobiography, between remarks on gardening and a meditation on the fall of man. The spatial qualities of romance territory provide the ideal setting and an imagistic analogue for the kind of interchange that Hawthorne invents with the reader. What kind of experience does an invitation into this "neutral territory" make available to us?

Given the disregard for boundaries characteristic of Hawthorne's romance territory, one would expect the organizing principle of "The Old Manse" to be digressive. The passage that seems to me to provide the most revealing version of the conceptual meaning of romance is Hawthorne's description of a fishing excursion with Ellery Channing. As the mingled light and the confusion of actual and virtual suggest, they have paddled into deepest neutral territory:

> [The river] comes flowing softly through the midmost privacy and deepest heart of a wood, which whispers it to be quiet, while the stream whispers

back again from its sedgy borders, as if river and wood were hushing one another to sleep. Yes; the river sleeps along its course, and dreams of the sky, and of the clustering foliage, amid which fall showers of broken sunlight, imparting specks of vivid cheerfulness, in contrast with the quiet depth of the prevailing tint. Of all this scene, the slumbering river has a dream-picture in its bosom. Which, after all, was the most real—the picture, or the original? (*MOM* 22)

This pure borderland, by eliding distinctions, calls into being a freedom of conversation between the two friends akin to the familiar interchange between river and bank: "It was the very spot in which to utter the extremest nonsense, or the profoundest wisdom—or that ethereal product of the mind which partakes of both, and may become one or the other, in correspondence with the faith and insight of the auditor" (24). The place of romance, then, issues in a freedom of mind that answers its atmospheric qualities: the conventional boundaries that confine thought dissolve, and the kind of risky interchange between speaker and listener— where the value of what is said depends on how it is taken in—upon which Hawthorne stakes his art becomes possible.

Hawthorne's romance, then, is a conceptual place, less a "form" than a condition of mind that makes possible the reseeing of experience. Hence Hawthorne's description of the wages of their foray into the heart of romance: "the chief profit of those wild days, to him and me, lay—not in any angular or rounded truth, which we dug out of the shapeless mass of problematical stuff—but in the freedom which we thereby won from all custom and conventionalism and fettering influences of man on man. We were so free to-day, that it was impossible to be slaves again tomorrow" (25). To enter romance's neutral territory, Hawthorne suggests, is to effect a revolution of mind; one emerges with the capacity to overturn customary and conventional ways of seeing. It becomes "impossible to be slaves again tomorrow." It is typical of Hawthorne's understanding of conceptual freedom—which seems to consist in the ability to hold two opposed knowledges nonchalantly in mind at once—that his subversive excursion leads, in the following paragraph, to a tribute to the civilized life. "How sweet," he remarks, "was it to return within the system of human society, not as to a dungeon and a chain, but as to a stately edifice, whence one could go forth at will into statelier simplicity." The Old Manse "had grown sacred, in connection with the artificial life against which we inveighed; it had been a home, for many years, in spite of all; it was my home, too;—and, with these thoughts, it seemed to me that all the artifice and conventionalism of life was but an impalpable thinness upon its surface, and that the depth below was none the worse for it" (25). Under the influence of romance, even the revolutionary impulse can be subverted; the absolute juxtaposition of opposite perspectives can be tolerated. This return to the Old Manse also suggests that romance has its work to do inside the inherited edifice, protecting our depths from the encroachment of an accustomed surface, saving us from the mental rigidity typical of Hawthorne's anxious males. The Old Manse itself must be made—and becomes in the essay—a distinctly domestic outpost of romance.

Later in the essay, Hawthorne entertains in his depiction of the effect of the Old Manse on its guests a comic vision of romance in action. His visitors, he remarks, exhibit a universal tendency to fall asleep; yet he finds their dozing the most "acceptable compliment" to his "abode" and to his own "qualities as a host": "Others could give them pleasure and amusement, or instruction—these could be picked up anywhere—but it was for me to give them rest—rest, in a life of trouble." He argues that, in point of fact, mankind in general, "distracted through a morbid activity" and "tormented" by unreal visions, needs sleep. Such mass repose "is the only method of getting rid of old delusions, and avoiding new ones—of regenerating our race, so that it might in due time awake as an infant out of dewy slumber—of restoring to us the simple perception of what is right, and the single-hearted desire to achieve it" (29–30). The curiously active "rest" offered by romance, like the apocalyptic slumber Hawthorne envisions here, aims at regenerating and revising consciousness. Romance seems to offer not simply speculative latitude but a restored inner vision. For the visitor to the Old Manse, anxious visions assume "their true aspect and character," and the grip of the psyche's customary ambivalence is broken, restoring, for a curative interlude, "simple perception" and "single-hearted desire"—and with them the possibility of self-transformation and moral action.

The territory of romance that Hawthorne calls into being in his fiction and describes most fully in his prefatory writing is "neutral" but not inactive. Hawthorne conceives of romance as the place of mind where boundaries are blurred and the capacity to resee the mind—and by that reseeing to revise it—is recovered. This loosening of rigid habits of thought and feeling is made possible by, and in turn encourages, a corresponding literary strategy, the substitution of an aesthetic of interchange for the customary forms of authority that writers exercise over their willing readers. Such a genre of boundary breaking and interchange is precisely the conception of his work that Hawthorne needs to invent to elude entrapment by his own ambivalence. Romance makes expression possible because it allows Hawthorne to establish his presence not by imposing himself but by a veiling that teases the reader into freedom of mind. We in turn may stop seeing ourselves as guilty or innocent, impotent or all-powerful, fully known or absent, and tell different, more fluid stories about the nature of the psyche. In the story of romance's discovery that the prefaces tell, both author and reader escape from self-enclosure and the compulsions it breeds into a significance not extorted but jointly invented.

Hawthorne conceives of romance as a cure by narrative; the stories he tells are designed to break the fixity of our attempts to establish an authoritative self. An analogy that for me illuminates the curative logic of Hawthorne's conception of romance—and one that is perhaps unsurprising given Hawthorne's interest in revising the mind—is between the "place" of reading that romance establishes and what is said to happen in psychoanalysis. In an essay called "Recollection, Repetition, and Working Through," Freud describes a crucial moment in the development of analytic technique. What Freud discovered was transference, the patient's tendency to reproduce his illness in his relation to the analyst. Such reproduction frees analyst and patient alike from the often impossible burden of recovering a hidden, traumatic past through actual recollection, for the "transference-neurosis" represents the patient's difficulty in a way that makes it accessible to treatment. Instead of remembering what has been repressed, the patient "repeats" it by expressing it in action. This therapeutic technique, Freud notes, is an art of representation: it "constitutes a conjuring into existence of a piece of real life" (162). And the conceptual place established in analysis has a remarkable affinity to the "neutral territory" of Hawthorne's romance:

> The transference thus forms a kind of intermediary realm between illness and real life, through which the journey from the one to the other must be made. The new state of mind has absorbed all the features of the illness; it represents, however, an artificial illness which is at every point accessible to our intervention. It is at the same time a piece of real life, but adapted to our purposes by especially favourable conditions, and it is of a provisional character. From the repetition-reactions which are exhibited in the transference the familiar paths lead back to the awakening of the memories, which yield themselves without difficulty after the resistances have been overcome.

It is the mixed, boundary-breaking nature of these two places of mind— Freud's "intermediary realm," Hawthorne's "neutral territory"—that lends them their power to remove "resistances" and recover the clearer self-perception that moves us toward freedom of mind. In both techniques an interchange between an act of representation and an answering act of interpretation overturns the mind's entrapping conceptions of itself.[7] At the center of Hawthorne's practice, as at the center of Freud's, is an aspiration to cure. And it is finally the invention of romance as a cure for the reader that makes possible its therapeutic effect on Hawthorne himself, for such a conception of his relation to his audience permits Hawthorne to forgive himself his ambitions and find a place and a presence from which to speak.

The story about literary authority that Hawthorne tells in his prefaces seems, in its focus on the worries and longings of the writer, a particularly private and psychological one. But, like the other emotions or trends of mind that we have been encountering in his work—guilt, ambition, anxiety, projection—the emergence from isolation into significance that he dramatizes here carries a cultural force we need to recover. As with his tales of ambition's entrapments, Hawthorne is telling on his own behalf a story that his community has a pressing need to hear, for finding ways to negotiate a newly alienating cultural terrain without losing the self is one of the definitive ideological tasks of middle-class culture in antebellum America. The work of cultural historians helps us recognize the figure of himself that Hawthorne invents here—anxiously guarded, intensely scrupulous, longing for intimacy—as the character called into being by the changing conditions of American social and economic life and by the emphasis on self-scrutiny and moral discipline that came to constitute the characteristic middle class response to these changes. Hawthorne sets out to liberate that figure from an alluring but entrapping privacy by practicing the arts of romance, calling into being a cultural terrain—intimate, restful, clarifying—where anxiety might be penetrated, uncertainty accommodated, and pleasure rescued. We might recognize in his evocations of the "place" of romance an appropriation, expansion, and complication of the conception, canonical to middle-class culture, of the "domestic sphere" as a curative refuge from the pressures of the marketplace. Another way to describe, then, the invention of romance: Hawthorne discovers in his near-isolation from the community the very ground of his significance to it, and he moves, by telling the story of his rescue, from privacy into representativeness, from self-enclosure into engagement, from self-doubt into authority.[8]

PART TWO

The Practice of Romance

Chapter Four

ROMANCE AS REVISION:
THE SCARLET LETTER

IN THE TERRITORY of *The Scarlet Letter* and in the precinct of "The Cus-tom-House" appended to it, things happen at least twice. Most strikingly, the plot of the romance ends by returning Hester and Dimmesdale to the moment of transgression that has generated its action. Attached to this pattern of return is a whole set of recurrences, from the famous trips to the scaffold, to Dimmesdale's pseudoconfessions, to Pearl's persistent questions about the letter, to the ghost stories that link the musings of "The Custom-House." Together, these circlings back make manifest a drama of cultural affiliation; the book's remarkable examination of the psychology of guilt is best understood as an attempt to locate, between the pulses of private feeling, the meaning of living within a community. *The Scarlet Letter* begins the work of romance by raising a question about the career of the self within a culture: is a life the repetitive playing out of the constrained relation between a given inner nature and the struc-ture of the community one inhabits, or is there some room for freedom in our place of mind and in the forms of relation that constitute our social life? Our attempt to understand the particular answer that *The Scarlet Letter* poses to it might start from the shape of the plot: when the originat-ing moment of transgression, itself elided from the book, returns, it re-turns with a difference. Its consequences have been lived out, fully re-vealed, and its meaning for Hester and Dimmesdale and for us as readers will be defined by acts of choice and interpretation rather than the inartic-ulate logic of passion. This essay argues that the working out of this dis-tinction between constraint and choice—and the establishment of a possi-bility I will be calling revision—is at the heart of the book and the essence of Hawthorne's practice of romance.

INTRODUCTORY TO *THE SCARLET LETTER*

I will introduce my account of the kind of attention *The Scarlet Letter* asks of us by turning over once again the question—like the letter itself, worn but still generative—of the way "The Custom-House" is "introduc-tory" to the story proper.[1] My claim is this: "The Custom-House" at once enacts and recommends a particular stance toward the experience of inhabiting a community, a way of thinking that I will be calling "revision-ary." It establishes, that is, the spirit in which the book it introduces should be read. Hawthorne's essay begins with the fact of cultural attach-ment; his reasons for taking the job of Surveyor lie "chiefly" in a "strange, indolent, unjoyous attachment for my native town" (12), a rela-tion not of "love, but instinct" (11). The gap between his actual reasons for taking this post—a desperate need for cash—and the version we en-counter here should remind us that the Hawthorne of "The Custom-House" is himself an invention, and that his creator is introducing us to *The Scarlet Letter* by constructing a story about his affiliation to the com-munity that enfolds him, and by asking whether the joyless and unchosen forms of his attachment might be revised. This interrogation unfolds along two axes: what forms of connection to its past does the community make possible; and what configurations of selfhood does it allow? In each case, a significant, freeing way of living one's cultural attachment must be rescued from the dangers of constriction and enervation that characterize the life of the customhouse. In performing this work of rescue, the tactics of the essay—the acts of mind it performs and invites—are as important as the stories it tells.

"The Custom-House" unfolds as a series of ghost stories, and it is through these recurrent hauntings that our possibilities for significant connection to the past are explored. In the first of these encounters, the character Hawthorne invents for himself meets his Puritan ancestors. His willingness to take upon himself and expiate the "shame" of their perse-cutory excesses—an offer that implies a significant moral connection be-tween generations—yields only inhibition in return, as his ghostly for-bears deliver an authoritative condemnation of story telling as a form of work. Despite this repudiation, Hawthorne persists in claiming that a link to these censorious ancestors remains: "strong traits of their nature have intertwined themselves with mine" (10). One of the central tasks of "The Custom-House" is to work out the form of the writer's engagement in his familial and communal history.

To enter the customhouse proper is to enter the order of life implied by the unchosen form of cultural affiliation—"not love, but instinct"—that attaches Hawthorne to Salem. The aged officers of the customs live out an evacuated selfhood held in place by the pointless repetition of stories and jokes that have been stripped of meaning, denatured to "pass-words and countersigns." This aspect of the customhouse is presided over by the Permanent Inspector, who lives a life of instinctual gratification and for whom memory is reduced to the afterglow of past meals. His one unhap-piness, in a parody of Hawthorne's ancestral haunting, is the memory of a promising-looking goose that proved to be too tough to cut. Like their leader, the aged functionaries have been unable to summon any meaning from the past: they "had gathered nothing worth preservation from their varied experience of life" (16).

The other patriarch of the customhouse is haunted by himself. Within the customhouse's archives of self, the General represents both the achievement of meaningful action and the fear that such a possibility is lost. He lives a rich but incommunicable inner life, full of the memories of a heroic past. His access to the present—and its access to him—is obscured by age's "veil of dim obstruction" (22). For Hawthorne the Surveyor, trying to reconstruct like an archaeologist the structure of his character, General Miller comes to represent, through the legend of his battlefield heroics, the revolutionary generation and the circumstances that so adequately answered their ambitions: he is as out of place among the "inkstands" and other writerly paraphernalia of the customhouse as "an old sword." He thus haunts Hawthorne as well as himself, his inward-turning presence a reminder, along with the essay's parodies of fame and hints of literary oblivion, of the dwindling scope of the present.

These customhouse portraits imply a culture of enervation and a form of affiliation to its history reduced to empty repetition on the one hand and a frustrating sense of loss on the other. But out of these materials the essay composes a different story about our relation to the past, a form of connection not inhibitory, empty, or elegiac but—at least potentially— invigorating. The story of the genesis of *The Scarlet Letter* that Hawthorne tells is in striking ways a revision of the stories of lost connection he has been telling. In a story told under the protection of a liberating "as if," he substitutes his official predecessor, Surveyor Pue, for his skeptical ancestors, and an energizing reconstruction of the past for the repetition and nostalgia we have witnessed.

Hawthorne's discovery of what will become *The Scarlet Letter* begins with the kind of emotional enervation that marked his return to Salem. He glances through the customhouse's detritus of discarded papers "with the saddened, weary, half-reluctant interest which we bestow on the corpse of dead activity" (29) until he locates a different kind of document, not "official" but "of a private nature" (30). This relic of the unofficial activities of his "official ancestor"—his work as a preserver of stories— animates a form of connection between them that evades the intellectual practices and emotional range of the customhouse. As he examines the letter itself, he moves from "accurate measurement," the mode of attention that belongs to the customhouse, to visual inspection and intellectual analysis, and finally to a form of connection that leaves mere "Surveyorship" entirely behind: placing the letter on his breast, he experiences "a sensation, not altogether physical, yet almost so, as of burning heat" (32). Hawthorne is careful to identify this moment of sympathetic exchange, in which the external becomes internal, as the indispensable moment in his account of the origin of his book: "the reader may smile, but must not doubt my word" (32).

This moment of connection not only generates *The Scarlet Letter*, which Hawthorne represents as a completion or filling out—a revision, in effect—of the "outline" he inherits from Surveyor Pue; it produces the appearance of the Surveyor himself. This newest in the essay's series of hauntings works to supply what the essay's previous versions of ancestral connection lacked. In place of the legacy of inhibition offered by his actual ancestors, Surveyor Pue offers through his manuscript a connection to the past that at once originates within the customhouse and offers a way out of its habits of heart and mind—a different cultural location, as it were. And the "I will" with which Hawthorne formally accepts Pue's commission reframes in its form General Miller's legendary act of heroic speech: "I'll try, Sir." Hawthorne's act of revision, then, animates the null relation to history that had belonged to the customhouse, and it covertly attaches the aura of heroic action to story telling.[2]

This sequence of hauntings provides, in several ways, a model for the transformation of a cultural attachment gone wrong. Hawthorne's invention of the story of Surveyor Pue and his literary legacy substitutes for the inhibitory authority of the Puritan forefathers a different kind of connection, a "private" relationship that keeps alive the direct experience of meaning—the heart's heat of the letter—almost lost among the repetitions, erasures, and dead documents that constitute history within the customhouse. Authority, we must notice, is being rewritten rather than erased, for Surveyor Pue makes his own demands upon the fidelity of his legatee: *his* story must be told, he must be credited as the source. More subtly, we might see in the rewriting of this tale of authority an answer to the question with which we began: how have those Puritan ghosts intertwined themselves into our storyteller's nature? Hawthorne's imitation of the General's heroic act of burden bearing—itself a version of his offer to take on his ancestral "shame"—implicitly claims that story telling is not idle but central, performing the crucial work of recovering or rescuing an evanescent meaning. By claiming, though by a liberatingly oblique route, a crucial cultural role for fiction, Hawthorne acknowledges that the ancestral question—"what mode of glorifying God, or being serviceable to mankind in his day and generation" is writing storybooks?—is in fact the right one to ask. Finally, the very method Hawthorne employs in composing the essay, with its movement away from inhibition and enervation by recomposing similar narrative elements, suggests that one's mode of life within a community and a freer form of cultural affiliation will be a reworked, reimagined, "revised" thing—not, *pace* Emerson, an act of untrammeled invention.

The striking and curious thing about this story of liberating revision, though, is that its immediate yield is not freedom but constraint, in the form of a writer's block. This block is dramatically illustrated by still another haunting. In an ironic take on the scene of ancestral repudiation, the characters of his would-be romance refuse animation, rejecting him for the taint of practicality that brought him to the customhouse in the first place: as a mere wage-earner, "the little power you might once have possessed over the tribe of unrealities is gone!" (34). And the essay's famous invocations of the moonlit "neutral territory" of romance, where imagination finds its scope and power, are all written as conditions contrary-to-fact: they record an imaginative reawakening that is *not* happening. Though the writer's relation to the past, and to the figures of authority who preside over it, has been successfully reimagined and reclaimed, the essay clearly has more work to do. Hawthorne thus turns his attention to the present condition of his relation to his community.

The Hawthorne of the essay is haunted by an anxiety about the effect of his sojourn in the customhouse upon his character. He notes, early on, that his imagination has been deadened by his surveyorship, and he wonders whether too much of the customary life might permanently alter his character. He immediately erases his worries with a curious claim of immunity from the influence of external circumstances: it lies entirely "at [his] own option" to recover his past imaginativeness. He accompanies this confident notion with the assertion of a kind of imaginative election: "There was always a prophetic instinct, a low whisper in my ear, that, within no long period, and whenever a new change of custom should be essential to my good, a change would come" (26). Implicit in these assertions is a theory about the nature of selfhood and its interactions with the community that surrounds it. The Surveyor assuages his anxiety about self-loss, that is, with the notion that there exists an inviolable margin of free selfhood, an unencumberable form of property in the self, immune from the effects of living in the customhouse of culture. The saving "change of custom" does indeed come with his dismissal from his post, but not before he suffers, in the shock of the writer's block, the loss of his absolutist fantasy about the inviolability of the private self.

Hawthorne's inability to write wrests from him a more chastened, complex understanding of the relation between self and culture. This revision emerges in a new account of the effects of inhabiting the customhouse: "I had ceased to be a writer of tolerably poor tales and essays, and had become a tolerably good Surveyor of the Customs. That was all. But, nevertheless, it is anything but agreeable to be haunted by a suspicion that one's intellect is dwindling away; or exhaling, without your consciousness, like ether out of a phial; so that at every glance, you find a smaller and less volatile residuum" (38). This enervation of the self, a kind of internalization of the prevailing customhouse atmosphere, is assigned interesting origins. The customhouse officer, as a viewer rather than a maker, "does not share in the united effort of mankind" (38). Hawthorne attributes his loss of self, then, to his sequestration from culturally valuable work—the kind of work that writing, in the Surveyor Pue vignette, had seemed. Moreover, a job in the customhouse places the officer in a dependent relation to the too-paternal government—like his relation to his ancestors, this is another bad authority relationship—and each payment extracts some of the self's "proper strength . . . its sturdy force, its courage and constancy, its truth, its self-reliance, and all that gives emphasis to manly character" (39). And here Hawthorne acknowledges that his previous belief in the easy recoverability of independent selfhood was too optimistic. He admits that a moment of no return will arrive, after which even ejection from office will only produce fantasies of reacquiring it. He finds himself calculating "how much longer I could stay in the Custom-House and yet go forth a man" (39–40).

Hawthorne's dismissal from office of course rescues him from this frightening fate. Once out of office, Surveyor Pue's story at last comes to life. With the resurgence of his imaginative powers, the sojourn in the customhouse becomes a healthy break from the literary life and the unimaginative Surveyor is revealed merely to be Hawthorne's "figurative" self; the writer regains his position as "the real human being," and *The Scarlet Letter* gets written. But a careful reading of the essay will insist that we notice that Hawthorne's rescue is an accident that, in the euphoria of his relief, is being celebrated as if it had been a choice—a choice, he is careful to point out, he would not have made. The ending of "The Custom-House," for all of its comic brio, reminds us of the narrowness of its author's escape and of the necessity of choosing—not merely acceding to—the forms our cultural attachments take. Hawthorne's close call, it seems to me, is acknowledged both in the description he supplies of the experience of writing *The Scarlet Letter*—its somberness is the mark of "the period of hardly accomplished revolution and still seething turmoil, in which the story shaped itself" (43)—which suggests a degree of struggle with his Surveyor-self that belies the serenity of the essay's account of his escape, and in the imagery of decapitation and death that finds its way into his comic ending.

A "real human being," a freeing, imaginative relation to the community and its history, and a valid form of work are all recovered during the course of the essay, but this vindication does not take place because that self was invulnerable to the power of the customary all along. Rather, the essay locates a significant relation to the community in the precarious balancing act I have been calling "revision," in acts of choice that do not leave the community behind but maneuver among its structures: in the way the essay proceeds by writing the inhibition out of the available stories about the past, or the way Hawthorne and Surveyor Pue meet on the ground of sympathetic connection created by the story of the scarlet letter. Hawthorne must indeed get out of the customhouse and its atmosphere of enervation in order to write his romance, but it would be a mistake to conclude that the essay is suggesting that there is an "outside" of cultural affiliation in which the writer and his reader might freely roam. For the story that points the way out of "The Custom-House" is found within it, and Hawthorne aspires to do work that will "share in the united effort of mankind." The essay recommends not romantic escape but a kind of revisionary aplomb; during the course of the essay, writer and reader, as it were, hold the experience of belonging to one's culture up to the light and see the forms of connection and meaning that are possible. Through this joint act of mind—through the acknowledgment that selfhood is not an inviolable essence but a form of relation, that freedom is achieved not by acts of transcendence but by acts of revision—the interesting terrain of choice, located in the interstices of the cultural field, becomes habitable. We become, in a phrase that balances fidelity and freedom, "citizens of somewhere else."

CULTURE AND THE CONDITIONS OF MEANING

I have suggested that *The Scarlet Letter* is engaged in providing a rigorous answer to the authoritative question that Hawthorne's ghostly ancestors asked in "The Custom-House": "A writer of story-books! What kind of a business in life,—what mode of glorifying God, or being serviceable to mankind in this day and generation,—may that be?" (10). Hawthorne answers that question by exploring, in a systematic and specific way, the relation between the shape of the self and the condition of the culture it inhabits. This first sustained romance promises to be "serviceable to mankind" by offering a lucid seeing of the conditions of meaning that attend social life, so that our relation to those conditions might become actively chosen, and so that we might see, in the fullest way, what connects us to the lives of others. While we have valuable accounts of many of the pieces or aspects of the book—the acuity of its analysis of the psyche and of the Puritan community, the social force of its themes, its generic inventiveness, its intellectual rigor—I do not think we have sufficiently seen how these elements together compose an exploration of how a particular culture creates and holds meaning and how the meaning of each private life belongs to that communal act.[3] It is thus worth emphasizing that the book begins by asking us to attend to the way Puritan Boston is organized and to the kinds of behavior and expression it sponsors or provokes. Its opening sequence provides us, that is, with an account of the Puritan community as a field of meaning. And animating Hawthorne's portrayal of this particular community is an overarching proposition about what a community is: not an inert framework but an animate system actively engaged in the generation of meaning.

Hawthorne begins his description of Puritan Boston with a theorem about the construction of communities: "The founders of a new colony, whatever Utopia of human virtue and happiness they might originally project, have invariably recognized it among their earliest practical necessities to allot a portion of the virgin soil as a cemetery and another portion as the site of a prison" (47). Along with its reminder of the nonnegotiable fact of death, this version of the act of establishment implies that the joint action that calls a community into being will inevitably include an act of suppression: that, as the life of a community unfolds, its meaning will in part be established and its boundaries in effect defined by what it chooses to punish. The prison, along with the larger "penal machine" (55) it represents, is thus a form of cultural expression—"the black flower of civilized society" (48)—that will yield to analysis. When Hester and Pearl emerge from the prison door, what we witness is most crucially a drama of cultural definition.

In Hawthorne's representation of Hester's punishment, her transgression is treated less as a genuine threat to the community than as an opportunity for Puritan Boston to define—and thus to fortify—itself. Her transgression thus opens to our view the structure of the community that responds to it and the process that bonds this people to their culture. Hester feels herself, during the course of her punishment, becoming a communal sign: "The unhappy culprit sustained herself as best a woman might, under the heavy weight of a thousand unrelenting eyes, all fastened upon her, and concentred at her bosom" (57). The letter is exposed to the gaze of the townspeople and the discourse of the authorities so as to establish its significance as a cultural boundary; the penal machine is engaged in the work of fixing Hester's new communal meaning. This punitive ceremony, then, strengthens the community by allowing it to proclaim again the kind of community it is. And the Puritan authorities continue to promote this opportunity for communal definition long after the initial ceremony is over, making Hester the text of sermons and the occasion for impromptu street-corner exhortations. Their sentence is thus said to be "undying" and "ever-active" (85). Even for those directly involved in the transgression—and this is a paradox I will be exploring later in the essay—Hester's exposure has the effect of both isolating them from the community and revealing the intensity of their affiliation to it, as though the transgression had itself become the site of a meaning too compelling to leave behind. Thus the one constant in Hester's, Dimmesdale's,

and Chillingworth's reactions to the letter is an odd loyalty to the scene
of their misery.

For all the power of this disciplinary ritual, the meanings it generates
are not univocal. Hawthorne makes it clear in this opening sequence, and
increasingly as the romance unfolds, that Hester's transgression and its
punishment reveal the existence of two crucially different forms of and
potentials for meaning within the community. The first of these ways of
meaning might be said to sponsor the punitive spectacle that I have been
discussing, and Hawthorne's spatial representation of the scene of punishment shows us its structure. Hester's meaning is established and enforced by the authority figures who occupy the meetinghouse balcony
that looms over her position on the scaffold; the townspeople assembled
below her give their assent, as members of this community, to the meaning implicit in her punishment. This version of communal meaning is,
then, hierarchical and protected by a power of enforcement. It establishes
one meaning by suppressing others, as the narrator's comment that a Papist in the audience might have seen Hester as a version of the Madonna
reminds us. To say that this form of meaning is the consequence of an act
of authority is not to claim that it is necessarily illegitimate, tyrannical, or
avoidable; the townspeople clearly share the vision of Hester that the
penal spectacle establishes. Thus many of the voices in the crowd that we
hear replicate—or even exceed—the punitive fervor of the Puritan elders,
and even the generally sympathetic narrator (best understood, here as
throughout Hawthorne's work, as an espouser of various cultural positions rather than a consistent voice) occasionally takes up the condemnatory view.

Even within this authoritative spectacle, though, we hear whispers of
other kinds of voices and notice traces of a differently constituted kind of
meaning. One of the first of these is the soft voice of the youngest of the
women Hawthorne places in the audience. Unlike her more vindictive
companions, who focus their attention on the outward sign and relative
severity of Hester's public punishment, this woman understands Hester's
experience in terms of its internal effect, claiming that Hester has felt each
stitch of the letter's embroidery "in her heart" (54). The act of sympathy
that produces this perspective implies a form of communal connection
that is not authorized from above but conducted on the same cultural
level and generated by an exchange of emotion. As befits its unofficial
status, this kind of meaning manifests itself as a barely articulated undercurrent: in the capacity for sympathy located in the "larger and warmer
heart of the multitude" (64) and absent from the Puritan elders; in the
"one accord of sympathy" (67) created by the latent emotional power of
Dimmesdale's plea that Hester reveal the father; later in the book, in the
acuity that lets the "uninstructed multitude," by virtue of the "intuitions

of its great and warm heart" (127), grasp the perversity of Chillingworth's attachment to Dimmesdale that official Boston cannot see; and,
most significantly, in the kind of response Dimmesdale's preaching awak-
ens, which depends not on the content of the sermons but on his capacity
to speak "the heart's native language" through the tones and rhythms of
his voice. This alternative form of meaning, which possesses significant
cultural power of its own, also emerges in certain "wild" or heterodox
meanings that the text occasionally puts in our way, like the beautiful
rosebush that grows by the prison door, reputedly in the footsteps of the
"sainted"—rambunctious adjective—Anne Hutchinson.

In his representation of the Puritan community as a system of meaning,
Hawthorne is not suggesting a simple opposition between these two
paths toward meaning, though *The Scarlet Letter* sets out to teach the
ways of sympathy and to discipline the authoritarian impulse. Rather,
their interpenetration within the life of this culture suggests that the original imposition of authoritative meaning that founded the community at
the same time gave shape to a striving to express or include what official
culture suppresses or discounts, as though to fill an empty communal
space and answer an ignored human capacity. This, I think, is the implication of one of the curious aftereffects of Hester's punishment, her capacity to sense the presence of "hidden sin" (86) or forbidden desires in
her fellow citizens; she has become attuned to the community of heterodox emotion that shares Boston with its official culture.[4]

A number of propositions crucial to our understanding of the life of a
culture accompany Hawthorne's theory of the "double" nature of communal meaning and emerge from his way of describing Puritan Boston.
Hawthorne's narrator is, in his insistence on cultural comparisons, an
anthropologist before his time. He continually imports into his narrative
the perspectives of different communities: the Papist's view of Hester as
Madonna, the Indians and mariners who observe the election day holiday, the many references to the folk traditions of the "Merrie England"
the Puritans have left behind. Most interesting in its effect is his ongoing
comparison of Puritan Boston to the middle-class culture of his nineteenth-century audience. He observes, for example, the differences between the public boldness, emotional bluntness, and physical vigor of the
Puritan women and the sensitivity and physical delicacy of their nineteenth-century descendants: "every successive mother has transmitted to
her child a fainter bloom, a more delicate and briefer beauty, and a
slighter physical frame" (78). He notices the difference in authority styles,
comparing the Puritan respect for experience and stability to his era's
admiration for the vagaries of "talent" (251). At times he uses a contemporary perspective to criticize the cruelty of Puritan social discipline, as in
his description of the horrible exposure inflicted by the pillory: "There

can be no outrage, methinks, against our common nature . . . more fla-
grant than to forbid the culprit to hide his face for shame" (83). An implicit act of comparison informs his tactics of representing character as
well, for some of these Puritan characters display distinctly nineteenth-
century characteristics. Thus the woman in the crowd able to sympathize
with Hester displays the delicacy of frame and sensibility that Hawthorne
has connected to his own era (she confirms her cultural advancement by
dying during the course of the book). Dimmesdale especially betrays
striking signs of nineteenth-century sentimentality (along with the requi-
site physical frailty), responding to Hester's refusal to name the father in
the canonical vocabulary of middle-class America's celebration of female
heroism: "Wondrous strength and generosity of a woman's Heart!"
(95).[5]

Taken together, the effects of this ongoing comparison between the
Puritan community and other cultural arrangements, especially those of
his own middle-class America, are complex and crucial to an understanding of what Hawthorne is up to in *The Scarlet Letter*. As the fair distribu-
tion of both appealing and unappealing characteristics indicates, the
book carries no brief for either the sixteenth century or the nineteenth.
Yet its perspective on cultural differences is not simply neutral or relativ-
istic. Any set of cultural arrangements will confer genuine gains and
losses, will sponsor or suppress different forms of pleasure, kindness, and
cruelty. The narrator thus admires the high seriousness of Puritan social
discipline *and* prefers the respect for private emotion accorded by the
middle-class notion of privacy; the complacent association of "progress"
with the present day is undermined by the evidence of declining energy
that suggests that our current enlightenment enforces its own hidden suppressions. These versions of cultural comparison finally produce in the
reader the sense that a culture is a structure of meaning that is not "natural" or automatic but locally variable, historically changing, and thus
both inescapable (one is always in relation to one's cultural system) and
humanly revisable—as the changing meaning of Hester's letter within the
Puritan community makes clear. And the final reverberation of Hawthorne's cultural portraiture is this: the nineteenth-century middle-class
culture that he writes from and to, and makes a presence within the book,
is also revisable and always also the subject of *The Scarlet Letter*.

The presence of identifiable nineteenth-century traits in these Puritan
characters, in addition to inducing readerly acts of cultural comparison,
suggests that character, at any given moment within the history of a community, will be in flux—that there will be a variety of places for people to
occupy within a particular cultural field. This range of responses or play
of structures of selfhood lets us identify another important aspect of
Hawthorne's account of the conditions of communal meaning: character

is portrayed throughout the book not as an independent "nature" or free-standing psychology but as a changeable form of relation to the community. In effect, character is another form of meaning within a community, a specific way of negotiating the cultural terrain. I will have much more to say about the specific working out of this relation in the cases of the book's main characters, but I want to observe here the consistent pattern of Hawthorne's representation of the self. A character's inner life begins with a given set of capacities—Hester's "rich, voluptuous, Oriental characteristic" (108); Dimmesdale's hunger for an authoritative creed; Chillingworth's analytic predilections—but this "nature" unfolds in response to the ideological structures and forms of expression available within the community one inhabits. This conception of selfhood as a relationship between a complex psyche and a complex culture implies neither determinism nor a transcendent personal freedom but a much more complicated transaction, in which both choice and limitation are real. One may choose one's forms and gestures of affiliation, be they pious or rebellious, but those gestures will always be given by, and will always mean within, the community's structure of meaning.

It is in Hawthorne's depiction of Pearl that this view of character as a form of meaning within a community is most evident, precisely because Pearl's link to her community is so loosely established. Her nature is said to lack "reference and adaptation to the world into which she was born" (114), like a sign unplaced within a language. The focus of her young life becomes precisely to determine the conditions of meaning in her immediate world. Her "hostile," embattled mode of play at once imitates the exclusionary behavior of the Puritan children she encounters, who play at "scourging Quakers" and "taking scalps" (117), and contains an account of the structure of the community that excludes her: she imagines the pine trees to be "Puritan elders" and "the ugliest weeds of the garden were their children, whom Pearl smote down and uprooted, most unmercifully" (118–19). Her fascination with Hester's letter and its origin and meaning is most deeply a question about herself, an attempt to locate the elements and fellow inhabitants ("Why does the minister hold his hand over his heart?") of a meaning system that might include her. For all her capriciousness and hostility to authority, Pearl is not a wild child; she is seeking, throughout the book, to find a way of meaning that can make sense of her experience.

One can see the various elements of Hawthorne's attention to the community's ways of meaning at work in the "The Governor's Hall" episode, where Hester fights to retain custody of Pearl. Hawthorne's depiction of the Governor's stately house makes it clear that Hester has entered the world according to authority. She is greeted by an indentured servant, a man, as the narrator reminds us, converted by decree into a piece of property, "as much a commodity of bargain and sale as an ox, or a joint-stool" (126). The most notable feature of the Governor's decor is the gallery of ancestral portraits that line the entrance hall. This display of ghostly "sternness and severity" produces an inhibitory effect reminiscent of Hawthorne's encounter with his own ancestral enforcers in "The Custom-House": Bellingham's forbears seem to gaze "with harsh and intolerant criticism at the pursuits and enjoyments of living men" (128). The most striking illustration of Hester's entry into the precincts of the authoritative and of the power of a culture's way of seeing to give its own twist to the local air is her reflection in the convex breastplate of the Governor's armor. She appears there exactly as she looks from the official point of view: all letter, as though her very shape had conformed to her new cultural function.[6] Hester receives a confirmation of the power of ideology to define the real when she encounters the Governor himself. As John Wilson jokes about the scarlet-clad Pearl's membership in the clan of elves and fairies they left behind in England, the Governor's magisterial interpretive grid descends, censoring Wilson's playfulness, erasing the culture of holiday he refers to, and producing his own reading of Pearl's significance: "Nay, we might have judged that such a child's mother must needs be a scarlet woman and a worthy type of her of Babylon!" (133).

In giving us this dispute over who might best take charge of Pearl's "Christian nurture," Hawthorne is placing us in the most revealing cultural territory, for it is through its way of nurturing and disciplining its children that a community works to preserve and replicate itself. We see the power of the Puritan cultural program in the comical but pointed glimpses we are given of their children at their peculiarly somber and exclusionary play. It is their interest in cultural replication that gives the matter of Pearl's upbringing such weightiness for those "of authority and influence" (133) in this newly founded and still-vulnerable community. And a sense of cultural mission motivates the Governor's authoritative question to Hester—"Were it not, thinkest thou, for thy little one's temporal and eternal welfare, that she be taken out of thy charge, and clad soberly, and disciplined strictly, and instructed in the truths of heaven and earth?" (133). What we witness is an encounter between the community's two ways of meaning, a battle, as befits Hawthorne's vision of a culture as a system of meaning, over how to interpret Pearl.

Hester's answer to the Governor speaks a truth out of Boston's other cultural dispensation, the community of meaning constituted by interchange rather than authority. She makes the extraordinary claim that her right to her child inheres in the very experience of wearing the letter: "See ye not, she is the scarlet letter, only capable of being loved, and so endowed with a million-fold the power of retribution for my sin?" (135). Hester's plea depends for its force on the logic of emotional exchange that

I have been describing. It is Pearl's capacity to receive love—to be more than the culturally inflected sign of sin that she is for the elders—that guarantees Hester's fidelity, in raising the child, to the ethical vision her adultery has violated. Hester's remark, cryptic though it is, suggests that she confronts in her daughter's wildness and alienation, at every moment, the costs of her transgression; and she measures, in her hopes for Pearl, the value of the human connection that she, through her sin, has forfeited. Hence Hester's feeling that Pearl is the only thing "keep[ing] her heart alive" (135).

It is a sign of the gap between Hester's way of meaning and that of the Governor and the Reverend Wilson that they find her statement utterly incomprehensible. We get an illustration of the real—rather than the official—importance of Dimmesdale to this community when Hester turns to him to plead her case on the grounds that he has "sympathies which these men lack" (136)—that he has access, that is, to the world of meaning from which she speaks. The argument that Dimmesdale mounts on her behalf is a remarkable piece of cultural mediation. He translates Hester's language of the "heart" into the vocabulary of authority: by presenting Pearl not as a sign of forbidden passion but as an expression of the divine intention, he recasts Hester's bid for emotional survival into a struggle to save her own soul. Dimmesdale thus accommodates Hester's need to the theocratic way of seeing, and he does so without simply violating or erasing her meaning.[7] Dimmesdale's successful mediation should be seen as a moment of cultural enlargement and strengthening, in which the authoritative vision that governs the community expands to include a difficult emotional truth. Wilson and Bellingham are not duped by Dimmesdale's plea, but given a way to discover and express their own capacity for sympathy. This moment looks forward to the community's awed and generous response to the tableau of suffering that closes the book, and it lets us see the complexity of the relationships and meanings that constitute, for Hawthorne, the life of a culture.

CHARACTER AND CULTURAL AFFILIATION

Hawthorne's representation of character in *The Scarlet Letter* should be understood not simply as psychological exploration but as an interrogation of the form taken by one's affiliation to a particular community: character is the subtlest and most complicated expression of the meaning that a culture makes. In portraying the different ways that Hester Prynne and Arthur Dimmesdale respond to their transgression, Hawthorne distinguishes between two structures of mind. Against Hester's persistent rebelliousness, speculative freedom, and capacity to love, he poses Dimmesdale's inner drama of self-entrapment: his compulsive acts of penance, his increasing passivity, his encompassing narcissism. These two psychologies simultaneously represent two forms of relation to the communal structure of Puritan Boston, for Hester's externally imposed punishment at last confers an inner freedom that makes her a profound critic of the community she inhabits, while Dimmesdale's guilt confines him ever more stringently to the authoritarian vision of the Puritan theocracy. *The Scarlet Letter*, then, is the history of two strategies available to consciousness in response to the guilt that expresses its affiliation to the community it inhabits: Hester's subversion of conscience, and Dimmesdale's entrapment by it—even his embracing of it.

In a beautiful sentence from the essay "On Narcissism," Freud writes, "A strong egoism is a protection against disease, but in the last resort we must begin to love in order that we may not fall ill, and must fall ill if, in consequence of frustration, we cannot love." I will be arguing that Hawthorne, as an analyst of emotion, represents the self-punishment that constitutes Dimmesdale's illness as bound up with "a strong egoism" and as marking out the path taken by the avoidance of love. In this sense, Dimmesdale is not only the inheritor of the overactive conscience that punishes Reuben Bourne, but the offspring of Hawthorne's egoistic male protagonists, for whom ambition is always a flight from love. We need also to see Dimmesdale's "illness"—the guilt-driven punitive spectacle that constitutes his inner life—as Hawthorne's examination of a particular cultural formation: through the Puritan conscience that is his ostensible subject, he explores the authority-ridden private sensibility that is the "black flower" of middle-class character formation.

To understand the complicated operation of guilt in Dimmesdale's psyche is to understand why he fails to confess his sin, and an answer to this question must begin with the illuminating reading of Dimmesdale proposed by Frederick Crews. Crews suggests that Dimmesdale nurtures his guilt because it offers him, by a devious psychic path, a way of gratifying the persistent libidinal impulse that generated the original act of adultery. "The original sexual desire has been granted recognition *on the condition of being punished*, and the punishment itself is a form of gratification"—hence the masochistic rituals that characterize his delusive attempts at penance.[8] What I wish to suggest is not exactly a refutation of this view, but a change in emphasis that seems to me significant. In Hawthorne's portrayal of Dimmesdale, it is clearly the elaborate process of concealment itself that transforms an understandable sense of guilt into a disease. The choice of concealment is determined by—and, in turn, fosters—the inward turning that shapes Dimmesdale's personality, and by the patterns of mind that have been established by his affiliation to the community that enfolds him. Certainly there is an odd gratification involved in Dimmesdale's attachment to his guilt, but it is a gratification even more devious and interesting than Crews's discussion implies.

I will begin my description of the path that guilt takes within Dimmesdale's mazy psyche with a detour through Freud's depiction of the relation between guilt and narcissistic gratification in the essay "On Narcissism." Let me first define the status of this Freudian model in my discussion. I do not mean to suggest that Hawthorne is right about the mind insofar as his account of conscience conforms to Freud's. I want rather to use Freud's essay heuristically, for Hawthorne's psychological portrait of Dimmesdale is so compressed and complicated that we need another lucid and complex narrative of mind to help us see what Hawthorne is up to. Repression in Freud's account begins with the establishment of an ego-ideal within the self. Originating in the image of his parents the child internalizes, and in the version of behavior enforced by parental criticism and endorsed by the cultural influences that surround him, the ego-ideal is that perfect self one learns to wish to be. This ideal version of self thus establishes an internal standard by which the actual ego is measured; when the ego generates an impulse that conflicts with this ideal, an attempt at its suppression ensues. "To this ideal ego," Freud writes, "is now directed the self-love which the real ego enjoyed in childhood"; by its capture of this "lost narcissism of childhood" the ego-ideal achieves extraordinary psychic power. The mental agency that performs the task of scrutinizing the actual self and measuring it against the ego-ideal is conscience. The purpose of conscience and of the guilt that enforces its dictates, then, is essentially a self-regarding one: to see "that narcissistic gratification is secured from the ego-ideal." According to the curious psychic economy that Freud identifies, the narcissistic psyche accepts the discomfort of the ego caused by guilt in order to claim the presumably more powerful gratification delivered by the fulfillment of the ego-ideal.

Freud goes on to picture the role that this conscientious self-seeking plays in the fate of love. When the ego looks for love where the ego-ideal fears to tread, a repression of the erotic impulse takes place. The loss of libidinal energy attached to this impulse, which is denied the satisfaction offered by requited love, depletes the ego's store of self-regard. The solution sought by the psyche, Freud speculates, is "the return of the libido from the object to the ego and its transformation into narcissism," which "represents, as it were, the restoration of a happy love"—since, one assumes, the ego-ideal does not play hard-to-get. Freud implies that not only does conscience function to protect narcissistic gratification by prohibiting certain impulses it deems unsavory, but the acts of suppression it enforces work to redirect libidinal energy, strengthening the ego-ideal by encouraging the mind to direct its supply of love toward its inward, idealized image of self. And, finally, by strengthening the ego-ideal, conscience in turn increases its own force and severity; the wages of guilt is guilt.[9] When we add to this depiction of conscience Freud's later observation—

which is part of Hawthorne's theory of the mind as well, as we saw in "Roger Malvin's Burial"—that conscience has access to, and punishes, unconscious and conscious impulses alike, we are ready to consider the case of Arthur Dimmesdale.

What is the course taken by Dimmesdale's capacity to love? What affinities exist between the emotions and practices that guilt produces in him and Freud's depiction of the narcissistic conscience? In the chapter entitled "The Interior of a Heart," Hawthorne provides his classic description of the strategies characteristic of a mind entrapped by guilt. Dimmesdale, moved by a recurring desire to confess his guilt to his adoring congregation, addresses them with self-vilifications that so ambiguously skirt his actual sin that they only increase his reputation for piety. Hawthorne writes that

> The minister well knew—subtle, but remorseful hypocrite that he was!—the light in which his vague confession would be viewed. He had striven to put a cheat upon himself by making the avowal of a guilty conscience, but had gained only one other sin, and a self-acknowledged shame, without the momentary relief of being self-deceived. He had spoken the very truth, and transformed it into the veriest falsehood. And yet, by the constitution of his nature, he loved the truth, and loathed the lie, as few men ever did. Therefore, above all things else, he loathed his miserable self! (144)

This passage is remarkable not only for its picture of the psychic house divided, but for the fluid mixture of levels of awareness and sources of motivation that expresses such an inner division. While part of Dimmesdale is moved to perform these gestures of penitence, another aspect of self remains fully aware of their emptiness and inadequacy. The self helplessly seeks to deceive a conscience that has, of necessity, been in on the deception from the start. It is as though conscience induces these impotent attempts at penitence in order to ensure the guiltiness of the self by increasing it. The mechanism of conscience seems, paradoxically, to have the effect of foiling the very confessional impulse it would be expected to encourage; something within Dimmesdale prefers the self-loathing that results from this pattern of behavior to the release from it that confession would provide.

But what, in Hawthorne's vision of mind, might motivate so destructive a preference? Part of the answer is suggested in the description of Dimmesdale's penitential rituals that follows the passage just cited:

> In Mr. Dimmesdale's secret closet, under lock and key, there was a bloody scourge. Oftentimes, this Protestant and Puritan divine had plied it on his own shoulders; laughing bitterly at himself the while, and smiting so much the more pitilessly, because of that bitter laugh.... He kept vigils, likewise,

night after night, sometimes in utter darkness; sometimes with a glimmering lamp; and sometimes, viewing his own face in a looking-glass, by the most powerful light which he could throw upon it. He thus typified the constant introspection wherewith he tortured, but could not purify, himself. (144–45)

We begin to understand the principle governing the division of self that Dimmesdale enacts in his rites of penance. In analogy to the deflection of self-love from the unworthy actual ego to the ego-ideal, Dimmesdale, as a defense against his guilt, has come to identify most powerfully not with his actual but with his desired self, not with the man who sinned but with the figure of authority who repudiates that sin. Like a child playing at being a harsh parent, the minister becomes, in imagination, the punisher rather than the punished.[10] Yet the fantasy is only an incomplete success, for part of Dimmesdale recognizes that victim he must remain—hence the bitter laughter he directs at his own penitential vignette. But in a frightening doubling of the inner conflict that tortures him, a still stricter version of the superego punishes even this dark levity, "smiting so much the more pitilessly"; the vision suggested is one of endless entrapment by an infinitely ramifying cycle of guilt and punishment. For Dimmesdale, as for the narcissistic psyche that Freud depicts, the need to fulfill the ego-ideal—to protect his position of authority, within the psyche as well as in the community—outweighs the freeing resolution that confession would make possible. Hawthorne's portrait of Dimmesdale gazing in the mirror at his guilty self not only emphasizes his identification with the forces of conscience within him, but establishes in its evocation of Narcissus the relation between self-punishment and self-gratification for which I have been arguing. And, in a noteworthy meditation on the penitential action he depicts, Hawthorne connects the minister's guilt-induced introspection to the intellectual manifestation of narcissism—the emptying out of external reality: "It is the unspeakable misery of a life so false as his, that it steals the pith and substance out of whatever realities there are around us. . . . To the untrue man, the whole universe is false,—it is impalpable,—it shrinks to nothing within his grasp. And he himself, in so far as he shows himself in a false light, becomes a shadow, or, indeed, ceases to exist" (145–46).

In the representation of moral psychology that Hawthorne offers here, conscience has become crucially misdirected. It prefers the continual punishment of the self to the route of penitence and forgiveness that would free the self from guilt. The diseased conscience has every interest in ensuring the minister's act of concealment, because that concealment, along with the doomed acts of half-repentance that conscience itself induces, is the continual sin that calls into being continual punishment. The narcissistic conscience, then, is not simply an agency of judgment within the self, but an appetite for punishment, and it is the intensity of Dimmesdale's identification with this inner tyrant that confines him to his penitential theater.

Still, the narcissistic gratification that the self finds in its identification with the punishing superego is only part of the explanation of Dimmesdale's refusal to disburden himself by confessing. The simplest way to account for his persistence in this painful concealment is to maintain that the minister suffers from an ethical lapse, a failure of moral courage. But I hope that the preceding discussion at least suggests that Hawthorne's presentation of the effect of guilt upon consciousness is too complex, and too infiltrated by suggestions of compulsion, to leave us contented by so unnuanced a notion. While it is certainly true that Dimmesdale is irritatingly passive, his lack of courage is determined not only by the power of conscience but by a fear of public exposure that marks the minister's affiliation to his culture. The existence of this kind of fear in Dimmesdale can be inferred from the fantasy that he composes as a defense against it. In disputing with Chillingworth on the benefits of immediate confession to the guilty soul, the frail divine offers this version of the day of judgment:

> There can be, if I forbode aright, no power, short of divine mercy, to disclose, whether by uttered words, or by type or emblem, the secrets that may be buried with a human heart. The heart, making itself guilty of such secrets, must perforce hold them, until the day when all hidden things shall be revealed. Nor have I so read or interpreted Holy Writ, as to understand that the disclosure of human thoughts and deeds, then to be made, is intended as a part of the retribution. That, surely, were a shallow view of it. No; these revelations, unless I greatly err, are meant merely to promote the intellectual satisfaction of all intelligent beings, who will stand waiting, on that day, to see the dark problem of this life made plain. A knowledge of men's hearts will be needful to the completest solution of that problem. And I conceive, moreover, that the hearts holding such miserable secrets as you speak of will yield them up, at that last day, not with reluctance, but with a joy unutterable. (132)

Improvising doctrine like a sectarian, Dimmesdale not only assumes the necessity of secrecy among the guilty, but imagines an utterly safe context for the exposure of shameful truths—a kind of retributionless seminar on the divine plan, in which one's guilty discourse is accompanied not by the shocked speech of others but by "joy unutterable."

The peculiar intensity of this fear and its dominion over the realm of the minister's emotions are suggested by the language of his response to Hester's revelation of Chillingworth's identity: "O Hester Prynne, thou little, little knowest all the horror of this thing! And the shame!—the indelicacy!—the horrible ugliness of this exposure of a sick and guilty heart to the very eye that would gloat over it!" (194). Notice the morbid emphasis on the act of looking that exposes him, conveyed in the reduction of Chillingworth to the gloating "eye," as well as the sexually tinged self-disgust implicit in the minister's hysterical modesty: the "indelicacy," the "horrible ugliness" of such exposure. There is more to this fear of exposure than a sense of the dangerous consequences of his guilt; in its curious intensity, Dimmesdale's anxiety reflects both the manifold disturbances of an ingrown psyche and the extraordinary power, within the minister's mind, of the idea of privacy. Moreover, the passage reveals that Dimmesdale's morality is entirely socially mediated: he thinks automatically and completely of the public effect of his exposure. Yet for all his attempts to keep his privacy inviolate, this self-absorbed minister in effect has no private self; his mind is utterly infiltrated by the presence of the community, as though there were a homology between the shape of his psyche and the authority structure of the town.

Hawthorne appropriately turns, in examining Dimmesdale's powerful fear of exposure before others, from the case history of "The Interior of a Heart" to a more dramatic narrative procedure. For the interaction between Dimmesdale and Chillingworth reveals the relation between the inner world of the conscience-ridden minister and the moral atmosphere of a community in which moral scrutiny has turned into a kind of guilt seeking. To a reader meditating upon the nature of conscience in *The Scarlet Letter*, Chillingworth begins to look like an embodiment, or projection, of the minister's diseased superego. Their relationship is the outward form of the guilty introspection whose inward character we have witnessed. Chillingworth begins his examination of the minister, he conceives, "with the equal integrity of a judge, desirous only of truth." The spirit of dispassionate investigation, however, soon gives way to compulsion, as "a kind of fierce . . . necessity seized the old man" (129). The physician moves from the passive, absolute judgment that would presumably characterize an ideal conscience to a variety of sadism: "He became, thenceforth, not a spectator only, but a chief actor, in the poor minister's interior world. He could play upon him as he chose. . . . As at the waving of a magician's wand, uprose a grisly phantom,—uprose a thousand phantoms,—in many shapes, of death, or more awful shame, all flocking roundabout the clergyman, and pointing with their fingers at his breast!" (140). Chillingworth's transformation from observer to punishing agent parallels Hawthorne's depiction of the authoritarian conscience, which in Dimmesdale and Reuben Bourne becomes not umpire but actor within the self. And the partnership of Chillingworth and the superego is implicit in Hester's observation that by means of Chillingworth's ministrations the minister's "conscience had been kept in an irritated state, the tendency of which was, not to cure by wholesome pain, but to disorganize and corrupt his spiritual being" (193).[11]

We need to move beyond Chillingworth's consciencelike function to consider the emotional quality of his attentions to Dimmesdale. Two descriptions of the physician's influence upon the minister—one the narrator's, one belonging to Chillingworth himself—are particularly striking.

> A man burdened with a secret should especially avoid the intimacy of his physician. If the latter possess native sagacity, and a nameless something more,—let us call it intuition; if he show no intrusive egotism, nor disagreeably prominent characteristics of his own; if he have the power, which must be born with him, to bring his mind into such affinity with his patient's, that this last shall unawares have spoken what he imagines himself only to have thought; if such revelations be received without tumult, and acknowledged not so often by an uttered sympathy, as by silence, an inarticulate breath, and here and there a word, to indicate that all is understood; if, to these qualifications of a confidant be joined the advantages afforded by his recognized character as a physician;—then, at some inevitable moment, will the soul of the sufferer be dissolved, and flow forth in a dark, but transparent stream, bringing all its mysteries into the daylight. (124)

I have quoted this passage at length because in it Hawthorne builds up a sexual rhythm—the periodic sentence with a vengeance—that is confirmed by the imagery of male orgasm in the closing lines. Chillingworth's penetration of Dimmesdale's psyche is imaged, then, as an act of sexual violation. Join to this passage the physician's description to Hester of the suffering he has caused his victim: "Never did mortal suffer what this man has suffered. And all, all, in the sight of his worst enemy! . . . He knew, by some spiritual sense,—for the Creator never made another being so sensitive as this,—he knew that no friendly hand was pulling at his heart-strings, and that an eye was looking curiously into him, which sought only evil, and found it. But he knew not that the eye and hand were mine!" (171). Chillingworth, like Dimmesdale, describes his power as one of the eye; he conceives of the minister's torment as an act of voyeurism and mastery. On the one hand, Hawthorne's evocation of the sexual content of Chillingworth's vengeful obsession, which suggests the vicissitudes undergone by the frustrated sexuality of the aging cuckold, is a remarkable piece of psychological analysis. Together Dimmesdale and Chillingworth constitute a kind of ingrown erotic system. The linked emotions that dominate this pair—voyeurism and morbid fear of exposure, sadism and masochism—are those described by Freud as "dependent on the narcissistic organization of the ego," and the turning round of forbidden libidinal impulses upon the self.[12] On the other hand, Hawthorne's analysis of this curiously eroticized punitive relationship reaches outward, suggesting how easily a community's forms of moral discipline become tinged by private fantasy and twist human connection. And this portrayal of the bond between the two men must have had a chill for his first readers that we might miss. He draws his language from the rhetoric that customarily celebrates the sacredness of human attachment in antebellum writing: "intimacy," a "sympathy" beyond the capacity of words, the "confidence" that makes self-revelation possible. Chillingworth and Dimmesdale thus ferociously parody an ideal at the center of middle-class culture's picture of itself: the intimate connection that was at once a refuge from the marketplace world and a sign of one's sensitivity to values beyond that world's ken.[13]

This link between psychological portraiture and cultural analysis is carried further in Hawthorne's account of Dimmesdale's relation to Puritan Boston. By both temperament and position, Dimmesdale, Hawthorne tells us, is uniquely susceptible to the internalization of communal structures of mind. He possesses an "order of mind that impelled itself powerfully along the path of a creed" and needs "to feel the pressure of a faith about him, supporting, while it confined him within its iron framework" (123). Moreover, "the minister . . . had never gone through an experience calculated to lead him beyond the scope of generally received laws. . . . At the head of the social system . . . he was only the more trammelled by its regulations, its principles, and even its prejudices" (200). These passages reflect what for Hawthorne is a central fact of our social life: every mind is susceptible to infiltration by the institutional forms of the cultural landscape that surrounds it. It is the peculiar tendency of Hawthorne's version of Puritan society to induce the combination of severity of conscience and self-absorption that we find in Dimmesdale, for it is at once a community ruled by the scrutiny of strict father figures and a community created out of the sense of its own inner superiority, its election. Hence the high volume of the voice of conscience, and the intense fear of the exposure of one's moral failures.

Hawthorne's sense of the mind's internalization of its culture's moral assumptions helps us read this intriguingly elusive allegorization of the working of Dimmesdale's conscience during the midnight vigil on the scaffold.

> No eye could see him, save that ever wakeful one which had seen him in his closet, wielding the bloody scourge. Why, then, had he come hither? Was it but the mockery of penitence? A mockery, indeed, but in which his soul trifled with itself! A mockery at which angels blushed and wept, while fiends rejoiced, with jeering laughter! He had been driven hither by the impulse of that Remorse which dogged him everywhere, and whose own sister and closely linked companion was that Cowardice which invariably drew him back, with her tremulous gripe, just when the other impulse had hurried him

to the verge of a disclosure. Poor miserable man! What right had infirmity like his to burden itself with crime? Crime is for the iron-nerved, who have their choice either to endure it, or, if it press too hard, to exert their fierce and savage strength for a good purpose, and fling it off at once! This feeble and most sensitive of spirits could do neither, yet continually did one thing or another, which intertwined, in the same inextricable knot, the agony of heaven-defying guilt and vain repentance. (148)

This passage invokes, in its overwrought psychomachia and its old fashioned personification of Remorse and Cowardice, a kind of superconventional sentimental psychology that, were it to be accepted uncuriously, might seem to refute the kind of moral complexity for which I have been arguing in Hawthorne's work. But let us look closely at the process of mind this allegory implies. First, the "ever wakeful" eye that observes this action reminds us that the vigil should be placed among the other theatrical acts of penance that conscience sponsors. We notice that the minister has been "driven hither" by Remorse; we do not witness, as it might at first appear, a familiar allegory of free moral choice but rather a fruitless struggle performed in obedience to the laws of compulsion. I find the relationship between Remorse and Cowardice, which would conventionally seem to be morally opposite psychological impulses, particularly curious. They are "sisters" and "closely linked companions," which implies that they together form a single structure of mind, which induces the very pattern of doomed penance and augmented guilt we noticed earlier. The "sisterhood" of Remorse and Cowardice seems to me to figure forth what for Hawthorne was a danger of the communal determination of moral vision. To submit passively, as Dimmesdale does, to the moral system enforced by the community is to transform remorse from a valid ethical emotion into a kind of cowardice—the mere sign of one's submission to authority.

Even more interesting is the sentence that suggests that "crime is for the iron-nerved." "Crime" here does not appear to denote a guilty action, but is rather something to be "endured" or "flung off" by an act of psychic strength. By "crime" Hawthorne seems to mean something like "a cultural definition of crime," which one can either accept and endure, or rebelliously fling off by denying its validity entirely. Dimmesdale, precisely because of the degree to which his mind has assumed the shape supplied by the Puritan community, is able neither to endure the consequences of confessing his sin nor to repudiate the sinfulness of his act by inventing a new significance for it. The courage Hawthorne attributes to the "iron-nerved" is the courage either fully to understand the meaning of their affiliation to their community, or to resist the community's definitions of transgression altogether. This passage is, moreover, an excellent example of the way Hawthorne characteristically correlates his tactics of narration with his thematic concerns. He uses a patently inherited, conventionalized language to expose and attack the socialization of mind that produces such conventions. This narrative strategy produces an unmooring of authorized moral categories, thus making possible the lucid interrogation of customary ethical thinking. The passage, in a most subtle way, commits the crime that it describes: it flings off a communal habit of mind, making possible the reexamination of the culturally authoritative, whether in Puritan Boston or antebellum America.

In his depiction of the entrapped mind of Arthur Dimmesdale, then, Hawthorne develops one account of the psychology of guilt, one version of cultural affiliation. The authoritarian conscience can be traced to a complex moment in the history of the individual consciousness, the hidden moment when the self chooses between two possible ways of loving—between engagement in the world and narcissism's creation of a more compelling world within. Love's inward turning institutes a tyranny of conscience, in which the self directs its capacity to love toward the fulfillment of its own inner ambitions. The severity of conscience becomes a source of gratification, the diseased extremity of self-love. Superimposed upon this choice of a way to love is another moment of decision, one that determines the degree to which the mind accedes to the forms of temperament that the community encourages and the moral categories that it establishes. Hawthorne's psychology posits a kind of interchange between the mind and the culture that surrounds it; in Dimmesdale's case there is no play, no room for freedom, in this relation, for the minister's psyche simply mirrors the authority structure of the community. His conscientiousness has been reduced to an authoritarian, self-sustaining system of compulsion. Thus for Dimmesdale the moments in the history of the psyche I have been calling "decisions" have been stripped of their quality of chosenness, and have come to look like dark necessities that govern the mind.

Against this knowledge of conscience's compulsive power, Hawthorne deploys an analytic intensity and a narrative strategy calculated to recover for these psychic choices precisely that quality of chosenness that compulsion steals from them. In exposing for his reader the tyranny of conscience and the logic of cultural affiliation, Hawthorne seeks to invent a chance for us to resee the self, to understand the meaning of our relation to our community, and to reclaim our way of loving. Yet he attempts this curative project by insisting that we see, as fully as possible, the power that our conditions of mind and culture array against such choice.

It is through his portrayal of Hester that Hawthorne considers the lineaments of a freer relation to the community than Dimmesdale can compass. The very publicity of her punishment—the community's interest in her solely as a sign of its coherent moral vision—seems, paradoxically, to have left Hester with a roomier, less trammeled inner life. Thus the language of ethical choice, which Dimmesdale's authority-seeking moral psychology empties of meaning, retains, though in a complicated way, its significance when applied to Hester. What elements of character and strategies of mind protect Hester from surrender to the guilt that expresses her affiliation to her culture? In Hawthorne's depiction of Hester, as in his account of Dimmesdale, the power of guilt is measured against the capacity to love. In Dimmesdale, love is deflected to the service of conscience; in Hester's case, the force of conscience is subverted by the persistence of love.

Let me begin with the processes of mind that Hawthorne associates with Hester's decision to remain, at so extreme a cost in suffering, in Boston. In "Hester at her Needle," Hawthorne offers a double explanation of Hester's "marvellous" choice.

> But there is a fatality, a feeling so irresistible and inevitable that it has the force of doom, which almost invariably compels human beings to linger around and haunt, ghost-like, the spot where some great and marked event has given the color to their lifetime; and still the more irresistibly, the darker the tinge that saddens it. Her sin, her ignominy, were the roots which she had struck into the soil. It was as if a new birth, with stronger assimilations than the first, had converted the forest-land, still so uncongenial to every other pilgrim and wanderer, into Hester Prynne's wild and dreary, but life-long home . . . . The Chain that bound her here was of iron links, and galling to her inmost soul, but never could be broken. (80)

The "fatality" that links Hester to the place of her sin seems to have the quality of fixation characteristic of the guilty mind; think of the scene of death in "Roger Malvin's Burial," or Dimmesdale's returns to the scaffold. But what distances Hester's emotion from Dimmesdale's is its curiously private quality. While for all his introspection Dimmesdale's psyche mirrors the public life of the community, Hawthorne represents Hester's sense of guilt not as an act of obedience to a culturally established ideal but as an act of fidelity to her personal history. Agency is not assigned to the conscience that compels but to the self that has acted, that "strikes" its roots into the soil by means of its sin. The metaphor of a "new birth" that Hawthorne chooses to describe Hester's transformed connection to the community implies that she has made her guilt into her identity—but not in the way the Puritan fathers intended when they sentenced her to wear the A. For Hester's new birth, with its "stronger assimilations," does not link her to the official community but to the marginal "forest-land," the wild place on the town's edge where she makes her home. Her guilt becomes in effect a "counterassimilation" that supplants the ties that held her before the adultery. She is bound to Puritan Boston by a "galling" chain, but it is a chain of her own construction, a pain that she chooses. While Dimmesdale comes to belong to his guilt, Hester's guilt—as the consequence of her deed—belongs to her.

Hester's guilt is thus linked to her establishment of a new form of affiliation to her community. It is also connected to the persistent love that is advanced as the second reason for her staying.

> It might be, too,—doubtless it was so, although she hid the secret from herself, and grew pale whenever it struggled out of her heart, like a serpent from its hole,—it might be that another feeling kept her within the scene and pathway that had been so fatal. There dwelt, there trode the feet of one with whom she deemed herself connected in a union, that, unrecognized on earth, would bring them together before the bar of final judgment, and make that their marriage-altar, for a joint futurity of endless retribution. Over and over again, the tempter of souls had thrust this idea upon Hester's contemplation, and laughed at the passionate and desperate joy with which she seized, and then strove to cast it from her. She barely looked the idea in the face, and hastened to bar it in its dungeon. What she compelled herself to believe,—what, finally, she reasoned upon as her motive for continuing a resident of New England—was half a truth, and half a self-delusion. Here, she said to herself, had been the scene of her guilt, and here should be the scene of her earthly punishment; and so, perchance, the torture of her daily shame would at length purge her soul, and work out another purity than that which she had lost; more saint-like, because the result of martyrdom. (80)

Hester is troubled by the inner division characteristic of Hawthorne's representation of guilt. She makes a conscious effort to suppress the fact of her continued love for Dimmesdale; she returns the serpent to its hole, the passionate idea to its "dungeon." Yet as the passage unfolds it becomes apparent that the love she attempts to sequester surreptitiously takes control of the mechanism of conscience that threatens to imprison it. While Dimmesdale's inner ambivalence results from his conscience's paradoxical diversion of the impulse to confess, Hester's subverted attempts to suppress her love express both her knowledge of what it would take to extinguish her love—to believe in its wrongness—and her refusal to perform that act of mind. Note the remarkable iconoclasm of the fantasy that happily accepts "endless retribution" as the price of a "joint futurity." Finally, in the elaborate story of temptation, purgation, purity, and martyrdom that Hester frames for her future life, love has managed to bring to its own rescue the narrative patterns that customarily belong to conscience and drive the behavior of Dimmesdale and Reuben Bourne. Guilt becomes for Hester a psychic disguise employed in the preservation of love, not in its repression; she transforms this scar of communal affiliation into a wound with a meaning all her own. Together these two passages imply the existence of a subversive psychological operation beneath Hester's public acquiescence: Hester's guilt becomes at once the ground of her private identity and the way she protects her love, so that to deny her guilt would be, paradoxically, a betrayal of the love that guilt seeks to punish, and of the self that has staked everything upon that love.

This tendency of Hester's mind to transform the operation of guilt into a strategy for the protection of a transgressive love is illuminatingly discussed by Richard Brodhead, who sees enacted in Hester's rejection of the pleasures of her needlework her sense that "her art might be a way of expressing, and thus soothing, her repressed passion, and in order to protect her love she rejects—and labels as sin—whatever might help her to sublimate it." She thus "employs Puritan terminology in a most un-Puritan strategy of consciousness, using it to perpetuate an inner need which she is unable to act out and unwilling to relinquish."[14] The art that Hester does allow herself, her adornment of Pearl, becomes a way of enacting the knowledge that is enfolded in the psychological equation I have just proposed: Hester's identity depends neither upon her sense of guilt nor her ability to love, but upon their linking, which is in turn embodied in the character of Pearl. As we have noted, Hester dresses Pearl as a version of the scarlet letter itself: she "had carefully wrought out the similitude; lavishing many hours of morbid ingenuity, to create an analogy between the object of her affection, and the emblem of her guilt and torture" (102). This "analogy" between affection and guilt, it seems to me, is the incontrovertible fact of Hester's emotional life, the consequence of her fidelity to the act of adultery through which she reinvents her identity. In a speech we have already looked at, Hester says that Pearl "is the scarlet letter, only capable of being loved, and so endowed with a million-fold the power of retribution for my sin" (113). Pearl emblematically joins the capacity to love beyond the self with the guilt the letter represents, saving Hester from the compulsion of conscience engendered by Dimmesdale's narcissism. But, as Hester's claim of a causal connection between the strength of love and the pain of retribution suggests, the constitution of mind that frees her from compulsion also denies her the protections, however tortuous, that the narcissistic psyche provides against experience.

It is, then, this capacity to love outside the self, to build her life upon her bonds to others, that crucially distinguishes Hester from Dimmesdale. Hawthorne uses this distinction between the lovers to establish the different ways an affiliation to a culture and its values might be lived out. Dimmesdale exemplifies, in his combination of ambition, narcissism, and hunger for the endorsement of the authority structure that names him as its own, the tendency of human character to shape itself unthinkingly to the configuration its culture supplies. Hester, freed by her transgression to devise an inner life of her own, invited by her punishment to suspect the authority of the Puritan fathers, and drawn by temperament and mother-hood to seek love rather than the endorsement of an internalized ideal defines for the reader the freedom available at the margins or within the interstices of a social structure.

It would be a mistake to assume that Hawthorne's interest in the rela-tion between the inner lives of his characters and the structure of the Puritan community is solely or even mainly historical. Rather, we need to notice some of the specific ways that Hawthorne's depiction of character as a culturally located form of meaning asked his nineteenth-century readers to notice the conditions of their cultural moment and to think through the ways a community speaks within the self. His emphasis on Hester's capacity to love as the source of her subversiveness and the es-sence of the distinction between her and her erstwhile lovers is Haw-thorne's contribution to the thinking about the nature of male and female character that was so absorbing a subject in antebellum America. Dim-mesdale and Chillingworth, careerists both, build their lives upon stories that are primarily about themselves, and in those stories emotional need assumes the guise of abstract principle and is fueled by ambition. For Dimmesdale the story of his adultery is not about him and Hester but about his private election and his right to public eminence. Chillingworth disguises his wounding and the career of his rage as a philosophical in-quiry into the manifestations of the guilty heart and adopts a determinism that diffuses personal responsibility for his vendetta. It is precisely Hes-ter's willingness to build her life upon her bonds to others that saves her from the self-absorption, despair, and abstraction that her isolation in-vites—that keeps her, from Hawthorne's point of view, alive as a woman and, paradoxically, freer in her relation to the community than her self-regarding lovers.

Hawthorne uses these established gender distinctions, it seems to me, to think about how cultural transformation might occur. Hester is just at the point of falling into a despair that might take the form of a rebellion against male authority conducted, like Anne Hutchinson's, on abstract grounds when Chillingworth's victimization of Dimmesdale at last gives her, along with her care of Pearl, a pathway for her passion, "an object that appeared worthy of any exertion and sacrifice for its attainment" (166). This moment, when Hester's "heart . . . come[s] uppermost," be-gins as a celebration, canonical to antebellum gender discourse, of the womanly capacity for sympathy, but we should notice where Hester's emotions take her. When Hester resolves to rescue the minister from the patriarchal camp, she moves from speculation to action, thus becoming subversive in a more dangerous way than in her theoretical musings. As she knows from her own experience, the authority structure of Puritan

Boston and the forms of male ambition it endorses depend upon love's subordination to abstract principles, and she is acting as though meaning were grounded not on principle but on love. And since the minister vividly represents the self-poisoning suppressions and closet egoism that attend the version of male character that paternalistic cultures—like antebellum America—seem to produce, Hester's attempt to steal Dimmesdale for her world is a step toward realizing her revolutionary vision of a transformed cultural life: a world in which "the very nature of the opposite sex, or its long hereditary habit, which has become like nature" (165) and the culture that supports that "habit" might be transformed and "the whole relation between man and woman" might be reestablished "on a surer ground of mutual happiness" (263). Hester, we might say, has understood that male personality is ideological—a habit of feeling that has come to look like "nature"—and thus vulnerable to attack and liable to change. Women, Hawthorne's portrait of Hester implies, because they are excluded from the authority structure that shapes the community, are more likely to envision, or exemplify, in their inner lives, a way to overturn it.[15]

Hawthorne's account of Dimmesdale's inner life, too, is more than another of his striking analyses of the deformation of male character by ambition. I have already suggested that some of the minister's most prominent characteristics, particularly his delicacy of frame and sensibility, invite us to see him as a precursor of the middle-class culture Hawthorne is addressing. Particularly in the curiously secular elements of Dimmesdale's self-torment—in the way hysterical modesty and a horror of public exposure replace fear of damnation as his chief emotion—we can see a distinctly nineteenth-century cast to his consciousness, an exemplification of the carefully guarded, but curiously empty private sensibility that for Richard Sennett emerges as the hallmark of nineteenth-century, middle-class personality.[16] In a seminal essay on the role of fiction in the formation of middle-class culture in antebellum America, Richard Brodhead has suggested that Dimmesdale's intense identification with the authority of conscience and his illustration of the operation of an utterly internalized form of cultural discipline (as opposed to Hester's older, public, external form of punishment) links the minister to the form of character formation—"disciplinary intimacy"—that was at the center of middle-class child-rearing practices, of its characteristic cultural productions, and of the moral vision that gave it coherence as a class.[17] Hawthorne is not only meditating, in his portrayal of Dimmesdale and Hester, on the history and condition of American selfhood; he is suggesting that the psychological and emotional resources of his culture—self-scrutiny, self-discipline, the heightened sensitivity that makes privacy a central value—can, in the absence of a clear seeing of the shape they give to experience, poison the world they define. We begin to recognize that the authoritarian has a protean resilience that did not die with the Puritan patriarchs, and that we, too, are characters in an ongoing drama of cultural affiliation.

ROMANCE AS INTERCHANGE

The dichotomy between Dimmesdale's life within his culture and Hester's life at its margins is explored and complicated when the lovers come together as *The Scarlet Letter* ends. In the disruption and repair of the minister's orthodoxy and in the flowering and chastening of Hester's rebellion, Hawthorne unfolds the full complexity of his understanding of the conditions of meaning that shape our lives within the community. Hawthorne builds this account around two linked concepts, both central to the practice of romance. The first we might call "interchange," by which I mean a form of meaning, exemplified by Hester's capacity to love, generated by neither private fiat nor authoritative imposition but produced by mutual acts of disclosure and response. The second, to be discussed in the closing section of this chapter, is "revision," a form of change, located in the interesting territory between the determined and the transcendent, that acknowledges the limitations upon freedom that attend the communal construction of meaning and the history that our choices make for us. It is through the elucidation of these two forms of relation that Hawthorne defines, for himself and for us, the way of engaging our culture that constitutes the art of romance.

We must begin our account of the resolution of *The Scarlet Letter* with the moment in the forest when the transgression that generated this story recurs. I have already suggested that this forest scene returns us to the unshown moment of transgression that began this story, but that the full orbit of the meanings of this act is now available to us—both because we have witnessed the characters living them out and because the book has taught us to read the overdetermined connections between character and culture. For Hester and Dimmesdale, too, this moment of connection makes the fullness of a life's meaning legible: "the crisis flung back to them their consciousness, and revealed to each heart its history and experience, as life never does, except at such breathless epochs" (190). We need to look closely both at this moment and at the consequences—for Hester, for Dimmesdale, and for Pearl—that flow from it.

This moment of transgression, in which Hester proposes that they flee Boston together and Dimmesdale acquiesces, is a complicated one, for it is both a moment of authentic connection, and contains, in Dimmesdale's covert resistance to such connection, the frustration of its still-genuine possibility. When Dimmesdale, in a heroic move outside the confines of his drama of self, forgives Hester for concealing Chillingworth's identity—and for the horrible scrutiny he has suffered under the doctor's gaze—the lovers recover the intimacy made possible by their earlier transgression: "Here, seen only by his eyes, the scarlet letter need not burn into the bosom of the fallen woman! Here, seen only by her eyes, Arthur Dimmesdale, false to God and man, might be, for one moment, true!" (195–96). Note that Hawthorne structures this moment so as to emphasize the connection between interchange and meaning, for the moment of mutual disclosure that love makes possible has the power to revalue Hester's letter and Dimmesdale's social presence. The bond between them has created a new context, and thus potentially a new meaning, for their act.

This new world of meaning comes briefly into being when Hester speaks the words—"Thou shalt not go alone"—that repeat the originating act of adultery. The beautiful description of the sexual flowering that attends Hester's removal of the letter reveals, excruciatingly, the possibility that her community's way of meaning has suppressed. And the answering awakening of the forest suggests that such a world of meaning is latent, there to be grasped by the two lovers. Our task as readers of romance is to understand what it is that despoils this moment of possibility. In consonance with the book's overlapping interest in character and culture, Hawthorne offers two answers to this question, two stories about the nature of freedom.

The first of these answers is located primarily in character. Hester's attempt to make out of this renewed transgression a new world of meaning fails because of the incompleteness of Dimmesdale's participation in it. The minister accedes to but does not fully share in Hester's vision of the meaning of their flight. His elusiveness is exemplified by the manipulative passivity that forces Hester to speak the transgressive words, as though the minister were preparing in advance an excuse for his behavior. Nor does it take long for the community's perspective to intrude on this moment of connection: Dimmesdale's first thought is that Chillingworth might expose him to his public. Most revealingly and, as the narrator suggests, most pathetically, the divine notes with relief that his departure will not prevent him from preaching the election sermon, the pinnacle of ministerial eminence and a chance to take a final bow before his adoring audience. Dimmesdale's acquiescence in Hester's plan, then, has hardly pried him loose from the authority structure of the community or from the order of ambition it sponsors. Unlike Hester, Dimmesdale has not found a moral vision alternative to the one he shares with his congregation; his acquiescence in Hester's plan of flight does not represent a freeing break with the ethical system that defines his life but, like the act of adultery itself, a betrayal of it that leaves it intact. He continues to conceive of his behavior, even at its most rebellious, as a battle with the fiend, and the language the narrator attaches to Dimmesdale's experience is accordingly Manichean: the minister's acquiescence is a second "fall," more serious than the prior act of passion because "he had yielded himself with deliberate choice, as he had never done before, to what he knew was deadly sin" (222). The minister's characteristically divided response fails to give Hester the partnership that might have ratified her redefinition of their transgressive act.[18]

Hester's dream of escape, then, is in part destroyed by the nature of Dimmesdale's character, by the extent of his entanglement in the official ideology of Puritan Boston and by his consequent violation of the possibility of interchange animated in this scene. But the most significant explanation for the failure of Hester's revolutionary project is implicit in Pearl's response to her mother's removal of the letter; Hester is thwarted not simply by Dimmesdale's inner orthodoxy but by the very conditions of meaning that her story illustrates. By claiming that she can by her own act free their transgression from the meaning that her community imposes upon it, Hester remains faithful to the force of her love but attempts to evade the force of the connection between guilt, love, and identity—between publically given and privately created meanings—that her symbolism of the letter has been acknowledging. These scenes at the brookside occasion Hawthorne's fullest exploration of the meaning for consciousness of its relation to the community that surrounds and shapes it.

I will focus on the remarkable moment when Pearl refuses to rejoin her parents until Hester has replaced the letter she has thrown off. The brook, with its direction "compelled" by the forest topography, its ability to reveal mysterious "tales out of the heart of the old forest," and its repetitive murmur of some "solemn experience" suggests, by the most subtle analogy, the shared psychic legacy of social discipline. It thus represents a threshold in the history of the self and its relation to the community. Pearl's actions can be explained both realistically, as a child's jealousy of a rival for her mother's affection, and emblematically, as a complex refutation of the beautiful autonomy that Hester imagines for herself and Dimmesdale in her vision of escape; I will discuss only the allegorical aspect of the scene.[19] Because the child bases her repudiation of Hester on the absence of the scarlet letter, we must begin by considering the significance of that "unlettering."

The tendency of Hester's solitary life, Hawthorne tells us, has been to free her from the restrictive ethical and conceptual frameworks to which her community subscribes. Her exhortation to "begin all anew," to "exchange this false life of thine for a true one" (198), reveals that Hester has become an Emersonian, and her conviction that each mind is free to establish its version of significance is the theology that underpins her reminder to Dimmesdale that their adultery "had a consecration of its own" (195).[20] If "consecration" can be established independently of a community of shared belief, then each individual is capable of inventing a sacrament. Thus Hester casts off the letter to the accompaniment of her own ritual discourse: "The past is gone! Wherefore should we linger upon it now? See! With this symbol, I undo it all, and make it as it had never been!" (202). For Hawthorne such freedom from the constraints of history and community is devoutly to be wished—as his beautiful description of the sexual flowering that attends upon Hester's act implies—but attainable only at the cost of an autonomy ultimately as self-enclosing as Dimmesdale's narcissism, and for the same reason: it refuses the act of interchange that must ground all human significance. Hester's attempt to erase her guilt, according to Hawthorne's understanding of the communal grounding of meaning, would, paradoxically, erase the meaning of her self-creating transgression, for only a shared convention of meaning can give to Hester's passion its quality of rebellion and to her relation to the community its liberating marginality. This scene in *The Scarlet Letter*, we might say, is Hawthorne's contribution to the debate about the nature of freedom that links together the most powerful writing of the American Renaissance.

This limitation placed by guilt—that is, by the fidelity to one's past choices that guilt, in Hester's case, expresses—upon the self's freedom to invent its own meanings is the hard knowledge conveyed by Pearl's insistence that Hester resume the scarlet letter. But how is it that Pearl, the anarchist, symbolically expresses the inevitable implications of the self's engagement in its community? Pearl pauses on the edge of the brook and regards her parents:

> Just where she had paused the brook chanced to form a pool, so smooth and quiet that it reflected a perfect image of her little figure, with all the picturesqueness of her beauty, in its adornment of flowers and wreathed foliage, but more refined and spiritualized than the reality. This image, so nearly identical with the living Pearl, seemed to communicate somewhat of its own shadowy and intangible quality to the child herself. It was strange, the way in which Pearl stood, looking so steadfastly at them through the dim medium of the forest gloom. . . . In the brook beneath stood another child,—another and the same,—with likewise its ray of golden light. Hester felt herself, in some indistinct and tantalizing manner, estranged from Pearl; as if the child, in her lonely ramble through the forest, had strayed out of the sphere in which she and her mother dwelt together, and was now vainly seeking to return to it. (208)

I wish to emphasize two aspects of this passage. The first is the suggestion that Hester's unlettering has uncannily robbed Pearl of her reality—has, in effect, turned her into the image, or type, reflected in the pool. Hence the child's "shadowy and intangible quality," her sense of exile to a sphere removed from the relationship to her mother that links her to a world outside of herself. The second is the weight that Hawthorne attaches to the idea of repetition in the attention he gives to Pearl's reflection in the brook. This motif of repetition is amplified as the scene of Pearl's insistence unfolds. "Assuming a singular air of authority," Pearl repeatedly points to her mother's unlettered breast and begins to shriek her increasing rage; each gesture, Hawthorne emphasizes, is repeated by her double in the pool, and each sound echoed through the woods, until "it seemed as if a hidden multitude were lending her their sympathy and encouragement" (210). It is precisely by means of repetition that Pearl becomes the representative of the idea of community in her refusal to accept Hester's sacramental undoing of the past. This undoing, which denies Pearl's existence by denying the consequences of her birth, accounts for the language of unreality that Hawthorne employs in describing her. Pearl's imagistic repetition—indeed, the idea of repetition itself—becomes the sign of the containment of the self within systems of significance that depend upon repetition for the institution of meaning, within the cultural discourse by which a community assigns meaning to the behavior of its members, and within history itself, in which one inherits not only such a cultural discourse, but the ramifying consequences of one's deeds.

The significance of this emblematic moment for Pearl as a character needs further meditation. Let me return to the narrator's observation that Pearl makes her defiant gesture with "a singular air of authority." This remark implies that Pearl has exchanged roles with her parents, and, in her attempt to reclaim her reality, comes to represent the dual necessity that Hester's sacrament seeks to overturn: one cannot deny the consequences of one's acts, and one cannot avoid the meaning assigned those acts by the culture to which one belongs. But Pearl has throughout the novel displayed a striking antipathy to such structures of significance. She especially abhors the idea of fatherhood—of being subject to a particular ancestry or history. Thus she insists that she was made by no heavenly father but was "plucked by her mother off the bush of wild roses, that grew by the prison door" (112), and, in a particularly graphic demonstration of "the freedom of a broken law," she dances on the grave of the great Isaac Johnson, a founder of the Puritan community itself (133). Throughout the book, Hawthorne repeatedly draws our attention to Pearl's uninterpretability, her excess of contradictory meaning. Up until this moment at the brookside, Pearl maintains the pure arbitrariness of utter freedom; at this moment she becomes fully interpretable, both as a child and as an emblem. When Pearl intuits that Hester's removal of the letter denies her very existence, she enacts the knowledge that her reality depends upon her relation to another, that her meaning is socially mediated, not solely whimsical. During this scene Dimmesdale speculates "that this brook is the boundary between two worlds" (208). When Pearl crosses the brook on the condition that Hester resume the letter, she, in order to protect herself from the unreality of mere self-reference, acquiesces in a future of communally determined meanings; she crosses the boundary between wilderness and culture. She destroys, as well, the fantasy of self-determination that Hester poses as a defense against the full meaning of her own affiliation to the Puritan community, no matter how rebelliously that affiliation has been expressed. The scene's proliferating repetitions, then, entrap Hester's dream of freedom within the limiting but fruitful systems of exchange that transform solipsism into shared significance.[21]

Pearl's refutation of Hester's fantasy of autonomy acknowledges that the meaning of a life depends in part upon its confinement by its community and its history; Hawthorne is working out, through the despoiling of Hester's dream, an account of the conditions of cultural meaning. What of Dimmesdale's career within the novel's closing pages? The minister's appearances in these final scenes are haunted by a question asked by the narrator, Hester, Pearl, Mistress Hibbins, even the minister himself: is this "the same man" who left Boston for his trip to the forest? With this question Hawthorne makes us consider the nature of Dimmesdale's self-transformation and the question that transformation implies: how might the inner freedom that makes change possible come about? For Dimmesdale, the answer is simple: he is an utterly different creature from the enfeebled, guilt-ridden man he had been and for whom he now feels scorn. Our own answer will be more complicated.

"Love," Freud writes, "has the power to remove repressions and restore perversions."[22] Is this what has happened to Dimmesdale when he returns from his encounter in the forest? Hawthorne displays the consequences of Dimmesdale's apparent moral rebellion in his most comic scene, in which the frail divine rolls through town, barely restraining newly awakened obscene and blasphemous impulses: "Before Mr. Dimmesdale reached home, his inner man gave him other evidences of a revolution in the sphere of thought and feeling. In truth, nothing short of a total change of dynasty and moral code, in that interior kingdom, was adequate to account for the impulses now communicated to the unfortunate and startled minister" (217). The momentary reawakening of the minister's love for Hester has, it seems, removed the restraints that conscience and community enforce. Thus Crews argues that the minister's moment of revelry is the beginning of a change in his psychic strategy: he begins to sublimate rather than repress his libidinal energy. He thus employs this newly liberated sexual energy in writing the election sermon and manages, finally, to confess his guilt.[23] Such a Dimmesdale would, indeed, be a "different" man.

While I agree that Dimmesdale's deliberate rebellion against communal moral authority has broken the capacity of his diseased conscience to restrain his impulse to confess, he has hardly been freed from a compulsive psychology. We should notice that the misbehavior that seems like a psychic carnival amounts to a new kind of authoritarianism, a tyranny of the id. The minister is pulled through town by his new, nasty impulses like an old lady walking a mastiff. Instead of freedom of consciousness, we have a change in "dynasty," and an explicit invocation of the psychology of compulsion: Dimmesdale's acts are "at once involuntary and intentional," "in spite of himself, yet growing out of a profounder self than that which opposed the impulse" (217). There is, moreover, an important link between this new Dimmesdale and the old. What has not changed is his fascination with eminence: just as a vision of a devastated congregation had justified his failure to confess, so his ribald urges reveal the persistence of a fantasy about his power to destroy the community that worships him ("the minister felt potent to blight all the field of innocence with but one wicked look" [220]). On the one hand, Dimmesdale's transgression seems to have loosened his ligature to the Puritan authorities, exposing it as a revisable thing; on the other, his ostensible liberation is governed by the mere inversion of authority that makes witchcraft this community's orthodox form of deviation.

As the closing scene of the book unfolds, it becomes clear that Dimmesdale has undergone not a simple transformation or self-liberation but a kind of splitting that completes the inner division we have already examined. He returns to town both as a man who has committed an act of love and as an unreconstructed narcissist intent on a last dose of celebrity. The scene of the election sermon and the revelation of the letter thus tells two stories at once; we see both what would make possible the minister's self-liberation and what frustrates that possibility.

When Dimmesdale returns to the chamber that has been the site of his penitential rituals, his first act is to measure the distance between the tormented minister and the man he has now become: "He knew that it was himself, the thin and white-cheeked minister, who had done and suffered these things, and had written thus far into the Election Sermon! But he seemed to stand apart, and eye this former self with scornful, pitying, but half-envious curiosity. That self was gone! Another man had returned out of the forest; a wiser one; with a knowledge of hidden mysteries which the simplicity of the former never could have reached" (223). The language of scorn, surveillance, and initiation that the narrator uses here strongly suggests that this new Dimmesdale has become a kind of Chillingworth; or, to put this more precisely, his narcissistic identification with the superego, which the physician bodies forth, has been strengthened by his renewed transgression, while his identification with the sinful, suffering ego seems almost to have disappeared, reduced to the condescension this passage records. This second, more deliberate sin, moreover, has stripped the ministerial psyche of its veneer of moralism and revealed its self-regarding core, for Dimmesdale experiences the extraordinary burst of energy that produces the new election sermon less as an influx of divine grace than as an efflux of high romantic imaginative power: "he wrote with such an impulsive flow of thought and emotion, that he felt himself inspired" and as "he drove his task onward with earnest haste and ecstasy . . . the night fled away, as if it were a winged steed, and he careering on it" (225). In Hawthorne's interesting economy of mind, the energy that had been spent in remorseful self-torment, apparently freed by Dimmesdale's second sin, is translated into "aspiring ambition," paradoxically keeping the rule of the ego-ideal in place.

This is the transformation that provokes Hester to ask her version of the "same man" question. For the price Hester pays for her vision of autonomy in the forest is to witness the man she thought she had reclaimed gone over to the camp of the "majestic and venerable fathers." The Dimmesdale who passes her by in the magisterial procession is lost in an inner world that merely echoes the celebration of authority of which he is a part: his mind is "deep in its own region, busying itself, with preternatural activity, to marshal a procession of stately thoughts that were soon to issue thence" (239). Hester feels the minister's defection as a betrayal of the moment of interchange that had bound them in the forest—"How deeply they had known each other then! And was this the man? She hardly knew him now!" (239)—while Hawthorne's language marks Dimmesdale's absorption as a death blow in the nineteenth-century battle of the genders. Feeling her inability to penetrate Dimmesdale's "unsympathizing thoughts," Hester concludes that "there could be no real bond betwixt the clergyman and herself": "And thus much of woman was there in Hester, that she could scarcely forgive him . . . for being able so completely to withdraw himself from their mutual world" (240). The result of Dimmesdale's transgression, it seems, has been to reclaim him for the public, paternalistic world that sponsors his ambition. Male narcissism proves, in Dimmesdale's case, to be stronger than sin—and certainly stronger than love. Hence Pearl can only echo her mother's puzzlement: "was that the same minister that kissed me by the brook?" (240).

But even as this story of the resilience of the authoritarian unfolds, another tale, about a different minister, begins to take shape. The "relational" Dimmesdale—the man formed by his capacity to connect with others—is, it turns out, not dead but sleeping. He, too, has been strangely strengthened by the splitting of self we have been noticing, as though

Dimmesdale the minister and Dimmesdale the sympathizer were each getting a share of the energy they had been spending containing one another.
The two Dimmesdales in effect produce two different election sermons
that share the same text. The ambitious minister delivers a vaunting address that gives communal shape to his private fantasies of personal eminence. He presents New England as the most elect of "the communities of
mankind" and foretells "a high and glorious destiny for the newly gathered people of the Lord" (249). And this magisterial discourse yields a
corresponding effect of social power: "the admirable minister was looking down from the sacred pulpit upon an audience, whose very inmost
spirits had yielded to his control" (246–47). Yet at the same time the
covert Dimmesdale, through the cadences of his voice, produces a subtext
of private disclosure that generates a link of sympathy between him and
his audience, and it is this emotional connection—a "plaintiveness . . .
that touched a sensibility in every bosom" (243)—that accounts most
deeply for the sermon's extraordinary effect on its auditors:

> But even when the minister's voice grew high and commanding,—when it
> gushed irrepressibly upward,—when it assumed its utmost breadth and
> power, so overfilling the church as to burst its way through the solid walls,
> and diffuse itself in the open air,—still, if the auditor listened intently, and
> for the purpose, he could detect the same cry of pain. What was it? The
> complaint of a human heart, sorrow-laden, perchance guilty, telling its se-
> cret, whether of guilt or sorrow, to the great heart of mankind; beseeching its
> sympathy or forgiveness,—at every moment,—in each accent,—and never in
> vain! It was this profound and continual undertone that gave the clergyman
> his most appropriate power. (243–44)

The two Dimmesdales and the two simultaneous sermons they deliver
correspond, we should notice, to the two opposed forms of meaning that
constitute the Puritan community: meaning produced by an act of power
and control, and meaning generated by disclosure and exchange. The
split within Dimmesdale has become a battle between two forms of cultural engagement.

While the sermon goes on in the meetinghouse, in the marketplace
Hawthorne reassembles the elements of the book's opening scene. Hester,
standing at the scaffold as she listens to the sermon, feels her life as an
"orb" centered on this one punitive spot, and she suffers the repetition of
her earlier sentence when a curious crowd gathers to refix the letter with
its gaze. Pearl skitters randomly around the marketplace, reminding us of
her exile from the system of exchange that produces communal meanings;
following the play of her curiosity, she seizes "upon that man or thing as
her own property, so far as she desired it; but without yielding the mi-
nutest degree of control over her motions in requital" (244). And when

Dimmesdale reenters this scene and once more makes his way toward the
scaffold, the task of our reading becomes to measure the meanings that
have been generated in the interim.

In the aftermath of the sermon, and as though liberated by the expenditure of psychic energy that had produced it, the covert Dimmesdale
emerges to join his ambitious twin. Wavering like "an infant, with its
mother's arms in view" (251), this newly amalgamated minister ascends
the scaffold, drawing Pearl and Hester with him and displaying signs of
a new balance of power between the narcissist and the lover. His look is
thus "at once tender and strangely triumphant" (252), and his behavior
an odd mix of dependence and willfulness as he relies on Hester to support him on the scaffold but requires that his last appearance be carried
out according to his exact instructions. There are thus two aspects to his
final scene, two meanings enacted before the assembled community.

In part, Dimmesdale's appearance on the scaffold represents a triumph
for the order of sympathetic interchange that has all along been an alternative to the community's hierarchical way of meaning. When Dimmesdale decides to assume his full communal meaning by acknowledging his
relation to Hester and Pearl and exposing his fleshly version of the letter—"let me . . . take my shame upon me" (254) he says, echoing Hawthorne's offer to bear the shame of his ancestors in the customhouse—he
takes his place in the order of disclosure and response, thus relinquishing
the control of his audience that had vitiated his earlier confessional cha-
rades. His revelation of his letter cedes to the community of onlookers the
power to determine, through their response, his meaning. He fully enters,
that is, the structure of communally determined meaning that Pearl identifies when she insists that Hester resume her letter. And just as it was
Pearl who had insisted on the inadequacy of Dimmesdale's entry into
communal discourse in his midnight vigil, speaking gibberish to him to
mark his evasiveness, so it is Pearl who ratifies the minister's new meaning by her sympathetic response to him. Her tears, the narrator observes,
in turn move Pearl herself fully into the community: this "scene of grief"
develops "all her sympathies" and promises that "she would grow up
amid human joy and sorrow, nor for ever do battle with the world, but be
a woman in it" (256). The minister shares, through this revision of his
earlier, truncated acts of mock disclosure, in a moment of genuine exchange, of jointly created significance.

Without denying the heroism of Dimmesdale's self-disclosure or the
inner freedom, however temporary, to which it attests, we must notice a
countertrend in this closing scene. Even as the minister takes his place in
the order of interchange, he begins to reconstrue his self-exposure, erect-
ing his self-torment into a kind of ultimate, solo election as that sinner
most interesting to God: "behold me here, the one sinner of the world!"

Throwing off the assistance of Hester and Pearl, he steps to center stage, and his last words to Hester suppress her vision of a heavenly reunion and substitute his own apotheosis: "God . . . hath proved his mercy, most of all in my afflictions. By giving me this burning torture to bear upon my breast! By sending yonder dark and terrible old man, to keep the torture always at red-heat! By bringing me hither, to die this death of triumphant ignominy before the people! Had either of these agonies been wanting, I had been lost for ever! Praised be his name! His will be done! Farewell!" (256–57). Ridden by the personal pronoun, this last speech returns us to the theater of eminence from which the minister had been briefly rescued. Authority—and the narcissism that is its inner ally—reclaims its own.

The retelling of the story of transgression that Hester and Dimmesdale live out in the book's closing chapters completes Hawthorne's enormously complex account of the conditions of meaning within a community. The scenes and patterns of narrative we have been examining— reenactments, transformations, and repetitions: boundary moments in the history of the self—continually attach actions to the alternative shapes and possibilities they refuse or imply. Together they define this romance's crucial demarcation: between the discredited fantasies of autonomy and eminence on the one hand, and the order of disclosure and response that I have been calling interchange on the other. Hawthorne's narrative places romance on the side of this source of cultural value, always endangered by the authoritarian without and within; and he defines, as the book comes to a close, the chastened form of freedom that an understanding of interchange makes visible.

It is possible to lose, in the momentum of one's discovery of the book's analytic project, a sense of the extraordinary sadness of this closing scene. The pietàlike tableau upon the scaffold, which restores the familial connection for which Hester has fought only to take it irretrievably away, gives this ending, as its first readers felt, the force of tragedy. Years later, Hawthorne, who had "never overcome my own adamant in any other instance," wrote that as he read it aloud to Sophia his voice had "swelled and heaved, as if I were tossed up and down on an ocean as it subsides after a storm." A few days after the reading, which had sent her to bed with a broken heart and a headache, Sophia wrote to her sister that the book was "most powerful, & contains a moral as terrific & stunning as a thunder bolt. It shows that the Law cannot be broken."[24] Still, the analysis of the conditions of communal meaning that I have argued is that the book's chief interest helps us specify the source of this sadness and understand, I like to think, the acuity of Sophia Hawthorne's comment. For the "law" that Hester's story makes plain is the unyielding one that binds each private history to its culture and the meanings that culture makes possible. In Hester's case, that law obeys an economy we have come to call tragic: a life's meaning is discovered by transgression and measured in the form of loss.

ROMANCE AS REVISION

The Scarlet Letter proper might be said to end with the community's response to "the great scene of grief" presented on the scaffold: "The multitude, silent till then, broke out in a strange, deep voice of awe and wonder, which could not as yet find utterance save in this murmur that rolled so heavily after the departed spirit" (257). The actions that have led to the revelation of Dimmesdale's letter give way to acts of interpretation, attempts within the book to locate the meaning of the events that we, too, have witnessed. We thus become part of a community of interpreters trying to give "utterance" to the inarticulate voicing that attends Dimmesdale's disclosure. The conclusion of *The Scarlet Letter* thus returns us explicitly to the process by which a community makes sense of things and, through our own interpretive activity, turns our attention at last to the form of relation between writer and reader that the book has created. It is through this assembly of acts of interpretation that the act of mind I will be calling revision—and with it the communal function of romance—becomes fully defined.

Dimmesdale's own response to his revelation of the letter is in a sense the first of the interpretations that Hawthorne records. The minister's rendering of his own significance, as an illustration of the divine will, is an attempt to confine the meaning of the *A* upon his breast, to render an interpretation consistent with the authoritative creed he continues to espouse. Certain "highly respectable witnesses" follow the minister's lead by denying the presence of the bodily inscription and accounting for the minister's actions as a kind of farewell sermon, a comfortingly abstract lesson in the universality of sin. We witness, in this response, an instance of meaning by authority, an attempt to restore ideological stability by suppressing the uncomfortable complexity of the scene on the scaffold.

The desperate orthodoxy of this "respectable" response is transparent and easily dismissed, as the narrator cites the less defensive theories, more in accord with the evidence the text supplies us, offered by other members of the community. The narrator's own casting about for an adequate moral has the effect less of settling the question of this story's meaning than of alerting us to our need to interpret for ourselves. He throws up his narratorial hands—"We have thrown all the light we could acquire upon the portent, and would gladly, now that it has done its office, erase its deep print out of our own brain" (259)—and at last offers up a moral—

one among the "many" that come to mind—that is at once emphatic and equivocal: "Be true! Be true! Be true! Show freely to the world, if not your worst, yet some trait whereby the worst may be inferred!" (260). The narrator's "Be true!" at once reminds us of the dangers of leaving the community's order of disclosure for Dimmesdale's world of self-absorption, and curiously reanimates, when it shifts from disclosure to inference, the lure of self-protection.

The most revealing of the interpretations that bring *The Scarlet Letter* to its close remains unspoken. The moral debate that I have been describing suddenly gives way to the reticence of mere telling: Hester simply comes back. Hester's return is *The Scarlet Letter*'s salient moment of interpretive demand, its challenge to the reader. Our explanation of her act and her resumption of the letter throws us back upon our own interpretive resources and becomes the measure of our reading of the novel. It is a measure that we are left to take on our own, without the comfort of authorial confirmation.[25]

I have argued that the scene at the brookside is an emblematic acknowledgment of what limits the power of the private self to shape its world. It expresses as well the understanding that the cost of a significance that is not solipsistic is the guilt that signifies one's affiliation—however subversively expressed—to a community of human interchange and to one's own past deeds. Pearl's tears of sympathy for Dimmesdale on the scaffold confirm her entrance into the signifying limitation of social existence. It is this irretrievable location of meaning within a community that Hester, who holds fast on the scaffold to her transcendent vision of a reunion with the minister after death, at last acknowledges in her return to Boston. Her return thus becomes at once the occasion and the model for our own interpretation of her story.

To achieve a freedom of mind that avoids solipsism is, for Hawthorne, to understand the sense in which the meaning of one's own life—even to oneself—belongs to the community, but to refuse nevertheless to accede to the coercive patterns of mind that the community attempts to enforce. Hester, by her return, becomes the representative of this revisionary act of mind. By returning to the community and resuming the letter "of her own free will" (263), Hester joins an understanding of limitation to an act of choice; she remains faithful to her acts of rebellion by choosing again the cultural context that gave those acts their meaning. Her fealty, finally, is to the full meaning of her own story. Hester's return and her resumption of the letter is best understood, then, as an act of interpretation that takes as its text her own life. Hester locates, through her return (and in analogy to the Hawthorne of "The Custom-House"), a place of her own within the community, a story to tell, a margin from which to speak—"a more real life . . . here, in New England, than in the unknown region where

Pearl had found a home" (262–63). It is thus as an interpreter that she sets up shop in the Puritan community, explaining to fellow women the vicissitudes of love, forecasting a revolution in consciousness—the establishment of "the whole relation between man and woman on a surer ground of mutual happiness" (263)—accomplished not by private fiat but by communal change. Hester, then, discovers the chastened freedom of mind that is the characteristic object of Hawthorne's fiction by rereading and revising her own life. And it is in our answering act of interpretation—in the complex understanding of the conditions of meaning within a community that interpretation in this case carries with it—that the revisionary work of Hawthorne's romance is defined.

In contending that Hester's return at once models and is designed to occasion the achievement by the reader, via interpretation, of a substantially freer, authentically critical relation to the community, I am countering an influential body of readings, built upon the fact of her return and her assumption of the role of counselor to unhappy women, that accuse Hawthorne of attempting to contain or escape the radical possibilities let loose in Hester's character. Both Myra Jehlen and Amy Schrager Lang see in Hester's disqualification of herself as the immediate achiever of this world of transformed gender (and thus power) relations the invocation of a vague politics of patience and inaction. Sacvan Bercovitch, attentive to both the book's narrative practice and its historical context, argues, much more formidably, that Hawthorne's reader learns, in appreciating the balancing complexities of Hester's return, to practice—indeed, to choose—to arts of compromise that sustain America's liberal consensus. My resistance to this way of seeing the book is both local and general. Hester's moment of utopian prophecy provides iffy evidence for the sweeping claim that the book is recoiling upon itself or, more subtly, revealing its deepest ideological affiliations. Such readings assume that Hester's counsel—which we do not hear—is merely palliative; we *do* know that the Hester who tried to steal Dimmesdale has not repented that act ("Here was yet to be her penitence" [263]). They also fail to consider the immediate context: discussions of social transformation, especially ones based on an ideal of earthly happiness and a critical analysis of male personality, would hardly have been welcome to the Puritan authorities. These meetings clearly belong, moreover, to what I have described as the community's nonauthoritarian way of meaning making. Finally, Hester's sense (explicitly hers, not the narrator's) that she will not be the "angel and apostle" of this cultural renovation may indicate less her new quietism than an estimate of the limitations of her audience's sympathy. Is a utopian vision necessarily incompatible with a determination to act?

More largely, I do not think that one's estimate of the cultural effect or ambitions of the book depends upon answering the undecidable question of whether Hester is *really* revolutionary or upon Hawthorne's own political affiliations. Bercovitch's suggestion that Hawthorne is a remarkably canny proponent of the ideology of liberalism seems to me to discount the force of the book's portrait of Dimmesdale, with its appalling account of the effects of an unexamined conformity to a dominant ideology. In my view, his theory of containment through interpretive choice fails to appreciate the way the book makes the nature of our affiliation to the community its continual subject, insisting that we see our relation to that community, even in its deepest, most compulsive forms, as chosen and thus revisable. Hawthorne is recovering, then, an opportunity for choice that need not issue in appreciation, or inaction, or "compromise"—even if that is the choice that Hawthorne himself made on the question of abolition. Finally, this way of framing the issue of the book's designs upon its readers forecloses on another kind of possibility: that Hawthorne's exploration of the consequences and meanings of Hester's choices expresses an ethical vision that is not reducible to or contained by so local a set of power relations.[26]

I think that Hawthorne offers one of the novel's most curious passages as a test of our attainment of the kind of interpretive acuity that Hester achieves—a test of our own capacity to negotiate the vicissitudes of cultural meaning and to resist the coercions of the authoritative:

> It is a curious subject of observation and inquiry, whether hatred and love be not the same thing at bottom. Each, in its utmost development, supposes a high degree of intimacy and heart-knowledge; each renders one individual dependent for the food of his affections and spiritual life upon another; each leaves the passionate lover, or the no less passionate hater, forlorn and desolate by the withdrawal of his object. Philosophically considered, therefore, the two passions seem essentially the same, except that one happens to be seen in a celestial radiance, and the other in a dusky and lurid glow. In the spiritual world, the old physician and the minister—mutual victims as they have been—may, unawares, have found their earthly stock of hatred and antipathy transmuted into golden love. (261)

I am tempted to take this passage as a confirmation of an argument dear to this essay: that hate and love within the narcissistic psyches of Dimmesdale and Chillingworth *are* the same thing at bottom—that what looks like hatred, or self-loathing, is in fact the inward deflection of love. But I think that, upon reflection, these curious lines have quite a different effect. Hawthorne garbs these ruminations in the authority that we tend to attach to the abstract and the metaphysical—"Philosophically considered, therefore, the two passions seem essentially the same"—but the "truth" that the passage attempts to impose upon us is in complete opposition to one's experience of the novel, to which the ethical distinction between Hester and her erstwhile lovers is central. There is, moreover, a distinctly Chillingworthian tinge to these remarks: "philosophy" is a word attached, earlier in the book, to the physician's debased mode of inquiry into the identity of Pearl's father (116); and the erasure of an ethical distinction implicit here echoes his deterministic denial of responsibility for the minister's torment. This passage surreptitiously invites us to realize that what is important about hatred and love is not their metaphysical essence but their human effect. The further implication of the narrator's apparent espousal of this Chillingworthian view is that interpretation is itself an act of ethical choice. We are faced as readers with the task that confronts Hester; like her, we must find an understanding of *The Scarlet Letter* that eludes both acquiescence and self enclosure, that resists or revises the meanings that authority sponsors.[27]

I began this essay by suggesting that things happen at least twice within the world of *The Scarlet Letter*. From the vantage point of its close, this pattern of repetition becomes visible as a series of achieved and failed acts of revision: from Hawthorne's replacement of his inhibitory ancestors with Surveyor Pue; to Hester's opening gesture, in which she strides toward her punishment "as if by her own free-will" (52); to Pearl's verdant imitation of her mother's scarlet letter; to Dimmesdale's failed confessions and Chillingworth's refusal to forgive; to the displacement of Dimmesdale's midnight appearance on the scaffold by the tableau of disclosure that brings the action to its close. "The Custom-House" itself, from the standpoint of the end of the book, is as revisionary as it is introductory, for it rewrites Hester's tragedy of irretrievable loss as Hawthorne's comedy of escape.[28] This revisionary relation between story and introduction insists that our reading accommodate both the tragic stasis of the final scene and the resilience of the "decapitated" but vital Surveyor, that we locate in the overdetermined scene of cultural meaning both the scaffold of limitation and room to maneuver.

• • •

Late in *The Scarlet Letter*, as she prepares to depart for her meeting with Dimmesdale, Hester is struck by the notion that Pearl's ceaseless questioning about the meaning of the letter may express a potential for sympathetic understanding. Pearl might have been sent, Hester speculates, as a confidant to soothe her sorrow by hearing her confession. But Hester, finding herself unwilling to pay the price of this sympathy—to give up her control of the meaning of her act and enter interchange's terrain of disclosure—denies Pearl's intuitive linking of the letter and the minister and insists that she wears the letter "for the sake of its gold thread." Hester's deception prompts the narrator's most severe criticism of her: for the first time she is "false to the symbol on her bosom." Worse than this refusal to present herself truthfully to her daughter is the consequence of her denial. Hester responds to Pearl's continued questioning with a command of silence and a threat to shut her daughter into "the dark closet" (181); she thus threatens to replicate, in her relation to her own child, the self-protective version of authority that punishes her. Yet Hester finds a way out of this entrapment, a way of repairing her falsehood without violating the limits of her child's capacity for understanding, and it is the revisionary way of romance. As they walk to meet the minister, Pearl changes her strategy of inquisition, and asks her mother about the Black Man and her relation to him. Hester seizes upon the story Pearl supplies, and, in a most Hawthornian maneuver, turns it into an allegory: "Once in my life I met the Black Man! . . . This scarlet letter is his mark!" (185).

This improvisatory act of artistic invention redeems Hester's previous failure of candor; her fiction making—her experiment in romance—not only at last makes possible a truthful rendition of her situation but makes its admission in a style that is right for the young child, however precocious, who is its audience. The resources of fiction enable Hester to represent the complex meaning of her experience: she is faithful to the transgression that has defined her identity, and she balances Pearl's right to know with what she can be asked to understand. Her moment of artfulness frees her from falsehood and from perpetuating the pattern of repression that confines her. I take Hester's discovery of allegory as a miniature discourse on artistic method. Hawthorne, like Hester, needs to invent a fictive strategy adequate to the complex quality of our lives within culture, a form of story telling that acknowledges that the restrictions belonging to character and culture are inescapable, but that a nontrivial freedom of mind is nonetheless possible. Hester's successful improvisation reflects Hawthorne's confidence in his newly invented fictive method. Like Hester's inspired allegory, *The Scarlet Letter* exercises and teaches the art of revising the mind; it defines and accomplishes the work of romance.

Chapter Five

ROMANCE AS ENGAGEMENT:
THE HOUSE OF THE SEVEN GABLES

As *THE SCARLET LETTER* ends, Hawthorne offers us a glimpse of Hester's future. We are to imagine her as a figure of wisdom, offering counsel to a community of perplexed and sorrowful women, the casualties of love. Her bitter experience has at last become a source of authority; the marginal has become central. This vision of Hester anticipates Hawthorne's transformation of his fiction as he moved from *The Scarlet Letter* to *The House of the Seven Gables*. The "hell-fired" intensity of the former book generated in Hawthorne the wish to write something more genial, less gloomy, "a more natural and healthy product of my mind," a work he could feel less "reluctance" about publishing.[1] The lure of the central hinted at in Hester's reward and Hawthorne's remarks is at the heart of *The House of the Seven Gables*'s way of claiming authority, its attempt to reinvent and perform the work of the novelist.

The book's ambition to speak from the center of the middle-class culture it addresses has recently attracted readers interested in placing Hawthorne and his work within his historical moment and in defining the ideological force of his fiction. This seems to me precisely the kind of questioning that *The House of the Seven Gables* invites, but most of the readings I have in mind underestimate the extent to which Hawthorne has already performed their task for them. Let me take two influential examples. In *American Romanticism and the Marketplace*, Michael Gilmore reads the book as an allegory of Hawthorne's ambivalence about participating in the literary marketplace. Gilmore's analysis leads finally to an accusation: by giving in to his audience's demand for a happy ending, Hawthorne betrays the dark truths of his art, replicating the hypocrisy that he condemns in Jaffrey Pyncheon. Gilmore gives us a Hawthorne trapped in a simple dichotomy between his real beliefs and his desire for commercial success. Walter Benn Michaels's much subtler reading uncovers in Hawthorne's conception of romance a longing for an inalienable right of property, an attempt to escape the knowledge that the self, like any piece of property within capitalism, is subject to appropriation. Both these interpretations derive their éclat from an implicit claim about the limits of Hawthorne's range of vision—as in Gilmore's assumption that Hawthorne's understanding of artistic integrity could not include a complicated engagement in the values of his audience rather than a repudiation of them, and in Michaels's argument that the relation between selfhood and economic relations is being suppressed rather than interrogated.[2] My contention is that such readings miss the extraordinary way in which an interest in interpreting American culture informs the narrative logic of *The House of the Seven Gables*. The question of what the book is up to—what purposes shape its narrative strategies—needs fuller, more specific, and—patient Reader!—closer attention than it has yet received. One need not naively envision the artist as heroically above or outside ideology to grant Hawthorne something like the intellectual maneuverability—the range of perspective and capacity for analysis—that we think ourselves to possess. I will be arguing that Hawthorne's wish to establish his position at the center of his culture produced neither a straightforward celebration of shared communal values nor even such a celebration betrayed by "deeper" ambivalence, but an investigation of what it means to speak from the center of a community and an attempt to transform that center in the very act of occupying it.

The Play of Voices

The House of the Seven Gables in effect begins three times, assuming each time a new authorial voice and a correspondingly different kind of relation to the reader. In the relation between these beginnings, in the drama of voice enacted in that relation, what will become the work of the novel is at once defined and set in motion. The first of these authorial incarnations speaks the preface. The figure that emerges here—"the Author"—is the writer as public man, and the relation established with the reader is correspondingly circumscribed and correct. We figure corporately, as "the Public" and "the Reader," and the model for our engagement with the book is at once economic and legalistic.[3] With his first sentence the Author encases his relation to the Reader in the formality of a contract—"When a writer calls his work a Romance, it need hardly be observed that he wishes to claim a certain latitude, both as to its fashion and material, which he would not have felt himself entitled to assume, had he professed to be writing a Novel"—and spends the rest of the opening paragraph specifying his rights as a Romancer: this literary form implies, he avers, "a right to present that truth under circumstances, to a great extent, of the writer's own choosing or creation." He goes so far as to fend off an anticipated prosecution for excessive use of the marvelous: "He can hardly be said, however, to commit a literary crime, even if he disregard this caution" (1). The preface, then, conceives of authorship as above all the act of entering a contentious marketplace and suggests that one had better operate in the literary market as in any other, warily, with full awareness of one's rights and liabilities.

Having established his "immunities" (2), our Author begins to speak less guardedly, specifying—as a trustworthy kind of person to do business with—the particular way he intends to fulfill his end of our literary transaction. As Nina Baym's crucial work on nineteenth-century book reviewing lets us see, the Author follows an itinerary, established in reviews, of public expectations about how novels ought to behave.[4] He will operate within an established range of genres ("Novel," "Romance," "Tale," "Legend") and effects (the "picturesque"). He will, however, offer only a carefully modified assent to other expectations. "Many writers," he notes, "lay very great stress upon some definite moral purpose, at which they profess to aim their works." Though quite able to provide such a moral, he candidly admits his doubt that fiction can claim, "in good faith," to deliver this particular product in the expected way: "A high truth, indeed, fairly, finely, and skilfully wrought out, brightening at every step, and crowning the final development of a work of fiction, may add an artistic glory, but is never any truer, and seldom any more evident, at the last page than at the first" (2–3). In place of such overt moralizing, he offers something more elusive, perhaps riskier: "When romances do really teach anything, or produce any effective operation, it is usually through a far more subtle process than the ostensible one." There is more at stake here than sophistication. Hawthorne-as-public-man is not only giving the literary equivalent of good weight; he is accepting, though on carefully specified, idiosyncratic terms, the ethical role—as a purveyor of moral influence—that his audience demands. Book writing is dramatized as a bargain, in which both author and reader adjust to the desires and expectations of the other.

We thus begin *The House of the Seven Gables* with the drama of the book's own entry into the cultural marketplace that will determine, both ethically and economically, its success. Books, like other products, are subject to the risks of exchange, their claims to "title" and worth valid only if ratified by the public: "He trusts not to be considered as unpardonably offending, by laying out a street that infringes upon nobody's private rights, and appropriating a lot of land which had no visible owner, and building a house, of materials long in use for constructing castles in the air" (3). The scrupulous public voice that advances these claims hints, in the very care with which it conducts this transaction, that it conceives of the world of public interchange as dangerous place. And in the distance that bolsters its authority, in the exclusion of the private voice, we feel a corresponding constraint as readers, for this preface locks us within a marketplace relation to what we are about to read and to the person that produced it. Hawthorne begins the book, then, by reminding us of the atmosphere of inhibition that the modern marketplace imposes on human connection—the very constriction that we turn to novels to escape.

This lack of intimacy is repaired in the first chapter proper of the book, when we encounter a second authorial voice, an alternative way of conducting the transaction between writer and reader.[5] A much more genial voice welcomes us into the narrative of chapter 1. This version of the writer—let us call him the Historian so as to mark his relation to his materials and his full possession of the story he tells—begins life as an "I," locating the genesis of the book in his private experience—his walks through Salem—and his capacity to respond to the experience of others: "The aspect of the venerable mansion has always affected me like a human countenance, bearing the traces not merely of outward storm and sunshine, but expressive also of the long lapse of mortal life, and the accompanying vicissitudes, that have passed within" (5). His image of the legible countenance establishes a claim to his story quite different from that defended by the preface's Author; his authority is based not on contractual rights but on what he can see and understand. This "I" changes quickly into a "we," invoking the reader not as purchaser but as a member of a community of the thoughtful, the adequately responsive.

Confident of his sympathetic possession of the plenitude of meaning enfolded in the house itself, the Historian openly establishes the authority of his telling by letting us see his version being constructed, by defining his relation to the various versions of the Pyncheon story available to him. He begins his narrative with an act of scrupulous reconstruction, working from two often contradictory sources, an official history associated with a written record and a "tradition" preserved and transmitted by the human voice. This distinction between the authority of the document and the authority of the voice, which will be crucial throughout the book, replays the property dispute between Colonel Pyncheon and Matthew Maule. Maule's claim, based on original occupation and his own labor ("an acre or two of earth, which, with his own toil, he had hewn out of the primeval forest, to be his garden-ground and homestead") is endangered by Colonel Pyncheon's claim, which depends "on the strength of a grant from the legislature" (7). The dispute ends in the triumph of the written; Maule's claim is made moot when he is convicted of witchcraft, and, in an image that suggests being crossed off the human ledger, the authorities "drive the plough over the little area of his habitation, and obliterate his place and memory from among men" (7).

The way the narrator makes his way through this dispute is a guide to the dismantling of illegitimate authority. He is led to distrust the Pyncheon claim because Maule so successfully resisted it "at a period . . . when personal influence had far more weight than now" (7), which in turn argues on behalf of the "whispers" that saw self-interest in the zeal that made Pyncheon so prominent in Maule's prosecution. He enacts a critical relation to the official version of history, a sophisticated suspicion of the claims of the powerful. Yet these suspicions are tempered by a willingness to toss out many of the claims of "tradition" as well, "which sometimes brings down truth that history has let slip, but is oftener the wild babble of the time, such as was formerly spoken at the fireside, and now congeals in newspapers" (17). This "lettered" narrator's analysis of this title dispute forges an alliance with the claims of the "voiced" against the publicly enforced authority of the Pyncheons. Thus we find our Historian especially alert to the ways in which ideology works on behalf of the powerful: "There is something so massive, stable, and almost irresistibly imposing, in the exterior presentment of established rank and great possessions, that their very existence seems to give them a right to exist; at least, so excellent a counterfeit of right, that few poor and humble men have moral force enough to question it, even in their own secret minds" (25). A kind of counterauthority is achieved—resistant to the official and permeable to but open-eyed about the claims of gossip and legend—in the Historian's exercise of his analytic gifts. It is as though fiction, with its formal capacity to represent voices, might at last put the written at the service of the dispossessed.

Yet this narrator does not proceed by analysis alone. When he moves from the public history he has been reconstructing to the inner experience of its principal characters, he must invoke the constructive, generative powers of the imagination in order to tell his story:

> For various reasons, however, and from impressions often too vaguely founded to be put on paper, the writer cherishes the belief that many, if not most, of the successive proprietors of this estate, were troubled with doubts as to their moral right to hold it. Of their legal tenure, there could be no question; but old Matthew Maule, it is to be feared, trode downward from his own age to a far later one, planting a heavy footstep, all the way, on the conscience of a Pyncheon. If so, we are left to dispose of the awful query, whether each inheritor of the property—conscious of wrong, and failing to rectify it—did not commit anew the great guilt of his ancestor, and incur all its original responsibilities. And supposing such to be the case, would it not be a far truer mode of expression to say, of the Pyncheon family, that they inherited a great misfortune, than the reverse? (20)

Our Historian is engaged here in answering a question of cause that neither orthodox history nor the oral tradition, with its taste for determinism, can compass. Is Pyncheon history the consequence of a series of choices, of newly incurred guilt by appropriation, or an empty and inevitable pattern of repetition? The authority for his claim of ethical freedom is grounded solely in the narrator's capacity for reconstructing Pyncheon moral psychology, perhaps in his belief in moral responsibility itself. What the analytic and the legendary can only identify as pattern, the imaginative recovers as choice.

In this chapter's closing pages, the Historian returns to an image of the house as a plenitude of meaning: "But as for the old structure of our story, its white-oak frame, and its boards, shingles, and crumbling plaster, and even the huge clustered chimney in the midst, seemed to constitute only the least and meanest part of its reality. So much of mankind's varied experience had passed there—so much had been suffered, and something, too, enjoyed—that the very timbers were oozy, as with the moisture of a heart. It was itself like a great human heart, with a life of its own, and full of rich and sombre reminiscences" (27). There is comfort in the fullness of meaning that this image suggests and the promise of stability in our return to it. This narrator conjures up, in his adroit disposal of the authoritarian, in the sympathy through which he recovers the house of the seven gables as a place of connection as well as coercion, and in the openness with which he establishes his own right to tell this story, a world safe enough for the abandonment of the wariness dramatized in the preface. In the wisdom, urbanity, and measuredness of this voice we recognize a familiar figure, the narrator of classic Victorian fiction, in possession, as J. Hillis Miller suggests, of the sum of available communal wisdom.[6] Yet, as the Historian reminds us, his remarks are "preliminary" (26); the "real action of our tale" (6), the narrative proper, has not yet begun. As we shall see, the stability of this voice, its settled wisdom, cannot follow the narrative into the terrain of the "present day" (6). Its mastery belongs only to the historical, the finished; its uninhibitory authority and the sense of communal connection that it confers remain only possibilities, hovering at the threshold of the story we are about to enter, a goal rather than a possession.

After the urbanity of the Historian of chapter 1, the voice that opens the present-day narrative seems nearly hysterical. Public without the propriety of the preface's Author, inanely aggressive, this "disembodied listener" introduces us to Hepzibah by ridiculing her, working the exclamation point like a huckster: "Truly! Well, indeed! Who would have thought it! Is all this precious time to be lavished on the matutinal repair and beautifying of an elderly person who never goes abroad—whom nobody ever visits—and from whom, when she shall have done her utmost, it were the best charity to turn one's eyes another way!" (31). When we measure this voice, as we must, against the speaker of the preceding chapter, it comes to seem less a voice than a cultural position, something that is spoken rather than speaks, the dramatization of an unpenetrating unresponsiveness that is one aspect of the public culture the book depicts.

As Richard Brodhead has noticed, this is not the only voice that speaks in this opening chapter: "The cruel humor of this jaunty listener is supplemented by another voice, that of a more omniscient narrator who is privileged to know the interior of Hepzibah's heart and who can thus see her as an object worthy of compassion."[7] Brodhead observes that the chapter moves toward this second perspective—a voice like that belonging to the previous chapter's Historian—arriving finally at an assertion of the significance of everyday life despite the triviality or grotesqueness of its surface. For Brodhead, this oscillation between two opposed voices and perspectives supports a belief in the value of the quotidian by guaranteeing that this claim has been subjected to some skeptical testing, and it moves the reader toward the sympathy that makes the significance of the day-to-day perceptible. I think this drama of voice works in other ways as well, helping us identify what this story is to be a story of, helping us grasp the "real action of our tale" (6). The narrative logic of this chapter and of the book as a whole becomes understandable through the connection between the action performed by the chapter's sole character and the treatment that action receives from the two voices that struggle over its representation.

As we are repeatedly reminded during the course of the chapter, the action it records is as prosaic as can be: down-at-heel aristocrat Hepzibah Pyncheon, forced by financial difficulties to open a cent shop in the family mansion, gets dressed, enters the shop, unbars the door and retreats to the parlor. By this act, she simultaneously enters the marketplace and the cultural mainstream, feeling this moment as a painful emergence into the public gaze: "She was well aware that she must ultimately come forward, and stand revealed in her proper individuality" (40). The bulk of this chapter is spent not in describing this minimal action but in deciding how it ought to be received. The "disembodied listener," whose voice we have heard ridiculing Hepzibah, focuses relentlessly on her physical appearance and can see only the ludicrous or grotesque aspects of her venture; it can only represent Hepzibah by misrepresenting her. This scoffing voice, in effect, gives expression within the chapter to what terrifies Hepzibah about entering the public gaze, the dangers inherent in being seen and judged—reminding us in the process of what the Author of the preface was defending himself against. It threatens to repel Hepzibah's move toward the center of her culture, to return her to the isolation of her aristocratic fantasies.

What unfolds during the course of the chapter is the dismissal of this voice, its replacement by a more capacious way of seeing and judging that can represent and respond to Hepzibah differently. Or, to put this another way, one might imagine a communal voice educating itself out of blunt-mindedness into perspicacity. This second voice begins by penetrating the off-putting misrepresentation that Hepzibah offers to the world and comes to believe in herself—her nearsighted scowl:

> We must linger, a moment, on this unfortunate expression of poor Hepzibah's brow. Her scowl—as the world, or such part of it as sometimes caught a transitory glimpse of her at the window wickedly persisted in calling it—her scowl had done Miss Hepzibah a very ill-office, in establishing her character as an ill-tempered old maid; nor does it appear improbable, that, by often gazing at herself in a dim looking-glass, and perpetually encountering her own frown within its ghostly sphere, she had been led to interpret the expression almost as unjustly as the world did. . . . But her heart never frowned. It was naturally tender, sensitive, and full of little tremors and palpitations; all of which weaknesses it retained, while her visage was growing so perversely stern, and even fierce. (34)

The narrative voice is reclaiming a true estimate of Hepzibah's character from the shallow but powerful misperception of the community. We should notice, too, that it is reclaiming her *for* the community by revealing what connects her to it despite her aristocratic pretensions: the tender and palpitating heart that links her to the sentimental consensus that holds the community together.

This reclamation of Hepzibah on behalf of the communal is conducted in other ways as well. Most crucially, we come to see her as representative, as culturally valuable despite or even because of her apparent marginality. Under the sympathetic scrutiny of the gentler narrative voice, Hepzibah's significance keeps expanding, and, as it does, the ridiculing voice that opened the chapter begins to apologize for its underestimation of her ("Heaven help our poor old Hepzibah, and forgive us for taking a ludicrous view of her position!"). This narrator begins by placing Hepzibah within the book's historical moment: "For here—and if we fail to impress it suitably upon the reader, it is our own fault, not that of the theme—here is one of the truest points of melancholy interest that occur in ordinary life. It was the final term of what called itself old gentility" (37). This invitation to sympathy yields a sense of her representativeness still more expansive: "In this republican country, amid the fluctuating waves of our social life, somebody is always at the drowning-point. The tragedy is enacted with as continual a repetition as that of a popular drama on a holiday, and, nevertheless, is felt as deeply, perhaps, as when an hereditary noble sinks below his order. More deeply; since, with us, rank is the grosser substance of wealth and a splendid establishment, and has no spiritual existence after the death of these, but dies hopelessly along with them" (38). Hepzibah, then, becomes the occasion for a meditation on the vicissitudes, economic and emotional, of American life. As we have seen, her reluctance to enter the public gaze captures the force of the anxiety that accompanies entering the cultural marketplace—an anxiety implicit in the preface as well and one of the identifying marks of middle-class sensibility—and her decision to open a cent shop is presented as an example of the narrow range of economic possibilities that this culture offers to women.[8] By the end of the chapter this claim of cultural significance has expanded into what might be called the democratization of the tragic, the narrator's claim that the problem of representing Hepzibah, of locating the significant within the trivial, has always attended the discovery of meaning in human experience:

> What tragic dignity, for example, can be wrought into a scene like this! How can we elevate our history of retribution for the sin of long ago, when, as one of our most prominent figures, we are compelled to introduce—not a young and lovely woman, nor even the stately remains of beauty, storm-shattered by affliction—but a gaunt, sallow, rusty-jointed maiden, in a long-waisted silk-gown, and with the strange horror of a turban upon her head! Her visage is not even ugly. It is redeemed from insignificance only by the contraction of her eyebrows into a near-sighted scowl. And, finally, her great life-trial seems to be, that, after sixty years of idleness, she finds it convenient to earn comfortable bread in setting up shop, in a small way. Nevertheless, if we look through all the heroic fortunes of mankind, we shall find this same entanglement of something mean and trivial with whatever is noblest in joy or sorrow. Life is made up of marble and mud. And, without all the deeper trust in a comprehensive sympathy above us, we might hence be led to suspect the insult of a sneer, as well as an immitigable frown, on the iron countenance of fate. What is called poetic insight is the gift of discerning, in this sphere of strangely mingled elements, the beauty and majesty which are compelled to assume a garb so sordid. (41)

The struggle over how to represent Hepzibah ends with her universalization. The act of reseeing Hepzibah that the chapter dramatizes through its vocal combat is, then, a crucial part of what Hawthorne is conceiving as the "action" of the chapter.

What I have described as the triple beginning of *The House of the Seven Gables* should have important consequences for us as interpreters of the book as a whole. To hear the different voices that introduce us to the book, to occupy or resist the various readerly roles—the buyer, the boor, the sympathizer—they assign us, is to become alert to narrative voice as a dramatization of a particular way of participating in a culture. A corollary of such an awareness is the realization that narrative voice within *The House* will be a deployed thing, likely not to represent, in any consistent way, "Hawthorne," or even a single narrative perspective, but a range of available cultural positions and responses and the discourses that articulate them.[9] As I will try to demonstrate, this understanding of voice solves some of the interpretive problems of *The House of the Seven Gables* by protecting us from condescending to the book by invoking a confused, hypocritical, or ambivalent Hawthorne instead of attending to the kind of cultural analysis his text is performing.

This play of voices helps us understand what is meant when "the real action of our tale" is said to begin in chapter 2, with its move from the historical to the present. This shift from voice to voices suggests that to enter the present is to enter a realm of ideological contest in which ideas of cultural value struggle with one another and no voice can possess authority with the certainty of the Narrator of chapter 1. Our understanding of the "action" of the book we are about to read, then, must expand to include this struggle over the meaning of the emotions, decisions, and movements of the book's characters as well as the events themselves. What this means, I will be arguing, is that *The House of the Seven Gables* is about the way the culture it addresses works; Hawthorne has invented what might be called the narrative of the cultural system. Thus chapter 2 records as its sole event a change in Hepzibah's cultural position—her move from the margins into the marketplace—and dramatizes a contest over how to understand its meaning for the community she enters. As we shall see, the work done by this invention in narrative form is at once descriptive and ethical, for it sets out not only to understand how this community works but to teach it what it ought to value, to reestablish its moral center.[10]

Narrative Form and Cultural Transformation

In what follows, I will be making the case that *The House of the Seven Gables* is the product of two related authorial ambitions: to invent a narrative form adequate to the representation of the life of a culture, not simply of a set of characters; and to reshape the consensus that constitutes the ethical and emotional center of the community it addresses. As my account of chapter 2 suggests, our customary notion of "action" or "plot" needs to be expanded if we are to produce an adequate understanding of this experiment in romance. Reading Hepzibah's entry into the marketplace has, in effect, provided us with a guide to reading the book as a whole. First, Hawthorne asks us to attend to character in a peculiar way. While the characters come equipped with motivations and the psychologies to go with them, our attention, in contrast to the tales and *The Scarlet Letter*, is drawn less to their internal condition than to the cultural positions they occupy. The narrative tends to notice changes in a character's relation to his culture and in what that character represents to others rather than changes of heart or mind. This is why, it seems to me, the imagery of thresholds is so prominent in the book: the narrator continually asks us to watch characters as they move from one kind of relation to the community to another. Second, the play of voices continues. We need to attend, therefore, to the kind of treatment characters call forth from the narrator—or, to put this more exactly, we must ask what kind of narrator each character summons from the cultural pool. Finally, the "story" of the responses implicitly orchestrated by the narrative to what it presents to us becomes a significant element of the book's action. By this I mean that Hawthorne assigns the reader a crucial role within this drama of the cultural system: we represent the community. Through our responses to the book's characters and events, we are the definers of centrality and the determiners of cultural meaning, and it is finally changes in the reader's vision of culture that *The House of the Seven Gables* is most interested in.

Because it consists of so many layers, each of which needs attending to as we produce a reading, the larger "action" of *The House* is a little cumbersome to describe. I will organize my account of the book by examining in turn its central characters, describing the unfolding cultural drama by identifying each character's role within it. Phoebe Pyncheon arrives at the Pyncheon doorstep trailing clouds of rustic glory. Displaced by her mother's remarriage, she comes from a New England village "where the old fashions and feelings of relationship are still partially kept up" (69), and she is determined to fill a useful place in the city of Salem. In one sense, then, she represents a moment of cultural transition, the shift in population that accompanied the growth of an urban-centered market economy in antebellum America, and her behavior, especially her relation to the marketplace, suggests that she has preserved some of the values associated with the "face-to-face" transactions of a small-town economy.[11] Unlike her land-grabbing relatives, she conceives of the market as a place of fair exchange rather than as a field for appropriation; she has "a self-respecting purpose to confer as much benefit as she could anywise receive" (74). Interestingly, her first transaction in the shop is conducted by barter with the last woman in Salem who uses a spinning wheel. Still, the aplomb with which Phoebe adapts to Salem suggests that this change in cultural location is less significant than the fact that she already embodies the domestic values that the book invokes as the moral center of community life. Hawthorne makes her centrality manifest by celebrating her mastery of the domestic arts and her consequent capacity to transform the dingy Pyncheon mansion into a version of the middle-class home. No sooner has Phoebe awakened on her first Salem morning than she displays

> the gift of practical arrangement. It is a kind of natural magic, that enables these favored ones to bring out the hidden capabilities of things around them; and particularly to give a look of comfort and habitableness to any

place which, for however brief a period, may happen to be their home. A wild hut of underbrush, tossed together by wayfarers through the primitive forest, would acquire the home-aspect by one night's lodging of such a woman, and would retain it, long after her quiet figure had disappeared into the surrounding shade. (72)

A description of Phoebe, prompted by Hepzibah's notion that, for all her useful qualities, she is not quite a lady, ascends to a full-dress codification of the ideology of woman's sphere:

> She was very pretty; as graceful as a bird, and graceful much in the same way; as pleasant, about the house, as a gleam of sunshine falling on the floor through a shadow of twinkling leaves, or as a ray of firelight that dances on the wall, while evening is drawing nigh. Instead of discussing her claim to rank among ladies, it would be preferable to regard Phoebe as the example of feminine grace and availability combined, in a state of society, if there were any such, where ladies did not exist. There, it should be woman's office to move in the midst of practical affairs, and to gild them all—the very home-liest, were it even the scouring of pots and kettles—with an atmosphere of loveliness and joy. (80)

I quote so much of this orthodox domestic utopianism to make the point that Hawthorne is quoting it too, thus establishing—for anyone who had read *Godey's Lady's Book* or the domestic fiction of the time—Phoebe's representativeness, drawing our attention to her familiarity as a type in order to make her, as the book progresses, the occasion for an exploration of the cultural possibilities and values, constitutive of middle-class culture, that she stands for: the home as refuge from the marketplace; woman as exponent within that refuge of a set of values that counter the cutthroat market; sympathy and moral influence as forms of power alternative to the domination and appropriation that infect the economic sphere. It is to this home-centered but not inevitably homebound system of values and strategies of social transformation that I refer when I speak of "domestic" and "sentimental" ideology during the course of this chapter.[12]

Having established this connection between Phoebe and domestic ideology, Hawthorne begins, when he depicts her effect on other characters, a complex celebration and examination of her cultural role. Phoebe possesses two kinds of power in the book. Her innocence of ulterior motive and her absolute sincerity make her a kind of cultural solvent, exposing attitudes that threaten the communal. She needs only to see the Malbone miniature of Clifford to grasp his innocence, and her juxtaposition to Hepzibah exposes the silliness of the latter's aristocratic fantasies. Her instinctive refusal of her cousin Jaffrey's kiss unmasks the "cold, hard, immitigable" character beneath the unctuous exterior (118–19), and she senses the tendency toward cold observership that threatens to keep Holgrave alienated from the community: "Phoebe felt his eye, often; his heart, seldom or never" (177).

More significantly, Phoebe exemplifies the operation of "influence," middle-class culture's way of imagining the transformative power of a morality exercised (and enforced) through love, especially love possessed by women. Hawthorne could not be more direct in alerting us to Phoebe's cultural meaning, citing her "purifying influence" on the household atmosphere and comparing her effect to "a minute quantity of attar of rose" in a trunk of clothing (137). In essence, Phoebe cures the culturally outcast by moving them from the margins of the community toward its domestic center. Her presence, along with Clifford's return, elicits displays of more canonical womanly behavior from the prickly Hepzibah: "At such moments, Hepzibah would fling out her arms, and enfold Phoebe in them, and kiss her cheek, as tenderly as ever her mother had" (101). Her effect on Holgrave is to make "the House of the Seven Gables like a home to him," and her sympathy moves him from alienation to self-disclosure: "He poured himself out as to another self" (182). The operation of "influence" receives its fullest depiction in Hawthorne's account of Phoebe's effect on Clifford:

> To this man—whose whole poor and impalpable enjoyment of existence, heretofore, and until both his heart and fancy died within him, had been a dream—whose images of women had more and more lost their warmth and substance, and been frozen, like the pictures of secluded artists, into the chilliest ideality—to him, this little figure of the cheeriest household-life was just what he required, to bring him back into the breathing world. Persons who have wandered, or been expelled, out of the common track of things, even were it for a better system, desire nothing so much as to be led back. They shiver in their loneliness, be it on a mountain-top or in a dungeon. Now, Phoebe's presence made a home about her—that very sphere which the outcast, the prisoner, the potentate, the wretch beneath mankind, the wretch aside from it, or the wretch above it, instinctively pines after—a home! She was real! Holding her hand, you felt something; a tender something; a substance, and a warm one; and so long as you should feel its grasp, soft as it was, you might be certain that your place was good in the whole sympathetic chain of human nature. The world was no longer a delusion.
> (140–41)

Hawthorne is both imitating and, in an extraordinary way, extending and clarifying the claims made on behalf of female power within the sentimental ideology he is examining. He is careful, for example, to distinguish this admiration for Phoebe from the kind of idealization of women that aestheticizes and appropriates them; she is a power, not a "frozen" image. By conceiving of the potentate, the prisoner, and the artist as equally wretched, the passage identifies being "inside" domestic culture, "at home," as the greatest good, upsetting in the process the romantic hierarchies of power and spirit. Most striking is the metaphysical force given the domestic here. Phoebe is at once the creator of the home and the guarantor of the real; her touch ensures not simply one's comfort but one's place within the human community, one's escape from the meaninglessness, the "delusion," of a merely private selfhood. This celebration of womanly "influence" has become an ontological claim; being is conferred by the communal connection presided over by women and beginning in the home.

The House of the Seven Gables gives us no reason to question the sincerity of this claim about Phoebe's significance, and the power that Hawthorne's letters repeatedly attribute to his wife to make him real by loving him argues that he conceived of his own life story in just these terms.[13] What is curious, though, is that the book assigns this power and meaning to Phoebe without losing a sense that, in crucial ways, she is a very limited creature. For if Phoebe represents the domestic life that is the ground of meaning in this world, she also represents the tendency of the sentimental habit of mind to protect itself by excluding the complex or the difficult. Phoebe's tendency is "to think the thought proper for the moment," and, we are told, this capacity for "facile adaptation" is "at once the symptom of perfect health, and its best preservative" (137). But the way in which Phoebe's mind goes to work on her intuition that Judge Pyncheon is not what he seems suggests that this version of health is endangered by the very constriction that protects it.

> A doubt of this nature has a most disturbing influence, and, if shown to be a fact, comes with fearful and startling effect, on minds of the trim, orderly, and limit-loving class, in which we find our little country-girl. Dispositions more boldly speculative may derive a stern enjoyment from the discovery, since there must be evil in the world, that a high man is as likely to grasp his share of it, as a low one. A wider scope of view, and a deeper insight, may see rank, dignity, and station, all proved illusory, so far as regards their claim to human reverence, and yet not feel as if the universe were thereby tumbled headlong into chaos. But Phoebe, in order to keep the universe in its old place, was fain to smother, in some degree, her own intuitions as to Judge Pyncheon's character. (131–32)

Phoebe's view of the world, then, is temporarily comfortable but quite fragile; it takes a fair amount of intrapsychic labor—a glimpse of ideology in action—to keep her vision of orderliness in place, and that sense of order will not be adequate to the experiences and perspectives she will encounter within the Pyncheon house. As she will later tell Holgrave, "It makes me dizzy to think of such a shifting world!" (184). Phoebe, as the maker and protector of human connection, represents what this culture cannot do without. But her limitations and the vulnerability that attends them suggest the need for other kinds of capacity, like Hepzibah's rage or Holgrave's criticism, if the domestic is to survive its inevitable encounter with the authoritarian. Phoebe, then, does not need to change her cultural position because she is already central; her task, we might say, is to suffer expansion, to make a home for the marginal.

I have suggested that an account of the action of the book needs to notice the kind of treatment the characters call forth from Hawthorne's team of narrators as well as what they represent through their actions, habits of mind, and cultural associations. We must be alert to both the method of their representation and the way in which representation as a cultural act becomes one of the book's consistent interests. For one of the striking things about *The House*, and a sign of the sophistication of its cultural analysis, is the way that each character is associated with a particular strategy of representation. Thus Phoebe attracts not only the language of domestic celebration but, curiously, the jargon of contemporary book reviewing.

> The young girl, so fresh, so unconventional, and yet so orderly and obedient to common rules, as you at once recognized her to be, was widely in contrast, at that moment, with everything about her. (68)

> She shocked no canon of taste; she was admirably in keeping with herself, and never jarred against surrounding circumstances. (80)

By presenting Phoebe as a kind of aesthetic production, obeying certain standards of decorum but still "fresh" and "unconventional," the narrator connects Phoebe as a character to a particular kind of writing, the "domestic fiction" that reviewers admired for faithful observation and celebration of home and family, for a version of realism "in keeping" with the middle-class valuation of the home.[14] Clifford, significantly, receives the benefits of Phoebe's influence by reading her: "He read Phoebe, as he would a sweet and simple story; he listened to her, as if she were a verse of household poetry" (142). Hawthorne is suggesting, it seems to me, that Phoebe not only embodies womanly influence but represents, in her pleasing limitations, the kind of cultural production generated by her ideological position. The narrative logic of *The House of the Seven Gables*, then, insists that we see character as one "layer" within a larger cultural drama in which moral values, emotional needs, and the strategies of representation that give them expression compete and connect with one another, producing the culture that the book addresses and seeks to shape.

As my account of the representation of Hepzibah has already suggested, *The House* makes the operation of this cultural system dramatic through its orchestration of narrative voices. Phoebe calls forth a particular narrative voice, in possession of a set of rhetorical strategies and figures appropriate to her role as guarantor of meaning and borrowed from the kind of fiction with which she is associated. This voice, which we have already heard celebrating some of Phoebe's domestic accomplishments, welcomes her appearances in the novel by deploying the canonical tropes of domestic fiction, creating a set of nineteenth-century topoi that identify Phoebe's cultural habitation. Phoebe does not wake up but is kissed into sentience by her sister the Dawn (70) or greeted by "the early twittering of the conjugal couple of robins, in the pear tree" (98). She attracts countless comparisons to a sentimentalized nature and to the talismans of domestic life: "This natural tunefulness made Phoebe seem like a bird in a shadowy tree; or conveyed the idea that the stream of life warbled through her heart, as a brook sometimes warbles through a pleasant little dell" (76); she resembles "an earthly rosebud" (142), a garden flower (143), "the fire upon the hearth" (140).

What is the effect of these homey arias? We need to disabuse ourselves of the notion that Hawthorne is nodding here, unaware of the all-out sentimentality of these passages, or merely marketing a piety in which he does not fully believe. These assumptions have generated readings that too easily see *The House of the Seven Gables* as a desperately orthodox, muddled, or insincere work. The figurative range that Hawthorne displays within the book—Clifford's confronting Jaffrey, for example, "would be like flinging a porcelain vase, with already a crack in it, against a granite column" (242)—not to mention his other work, ought to be enough to convince us that these passages are performances. If we need a reminder that literary styles and effects are chosen and deployed things, we get one in Holgrave's remarks on the pieces he has written for "Graham and Godey": "In the humorous line, I am thought to have a very pretty way with me; and as for pathos, I am as provocative of tears as an onion!" (186).

It would be a mistake, though, to conclude that such passages, in their effect of "quotedness," aim at irony. They work, rather, to mark Phoebe's centrality by calling into being, in an identifiable way, the voice of the communal, which names her as its own. These topoi, through their use of a rhetoric that is familiar, already jointly possessed, give linguistic form to the experience of centrality. Figurative originality is beside the point here—even, arguably, a threat—because it does not participate in the building of the communal consensus that gives a culture its center of gravity. The way a shared rhetoric both marks and creates the central is intriguingly illustrated when the narrator represents himself as borrowing a figure, already canonical, from Uncle Venner, himself a walking miscellany of the vernacular wisdom:

> "I'm free to say, Miss Hepzibah, that I never knew a human creature do her work so much like one of God's angels, as this child Phoebe does!"

> Uncle Venner's eulogium, if it appear rather too high-strained for the person and occasion, had nevertheless a sense in which it was both subtle and true. There was a spiritual quality in Phoebe's activity. The life of the long and busy day—spent in occupations that might so easily have taken a squalid and ugly aspect—had been made pleasant, and even lovely, by the spontaneous grace with which these homely duties seemed to bloom out of her character; so that labor, while she dealt with it, had the easy and flexible charm of play. Angels do not toil, but let their good works grow out of them; and so did Phoebe. (82)

This rhetorical relay becomes the occasion for our participation, along with the narrator and Uncle Venner, in the construction of a community of sentiment. And this already-established rhetoric surfaces in the book whenever Hawthorne wants to notate a successful move toward the domestic center of middle-class culture. Thus Phoebe's curative effect on Clifford is acknowledged by an eruption of familiar figures that go to work to welcome Clifford into the sentimental consensus:

> But we strive in vain to put the idea into words. No adequate expression of the beauty and profound pathos, with which it impresses us, is attainable. This being, made only for happiness . . . this poor, forlorn voyager from the Islands of the Blest, in a frail bark, on a tempestuous sea, had been flung, by the last mountain-wave of his shipwreck, into a quiet harbor. There, as he lay more than half-lifeless on the strand, the fragrance of an earthly rosebud had come to his nostrils, and, as odors will, had summoned up reminiscences of visions of all the living and breathing beauty, amid which he should have had his home. (142)

This voice's deployment of sentimental rhetoric—even its doubts about language's capacity to render emotion are orthodox fare—alerts us to still another form of action within *The House of the Seven Gables*: a culture engaging in the ongoing work of its own construction.[15]

Hawthorne's many-layered representation of Phoebe, with its simultaneous attention to character, cultural position, and forms of representation, casts the reader as an analyst of culture and of the different discourses that shape and sustain it. We grasp our need for Phoebe as a source of meaning, and we observe, when Hawthorne shows us the ideological operations that establish her significance, how a cultural consensus is held in configuration. Yet Phoebe's limitations, like the constraints of the sentimental rhetoric that represents her, also reveal the vulnerability of a consensus that can accommodate only the domestic vision. The act of faith that *The House of the Seven Gables* performs in its celebration of Phoebe says that we cannot be at home in the world without her; the act of cultural analysis that the book simultaneously induces suggests that the center that Phoebe calls into being is not safe without the inclusion of a more expansive vision—a vision, like that induced by *The House* itself, both faithful and probing. Hawthorne's treatment of Phoebe implies, finally, that the health of a culture must be measured by what it is able to include as well as by what it needs to exclude. Our work as readers is being defined as well: we are engaged in deciding what should form the center of the community we represent.

The character through whom this expansion of the central is most crucially accomplished, both for Phoebe, who is eventually deepened by her exposure to him, and for us as readers, is Clifford. While our task in interpreting Phoebe was to notice how richly representative she is, through Clifford Hawthorne raises the question of what can be represented—and thus included within the cultural consensus the book is rebuilding. We first encounter this question in its most literal form, for our first glimpse of Clifford makes us wonder whether he can be represented at all. Clifford's imprisonment has robbed him of a place within the community; he returns to the Pyncheon house unfurnished with the means of self-presentation. In a book in which voices are directly associated with particular cultural locations, Clifford's voice at first fails him. Phoebe hears this "unknown voice" as "strangely indistinct," "less like articulate words than an unshaped sound," "an indistinct shadow of human utterance" (95, 97). His liminality is dramatized by his inability to cross the threshold of the parlor (103) and by the way he flickers in and out of existence:

> Continually, as we may express it, he faded away out of his place; or, in other words, his mind and consciousness took their departure, leaving his wasted, gray, and melancholy figure—a substantial emptiness, a material ghost—to occupy his seat at table. Again, after a blank moment, there would be a flickering taper-gleam in his eyeballs. It betokened that his spiritual part had returned, and was doing its best to kindle the heart's household-fire, and light up intellectual lamps in the dark and ruinous mansion, where it was doomed to be a forlorn inhabitant. (105)

Hawthorne's use of the figure of the house to represent Clifford's inner life links the restoration of his selfhood to his finding a place within the domestic sphere presided over by Phoebe. Clifford's role within the book's cultural drama is to move from inarticulateness to self-recovery, from marginality to representativeness.

Phoebe restores Clifford to himself, insofar as that is possible, by making him a place within the home. In response to Phoebe's care, Clifford comes progressively into focus and provides glimpses of what he might have been. Yet Clifford comes to mean different things to the reader than he does to Phoebe. Just as Phoebe represents both womanly influence and the domestic fiction that advances its claims, so Clifford is both identified as a particular character type and associated with a way of thinking about art. When Phoebe sees the miniature of Clifford, she responds to it with a kind of intuitive acuity that is part of her womanly prowess. His child-like expression evokes both a conviction of his essential innocence, and the maternal urge to protect him: "He ought never to suffer anything. One would bear much, for the sake of sparing him toil or sorrow" (75). The narrator later expands Phoebe's intuition into a meditation on Clifford's cultural role. As Clifford emerges into selfhood, he becomes definable as a "Sybarite," a connoisseur and consumer of "the Beautiful." As the narrator defines this role, it carries with it both an exemption from moral obligation and an interesting claim on the protection of others. He "should have nothing to do with sorrow; nothing with strife; nothing with the martyrdom which, in an infinite variety of shapes, awaits those who have the heart, and will, and conscience, to fight a battle with the world" (108). He owes the heroic Hepzibah nothing in return for her devotion, for "a nature like Clifford's can contract no debts of that kind. It is—we say it without censure, nor in diminution of the claim which it indefeasibly possesses on beings of another mould—it is always selfish in its essence; and we must give it leave to be so, and heap up our heroic and disinterested love upon it, so much the more, without a recompense" (109).

Clifford, as a type, occupies a curious place in the cultural consensus. In a sense he remains outside the culture's center even as he is admitted into its range of types. He is exempt from the moral economy of this culture—he "can contract no debts of that kind"—and consequently is not a part of the "we" that is obligated to love and protect him. Though there are dangers associated with this type—the narrator wonders whether Clifford, without his sorrow, might have become an affectionless monster of taste (112)—the innocent Clifford has value as a communal luxury, reminding the more earnest that there are pleasures that need not trouble the conscience. He is connected, via the idealizing aesthetic terminology ("the Beautiful," etc.) and pictorial range of description ("the quivering play of sunbeams through the shadowy foliage" [108]) that

Hawthorne chooses, to an understanding of art as similarly removed from the moral marketplace. This association between Clifford and the notion that art is free of ethical designs is reinforced by the narrator's description of Clifford's reading preferences. What he most enjoys is the sound of Phoebe's voice as she reads to him; fiction with the most modest moral or emotional claims—"pictures of life, scenes of passion or sentiment, wit, humor, and pathos" (146)—is lost on him. He prefers poetry of the "flitting and ethereal" type to fiction, but he most enjoys Phoebe's descriptions, uninflected by any intent at all, of the goings-on in the garden where they sit.

Clifford's exemption from moral responsibility and his dependence on Phoebe and Hepzibah suggest that a morally earnest middle-class culture can accommodate Clifford and the version of the artist he represents precisely because of his abdication of any claim to moral power; indeed, his aestheticism helps demarcate the seriousness that establishes the moral authority of the domestic view. There is already a place for this version of the artist within sentimental culture, as the familiar figurative language that celebrates Clifford's recovery—"this poor, forlorn voyager from the Islands of the Blest, in a frail bark, on a tempestuous sea" (142, cited previously)—implies.[16] Yet Clifford also represents things within the world of *The House of the Seven Gables* that are much more difficult to accommodate. To engage that knowledge is the task that Hawthorne sets for the reader.

A narrator different from the celebrant of Clifford as wounded, ethereal artist takes over his representation at crucial moments in the novel, and insists that we notice not his difference from us but his connection to us. The most important of these passages occur during the depiction of moments in the Pyncheon garden, where Clifford, via the observation of cultivated nature and Sunday afternoon conversation, takes the domestic cure. The movement toward cure is strikingly disrupted and complicated when Clifford slips out of the role of the dependent aesthete and starts to mean something else:

> He himself, as was perceptible by many symptoms, lay darkly behind his pleasure, and knew it to be a baby-play, which he was to toy and trifle with, instead of thoroughly believing. Clifford saw, it may be, in the mirror of his deeper consciousness, that he was an example and representative of that great chaos of people, whom an inexplicable Providence is continually putting at cross-purposes with the world; breaking what seems its own promise in their nature; withholding their proper food, and setting poison before them for a banquet; and thus—when it might so easily, as one would think, have been adjusted otherwise—making their existence a strangeness, a solitude, and torment. (149)

There is a Clifford who cannot be contained by the aesthetic, to whom suffering has given the analytic force to see the implications of his victimization. Clifford is an "example and representative"—to himself, to the narrator, to the reader—of the threat of a meaninglessness that domestic—indeed, all—ideology exists to counter. Providence, as Clifford reflects its operations, may be "inexplicable," the world a "chaos." It may even, in its perversion of nurture and production of alienation, parody the domestic order that thinks of itself as a secular enactment of providential sympathy.

Clifford, in this aspect, tests the capacity of sentimental ideology to account for experience, and he himself, in his secret despair, struggles to sustain a view of reality that includes both himself and Phoebe, both the possibility of happiness and the fact of irremediable loss. At the end of this account of the domestic life of the Pyncheon garden, the narrator gives us a version of Clifford's representativeness—more, his centrality—even harder to accommodate. The taste of pleasure that Clifford gets in the garden leads him to make a moral claim on his culture: "I want my happiness! . . . Many, many years I have waited for it! It is late! It is late! I want my happiness!" Clifford's attempt to assert his place within his culture produces an extraordinary meditation by the narrator:

> Alas, poor Clifford! You are old, and worn with troubles that ought never to have befallen you. You are partly crazy and partly imbecile; a ruin, a failure, as almost everybody is—though some in less degree, or less perceptibly, than their fellows. Fate has no happiness in store for you; unless your quiet home in the old family residence, with the faithful Hepzibah, and your summer afternoons with Phoebe, and these Sabbath festivals with Uncle Venner and the Daguerreotypist, deserve to be called happiness! Why not? If not the thing itself, it is marvellously like it, and the more so for that ethereal and intangible quality, which causes it all to vanish, at too close an introspection. Take it, therefore, while you may. Murmur not—question not—but make the most of it! (157–58)

Despite its homey references, this endorsement of the domestic is conducted on strikingly queasy grounds. Clifford becomes the representative of an order of absolute loss, an order in which each of us—"partly crazy and partly imbecile, a ruin, a failure"—is said to share. Clifford's situation moves from marginal to central; we are linked to him by an irreducible feeling of alienation, which the passage reveals as the ground of our affiliation to the domestic ideology that the passage weirdly celebrates. And our participation in that consensus is further revealed as a precarious act of faith not in a certainty but in a semblance. Yet in its exhortative close the passage reminds us that it is just such an act of faith—expanded into a shared exercise of the communal will—that makes a culture's center hold. Such knowledge, for which Clifford has become the occasion, constitutes what we might call cultural maturity, and it is the kind of participation in culture toward which Hawthorne's book is leading its reader.

Our question about Clifford was whether he could be represented, in the full range of his difficult meaning, within the communal consensus that *The House of the Seven Gables* is constructing. In Jaffrey Pyncheon we encounter a character constituted by his command of the strategies of self-presentation, a walking image designed for public consumption:

> No better model need be sought, nor could have been found, of a very high order of respectability, which by some indescribable magic, not merely expressed itself in looks and gestures, but even governed the fashion of his garments, and rendered them all proper and essential to the man. Without appearing to differ, in any tangible way, from other people's clothes, there was yet a wide and rich gravity about them, that must have been characteristic of the wearer, since it could not be defined as pertaining either to the cut or material. His gold-headed cane, too—a serviceable staff, of dark, polished wood—had similar traits, and, had it chosen to take a walk by itself, would have been recognized anywhere as a tolerably adequate representation of its master. This character—which showed itself so strikingly in everything about him, and the effect of which we seek to convey to the reader—went no deeper than his station, habits of life, and external circumstances. One perceived him to be a personage of mark, influence, and authority. (56–57)

Jaffrey is a public "figure" in several senses. His public character consists of the costumes and manners through which he produces the effect of authority; because he is all figure and no ground, his character is easily representable by the synecdoche "the gold-headed cane." Unlike his Puritan ancestor, this contemporary Pyncheon has had to adjust his style of self-presentation to the political theater of democracy, as his exaggerated humility, his frequently deployed, all-embracing smile, and his wearing of a form of silk "resembling broadcloth" (116) attest. This benign, democratic version of authority is revealed as a mystification whenever Jaffrey is resisted, however. Then the appropriative urge that generates this public performance surfaces, wearing the lineaments of the Puritan ancestor, and expressing "not . . . wrath or hatred, but a certain hot fellness of purpose, which annihilated everything but itself" (129). Hawthorne's phrasing suggests that it is precisely the absence of emotion that renders this drive to possess so "frightful"—even hatred would be, comparatively, a comfort. This absence of emotion, in turn, makes another of Jaffrey's representational strategies even more insidious: Jaffrey is an adept in sentimental discourse. Here is Jaffrey talking that talk: "Ah, you little know me, Cousin Hepzibah! You little know this heart! It now throbs at the thought of meeting him! There lives not the human being— (except yourself; and you not more than I)—who has shed so many tears for Clifford's calamity! You behold some of them now. There is none who would so delight to promote his happiness! Try me, Hepzibah!—try me cousin!—try the man whom you have treated as your enemy and Clifford's!—try Jaffrey Pyncheon, and you shall find him true, to the heart's core!" (227). Power in democratic Salem, Hawthorne's depiction of Jaffrey's character suggests, consists of mastery of the means of representation. And because Jaffrey's command of sentimental discourse conceals an emotionless appropriativeness that makes him impermeable to "influence," this portrait reveals him to be what the domestic consensus must recognize and expel if it is to survive as a significant form of social power.

Jaffrey's version of authority calls forth, as the book progresses, a kind of counterauthority. This alternative point of view produces an account of Jaffrey that punctures the high respectability of the authorized portrait:

> But, besides these cold, formal, and empty words of the chisel that inscribes, the voice that speaks, and the pen that writes for the public eye and for distant time—and which inevitably lose much of their truth and freedom by the fatal consciousness of so doing—there were traditions about the ancestor, and private diurnal gossip about the Judge, remarkably accordant in their testimony. It is often instructive to take the woman's, the private and domestic view, of a public man; nor can anything be more curious than the vast discrepancy between portraits intended for engraving, and the pencil-sketches that pass from hand to hand, behind the original's back. (122)

The Pyncheon that emerges from this unofficial portrait—"bold, imperious, relentless, crafty; laying his purposes deep, and following them out with an inveteracy of pursuit that knew neither rest nor conscience; trampling on the weak, and . . . doing his utmost to beat down the strong" (123)—is, like his ancestor, an embodiment of the appropriative and the authoritarian. He is also connected to a degree of domestic tyranny and sexual violence—his wife is said to have gotten "her death-blow in the honey-moon" and spent her short life demonstrating her "fealty to her liege-lord and master" (123)—that identifies him as the enemy of the womanly power that makes the domestic the site of meaning. This passage identifies "the private and domestic view" as the source of a subversive perspective, preserved by gossip's communal voice rather than official document, which resists Jaffrey's form of power. It begins as well the creation of an alliance between this traditional perspective and the analytic, ideologically sophisticated narrator who becomes responsible for the representation of Jaffrey.

This alliance generates a series of ironies at Jaffrey's expense, notably the communal jokes attracted, like the flies, by his tropical smile. It yields, for example, a demystification of the authority style employed by the rich in a democracy, an exaggerated humility that proves "a haughty consciousness of his advantages, as irrefragably as if he had marched forth, preceded by a troop of lackeys to clear the way" (130). This combination of gossip and the analytic culminates in an extended analysis of Jaffrey's character conducted by the analytic narrator but informed in crucial ways by the communal voice. Men with Jaffrey's moral psychology, the narrator claims,

> are ordinarily men to whom forms are of paramount importance. Their field of action lies among the external phenomena of life. They possess vast ability in grasping, and arranging, and appropriating to themselves, the big, heavy, solid unrealities, such as gold, landed estate, offices of trust and emolument, and public honors. With these materials, and with deeds of goodly aspect, done in the public eye, an individual of this class builds up, as it were, a tall and stately edifice, which, in the view of other people, and ultimately in his own view, is no other than the man's character, or the man himself. Behold, therefore, a palace! Its splendid halls and suites of spacious apartments are floored with a mosaic-work of costly marbles; its windows, the whole height of each room, admit the sunshine through the most transparent of plate-glass; its high cornices are gilded, and its ceilings gorgeously painted; and a lofty dome—through which, from the central pavement, you may gaze up to the sky, as with no obstructing medium between—surmounts the whole. With what fairer and nobler emblem could any man desire to shadow forth his character? Ah; but in some low and obscure nook—some narrow closet on the ground floor, shut, locked, and bolted, and the key flung away—or beneath the marble pavement, in a stagnant water-puddle, with the richest pattern of mosaic work above—may lie a corpse, half-decayed, and still decaying, and diffusing its death-scent all through the palace! The inhabitant will not be conscious of it; for it has long been his daily breath! Neither will the visitors; for they smell only the rich odors which the master sedulously scatters through the palace, and the incense which they bring, and delight to burn before him! Now and then, perchance, comes in a seer, before whose gifted eye the whole structure melts into thin air, leaving only the hidden nook, the bolted closet, with the cobwebs festooned over its forgotten door, or the deadly hole under the pavement, and the decaying corpse within. Here, then, we are to seek the true emblem of the man's character, and of the deed that gives whatever reality it possesses, to his life. (229–30)

What makes this spectacular passage so interesting is its curiously mixed cultural provenance. The representation of Jaffrey as a glorious edifice concealing corruption borrows the analogy between the condition of the self and structure of the house that is at the heart of the image-structure of domestic ideology—a vocabulary deployed in the comparisons between the Pyncheon mansion and the human heart that are so prominent in the book's opening chapter. The link between architecture and the psyche connects this edifice to the tradition of the popular gothic as well, and gives this emblem of hypocrisy a familiar or customary quality. Yet the image, along with its accessibility, exerts a kind of analytic pressure, especially in its suggestion that Jaffrey has emptied out his character by coming to believe in the lineaments of his own public representation, that links it to the more difficult psychological allegory that defines Hawthorne's practice of romance in the stories and in *The Scarlet Letter*. The passage's figure of the solitary seer and its homage, I am convinced, to Melville's great excavation of the edifice of the self, the Hotel de Cluny passage in *Moby-Dick*, emphasize the "marginal" or "difficult" elements of the emblem.[17]

This allegory of Jaffrey's character, I am arguing, is at once a crucial account of the condition of Jaffrey's psyche and an enactment of an alliance, achieved through a mixture of popular and marginal styles of figuration, between the traditional and the sophisticated psychologies of power. The narrator's probing examination of Jaffrey's moral psychology provides us with some knowledge that the traditional portrayal leaves out or mystifies. Instead of interpreting Jaffrey's evil in the manner of legend, as the reincarnation of the appropriating Puritan, the narrator presents it as chosen, the consequence not only of the initial act of victimization but of the daily suppression of the voice of his conscience. Because this suppression of the "inner" experience of consciousness eventually erases character except as an external representation—the high-minded, official Jaffrey, in which he himself has come to believe—Jaffrey is completely outside the power of transformation by "influence" and must be resisted in another way: "A hard, cold man, thus unfortunately situated, seldom or never looking inward, and resolutely taking his idea of himself from what purports to be his image, as reflected in the mirror of public opinion, can scarcely arrive at true self-knowledge, except through loss of property and reputation" (232). Nevertheless, the knowledge available to the marginal seer and that possessed by the subversive voice of popular tradition are—as unmaskings of the authoritarian—ripe for combination.

Hepzibah's moment of resistance to Jaffrey, which immediately follows this extended exploration of his character, provides an instance of this alliance at work. Her enraged response to Jaffrey's chilling threat to put Clifford into an asylum combines an invocation of the domestic ("You have forgotten that a woman was your mother!") with an analysis that unmasks Jaffrey's behavior: "You are but doing over again, in another shape, what your ancestor before you did, and sending down to your posterity the curse inherited from him!" (236–37). Hepzibah's condemnation of Jaffrey generates, in turn, the narrator's meditation on Jaffrey's ultimate unhappiness ("it may be that no wearier and sadder man had ever sunk into the chair" [238]), an assertion of the ultimate superiority of sentimental values, and the prelude to the physical death that confirms the death-in-life revealed by the edifice emblem.

The Pyncheon urge toward economic appropriation and psychological domination generates, then, both at the center of this culture and at its margins, strategies of opposition. The effect of this alliance between gossip and romance is not to suggest the superior acuity of the marginal but to establish its value to the antiauthoritarianism latent in the community. The analytic narrator who makes common cause with "the woman's, the private and domestic view" can give both analytic force and legible public form to the communal opposition to Jaffrey's form of power, thus ending the unintended cooperation between the sentimental and the authoritarian that Jaffrey's politics of misrepresentation has brought about. And the democratic authority possessed by the communal voice in turn rescues the marginal view from the impotence of cultural isolation. *The House of the Seven Gables* is thus offering itself, through the reading of Jaffrey that it arranges, as a model for the construction of a new cultural center.

Jaffrey, who occupies a position of centrality within the official culture of Salem, is revealed, through the intimations of the communal voice and the analysis of the narrator, to be covertly marginal. His appropriation of both property and people, his immunity to influence, and his parodic mastery of the rhetoric of sincerity identify him as precisely what the sentimental consensus needs to expel if it is to protect its version of community. Holgrave, whose radicalism and marginality is made much of, turns out to be secretly central and becomes the focus of the book's attempt to build an alternative cultural consensus. Like the other characters, Holgrave is capaciously representative: a composite of one of the most talked about—and worried over—figures of antebellum society, the young man who moves from job to job and from city to city, looking, in effect, for a place within American culture or for a new vision of culture that might accommodate him. Thus at the age of twenty-two Holgrave has been a country-schoolmaster, a salesman, a newspaper editor, a peddler of Cologne water, a dentist in various factory towns, a foreign traveler, a member of a Fourierist community, and a public lecturer on mesmerism—all before assuming his present role as a daguerreotypist. His political activities have been equally omniverous; Hepzibah reports to Phoebe that Holgrave hangs around with assorted "banditti-like associates": "men with long beards, and dressed in linen bouses; . . . reformers, temperance lecturers, and all manner of cross-looking philanthropists; community-men and come-outers . . . who acknowledged no law and ate no solid food." The penny press has accused him of "making a speech, full of wild and disorganizing matter" (84). The historian Karen Halttunen calls these young men, set in motion by the shift from an agricultural and artisanal economy to a more urban and industrial market economy, "liminal."[18] For Hawthorne, too, Holgrave represents life on a cultural border or threshhold; he lives, in his own wing of the mansion, in proximity to but not within the sentimental consensus represented by Phoebe and in uneasy relation to his own family history. The book engages, through Holgrave, the question of what cultural place—historical, political, ideological—such a man might occupy.

Compared to the anxiousness occasioned by such liminal figures in contemporary writing and reform activity, Hawthorne's portrait of Holgrave is remarkable for its equanimity. Hawthorne seems less worried by the social ferment associated with figures like Holgrave than interested in imagining a counter to Jaffrey. In contrast to Jaffrey's manipulative legalism, Holgrave follows "a law of his own," the antinomian perspective that is the beginning (though never for Hawthorne the fulfillment) of resistance to the authoritarian. While Jaffrey's public representation has erased his conscience and evacuated his interior, Holgrave, despite his immersion in the social flux, has "never lost his identity" or integrity: "he had never violated the innermost man, but had carried his conscience along with him" (177). Where Jaffrey, in his obsessive quest to appropriate, is associated with repetition and the deterministic, Holgrave, with his "deep consciousness of inward strength" and enough ambition to make his "generous impulses" efficacious, is a figure full of possibility, though his ultimate success is "delightfully uncertain" (181), given the caprices of American social and economic life.

In order fully to understand Holgrave's cultural significance, we need to attend to the specific way in which Hawthorne places him within the Pyncheon house, and to the way—by now familiar to readers of this essay—that questions of character bear ideological fruit in this book. Within the small community created by the inhabitants of the Pyncheon mansion, Holgrave occupies, as he does in relation to the larger cultural mainstream, a cultural boundary, the threshold between participation and observation. In a number of ways, Holgrave is drawn powerfully toward the sentimental values at the center of domestic ideology. He discovers within himself a deep need for the self-revelation made possible by sympathetic connection to Phoebe; as we noticed earlier, the "home" she creates enables him to "pour himself out as to another self" (182). Despite his sense of the inhibiting force of the past, he retains a belief in the possibility of social transformation that is allied to the story of personal transformation at the heart of the idea of "influence": "He had that sense, or inward prophecy—which a young man had better never have been born, than not to have, and a mature man had better die at once, than utterly to relinquish—that we are not doomed to creep on forever in the old, bad way, but that, this very now, there are the harbingers abroad of a golden era, to be accomplished in his own lifetime" (179). Holgrave's urge toward the central is wittily underlined by the revelation that he is a closet cultivator. In a reversal of Jaffrey's concealment of inner rapaciousness by public benignity, Holgrave is discovered secretly to engage in the art of gardening. Holgrave is also the grower of the bean vines that produce "a vivid scarlet blossom," bringing an earthy beauty to the garden that delights and soothes Clifford; these bean seeds, generations old and found in a garret of the mansion, also suggest the possibility of a more fertile relation to the past than Holgrave is inclined to imagine.[19]

Yet Holgrave's potential for fruitful connection to the little community of the house and to the domestic values it represents is endangered by the allure of a different social role. This cultural position might be thought of as a kind of permanent marginality; its authority is based not upon communal alliance but on a solely private integrity maintained by withdrawal, upon the strict construction of a law of one's own. Thus Phoebe senses Holgrave's removal from the communal: "he was too calm and cool an observer. Phoebe felt his eye, often; his heart, seldom or never. He . . . never exactly made common cause with them, nor gave any reliable evidence that he loved them better, in proportion as he knew them more. In his relations with them, he seemed to be in quest of mental food; not heart-sustenance" (177–78). The language in which Hawthorne couches Holgrave's observership, in identifying him with the eye and mind rather than the heart, places him outside the rhetorical and cultural sphere of the domestic consensus.[20] If we remember the book's association of Jaffrey with surveillance, Holgrave's connection with the "eye" suggests a violation of the laws of sympathetic exchange that govern the domestic sphere; he becomes in this language a consumer of the experience of others rather than a sharer of emotional "sustenance." This kind of chosen marginality is not only isolating but, as we shall see, threatens to reproduce the appropriating relation to others that Jaffrey embodies.

There is a different, more complex kind of entrapment implicit in Holgrave's way of imagining his relation to history. Here are some excerpts from his well-known protest against the power of the Past:

> "Shall we never, never get rid of this Past! . . . It lies upon the Present like a giant's dead body! In fact, the case is just as if a young giant were compelled

to waste all his strength in carrying about the corpse of the old giant, his grandfather, who died a long while ago, and only needs to be decently buried. . . . A Dead Man sits on all our judgement-seats; and living judges do but search out and repeat his decisions. We read in Dead Men's books! We laugh at Dead Men's jokes, and cry at Dead Men's pathos! We are sick of Dead Men's diseases, physical and moral, and die of the same remedies with which dead doctors killed their patients! We worship the living Deity, according to Dead Men's forms and creeds! Whatever we seek to do, of our own free motion, a Dead Man's icy hand obstructs us! Turn our eyes to what point we may, a Dead Man's white, immitigable face encounters them, and freezes our very heart! And we must be dead ourselves, before we can begin to have our proper influence on our own world." (182–83)

Both at the start and at the close of Holgrave's harangue, the kind of attack on authority that was in the transcendental air is punctuated by a swerve into the bodily, into the personal imagery of the horrific, that marks Holgrave's speech as a symptom of private anxiety rather than a piece of political analysis. Hawthorne presents Holgrave's anxiety as a fantasy of determinism; he imagines that the Past has in effect erased the Present by robbing its inhabitants of agency. The fear at work in the passage is the fear of immobilization and erasure; what the young man reads in the face—literally in the gaze—of the authoritative is his utter powerlessness. Holgrave's Dead Man, moreover, recalls in striking ways the novel's depiction of Jaffrey Pyncheon, both in his occupation of most of the available seats of authority and in the emphasis on the bodily, which gives the passage its horrific kick. This intimation of abject powerlessness in the face of this Jaffrey-like figure, it seems to me, is what accounts for both the extremity and the odd literalism of Holgrave's desire to erase the past, and with it the authority that to him it represents. It is because authority, as it is represented by Jaffrey, can only be conceived of as domination that Holgrave must erase it before it erases him; hence Holgrave's claim that he lives in the Pyncheon house only so as to learn how to hate it and his requirement that no house or family should last more than a generation.

Holgrave's attitude toward Jaffrey has generally been left unanalyzed by critics of *The House*, who have used this statement of Holgrave's politics as a way of measuring his bad faith, or his taming by the domestic, when he moves into Jaffrey's country house at the book's close. The isolation and immobility that attend Holgrave's fantasy of Jaffrey's absolute power, together with the silliness of tearing down houses as a political program, argue that we should instead see Holgrave's harangue against the past as a kind of cultural immaturity, the consequence of a young man's anxieties about the power of the fathers. This way of seeing

Holgrave's position is confirmed when Hawthorne has Clifford repeat Holgrave's program verbatim as part of the delightfully loony transcendentalist pastiche he delivers during his childlike—and fruitless—attempt to escape from Salem in the aftermath of Jaffrey's death.[21] "To plant a family! This idea is at the bottom of most of the wrong and mischief which men do," says Holgrave. Holgrave's position here exposes his difficulty in thinking about authority. Holgrave is as yet unable to distinguish between two possible meanings of the desire "to plant a family": the impulse to cultivate, which he feels strongly; and the urge to appropriate, which he has learned from Jaffrey needs suppression. His response is to deny the impulse altogether. Or, to put this another way, Holgrave cannot yet see the possible fruitfulness of the alliance between his critical perspective and the domestic tradition that his own career within the book will call into being.

We can, then, understand the lure of observership for Holgrave as the manifestation of his reluctance to enter the field of Jaffrey's authority, a reluctance that betrays his anxiety about his own resources for resisting the authoritarian. This aspect of Hawthorne's portrayal of Holgrave becomes especially significant when we notice that, like the book's other characters, he is carefully associated with a particular kind of representation. By virtue of his present occupation and his familial heritage, Holgrave becomes the book's exemplar of the kind of art that Hawthorne himself practices in his earlier fiction—the probingly analytic or "psychological" romance that Hawthorne depreciates in his prefaces as more elusive and marginal than an everyday realism, but nevertheless identifies as characteristically his own. This connection is strongly established through Holgrave's description of his work as a daguerreotypist—for Hawthorne not at all a straightforwardly realistic art—and through the product of that work, the picture of Jaffrey that penetrates his public mask and reveals the true lineaments of his grasping character and his resemblance to his unscrupulous ancestor. "There is a wonderful insight in heaven's broad and simple sunshine," Holgrave tells Phoebe. "While we give it credit only for depicting the merest surface, it actually brings out the secret character with a truth that no painter would ever venture upon, even could he detect it" (91). Holgrave's unmasking of Jaffrey, moreover, links him to the "seer" who could penetrate the edifice of Jaffrey's public self-representation, and thus to the analytic narrator who joins the voice of tradition in its attack upon Jaffrey's authority. Finally, his Maule lineage associates him with the image-generating fountain that is this book's clearest invocation of the romance place, and with the occult arts of character penetration, reminiscent of the novelist, that give the Maules their power over the Pyncheons.

Through this connection between Holgrave and the practice of romance, Hawthorne's depiction of the daguerreotypist becomes an interrogation of the cultural role that might be played by an artist of the marginal. While the origin of Holgrave's art in sunlight—a medium associated with Phoebe—and its capacity to expose the true Jaffrey forecast the kind of alliance with the domestic suggested in the book's treatment of Jaffrey, Holgrave's observatory tendencies suggest that romance, as an artistic strategy and cultural role, is also liable to the self-entrapment of a willful marginality. During a conversation about Clifford, Phoebe tells Holgrave that she feels that too probing an examination of Clifford's interior life would be an act of aggression, a violation of the sanctity of the private self. Holgrave's response is striking: "I can understand the feeling without possessing it. Had I your opportunities, no scruples would prevent me from fathoming Clifford to the full depth of my plummet-line!" (178). The appropriativeness implicit in Holgrave's analytic interest in Clifford is revealed by the language Hawthorne gives him here: "fathoming" becomes a verb of consumption, its object the possession of the whole of Clifford's psyche. After he makes this statement, Holgrave's attempt to cover his tracks is still more revealing: "this is such an odd and incomprehensible world! The more I look at it, the more it puzzles me; and I begin to suspect that a man's bewilderment is the measure of his wisdom. Men and women, and children, too, are such strange creatures, that one never can be certain that he really knows them; nor ever guess what they have been, from what he sees them to be now. Judge Pyncheon! Clifford! What a complex riddle—a complexity of complexities—do they present!" (178–79). Here Holgrave covers over his intellectual consumerism with an appeal to a generalized interest in complexity that invests his voyeurism with the aura of objectivity. Holgrave's mystification of his behavior, by making a fetish of the complex, exposes one of the dangers of romance as a form of art and a stance toward the community: its tendency to devolve into an evasion of the culture it addresses, to take refuge in an analytic distance that unknowingly replicates—without the inconvenience of the actual exercise of power—the appropriativeness of the Pyncheon-style authority it attacks.

Holgrave, on the threshold between commitment to the life of the house and analytic appropriation of it, allows Hawthorne to meditate on the cultural role of his way of writing and the dangers that threaten to immobilize it at the margins of culture. Just as Holgrave's move from anxious isolation to cultural maturity can only come through the acknowledgment of his stake in the house, so the value of romance's analytic perspective depends upon its alliance with a set of values on behalf of which it can act. The powerful alliance between the sentimental and the analytic that the book imagines is endangered not only by sentimental ideology's intolerance for the complex and the inadequacy of its understanding of power—its tendency, that is, unthinkingly to cooperate in the oppression of marginal figures like Clifford—but by the lure of the authoritarian as it disguises itself in an elitism of the marginal.

I have been describing, in my discussion of the characters of *The House of the Seven Gables*, the behavior of a remarkable literary invention: a narrative strategy that, by incorporating both a synchronic and a diachronic view of its materials, manages to represent—with a degree of success that it has been my purpose to demonstrate—the action of a cultural system as it emerges into history. One apprehends this purpose at work most directly, I think, in the book's curious narrative rhythm: though the plot of the novel is amply furnished with events, the sense of an unfolding action that one gets from most novels is replaced by the notion that relatively tiny acts are being surrounded by the large orbit of their implications. Here, reduced to simplest terms, is the story that emerges from Hawthorne's extraordinary narrative practice. *The House of the Seven Gables* gives us American middle-class culture at a moment of crisis. Hawthorne's Salem reveals a society in which the center of meaning—the domestic life presided over by Phoebe—and the center of power—the public realm presided over by Jaffrey—are dangerously split. The result is a cynical political culture in which a parody of democratic representation keeps the community as much under the appropriative thumb as it was in Colonel Pyncheon's day, and a social life debilitated by the isolation of ethical values in the domestic sphere, by the trivialization of the artist, and by the exile of imaginative acuity to the cultural margins or into the underground of legend and gossip. The ambition driving *The House of the Seven Gables*, as my account of Hawthorne's many-layered narrative has been suggesting, is to attack this cultural illness by engaging the reader in the reconstruction of the communal center. Hawthorne sets out to forge an alliance between the vision of human connection located in the domestic sphere and the critical perspective that can penetrate and disrupt the strategies of representation that maintain the authoritarian. As the book moves toward its close, this alliance is fully established and examined. And in the process, Hawthornian romance is redefined as the cultural medium for the negotiation of such an alliance.

RESOLUTIONS

Just as *The House of the Seven Gables* begins several times, so it ends in several different ways, each constructing or defining some aspect of the new cultural alliance that the book envisions. And just as questions of character and action throughout the work are connected to issues of representation, so the book's movement toward resolution is, all along, providing a theory of the cultural significance of fictive representation that counters both the literalism of Jaffrey Pyncheon and the trivialization of art that domestic ideology is liable to. The most resonant of these resolutions is Holgrave's telling of his version of Pyncheon history, the tale "Alice Pyncheon," to Phoebe. In its content and effect the telling is at once a momentous event within the book and a meditation on the cultural role of an unmistakably Hawthornian fiction, for both its thematic force and the kind of reading it sets in motion identify Holgrave's tale as a piece of analytic romance. I am suggesting, then, that Hawthorne scrutinizes his own artistic practice in the same way that he analyzes the other strategies of representation identified in *The House of the Seven Gables*.

"Alice Pyncheon" is most Hawthornian in the way its allegory compresses the history that concerns the book as a whole into an emblematic interchange that makes possible the analysis of that history's causal logic.[22] Holgrave begins by establishing, as does the book itself, the distinction between the Pyncheon and Maule claims to the house. The Maule claim is allied to the domestic—"his grandfather had felled the pine-trees and built a cottage, in which children had been born to him" (192)—while the Pyncheon claim depends on legal authority for its enforcement. Gervayse Pyncheon attempts to put Matthew Maule to work on behalf of the legalistic; he and his lawyers are convinced that a deed exists establishing the Pyncheon claim to a vast amount of land in Maine and suspect that Maule possesses, as his sole inheritance from his grandfather, knowledge of the whereabouts of that deed. Maule enters into a bargain with Pyncheon—the house and its land in return for the deed—but he complicates the arrangement by insisting that he must use Pyncheon's daughter Alice as the medium for his mesmerical title search. The effect of this exchange between Maule and Pyncheon is to bring the book's competing cultural spheres, its two forms of power, into contact, defining in the process the desires and behaviors that most endanger the community.

"Alice Pyncheon" offers this crucial knowledge in return for an act of reading that works to recover the oblique logic that links the elements of the narrative. The swerve toward brutality taken by this bargain originates in the first encounter between Matthew Maule and Alice Pyncheon. We begin with a description of her social presence. Her combination of "cold stateliness" and latent "tenderness" produces a curious effect on the "man of generous nature": "[he] would have forgiven all her pride, and have been content, almost, to lie down in her path, and let Alice set her slender foot upon his heart. All he would have required, was simply the acknowledgement that he was indeed a man, and a fellow-being, moulded of the same elements as she" (201). Alice occupies the boundary between two cultural positions—the urge to dominate that characterizes the aristocratic Pyncheons and the humanity-conferring "acknowledgement" that is central to Hawthorne's account of domestic life. Her response to Maule, though, moves her definitively into the aristocratic: "A glow of artistic approval brightened over Alice Pyncheon's face; she was struck with admiration—which she made no attempt to conceal—of the remarkable comeliness, strength, and energy of Maule's figure" (201). Because Maule understands the glance so fully ("Does the girl look at me as if I were a brute beast!"), he cannot forgive it, and he determines to prove to Alice the strength of his "human spirit." Here, then, is the moment that generates the action of the tale: Alice's artistic appreciation of Maule turns him into a piece of property, and engenders the form of his revenge—the attempt, via mesmerism, to stake a claim to her spirit.

In the course of his simultaneous attempt to recover the deed and establish his possession of Alice's selfhood, Maule pauses to demonstrate to Gervayse Pyncheon the meaning of the Pyncheon way of life. Maule's demonstration of his complete power over Alice's body is calculated to draw out for Pyncheon the implications of his willingness to risk her in exchange for the deed. By establishing Pyncheon's inability to reclaim Alice from the trance he has induced, Maule makes literal the alienation that is implicit in Pyncheon's decision. He has irrevocably made her a piece of property, and consequently he cannot return her to sentience, even with his belated turn to the arsenal of sentimental connection ("He kissed her, with so great a heart-throb in the kiss . . ." [205]). As Maule insists, Pyncheon has sold his daughter. Maule's mesmerism—in analogy to the analytic penetration of romance—reveals that within the house of Pyncheon the property relation has cancelled out the familial bond; the ambition to "plant a family" (185) has destroyed a family. The vision that Maule finally evokes within Alice's psyche reveals not the deed but the ironic logic of the Pyncheon quest. Colonel Pyncheon, eternally prevented by the Maules from speaking the deed's location, has achieved, in the most literal way, its permanent possession: he has, in effect, swallowed it, experiencing primitive accumulation with a vengeance.

More subtle than Maule's analysis of the hidden logic of the Pyncheon way of life is the tale's depiction of the private transaction between Matthew Maule and Alice Pyncheon and of the way his revenge implicates him in the appropriation he criticizes. As I have suggested, Alice begins by claiming, with her glance, property rights to Maule's person. Her willingness to risk mesmerism depends, in turn, on her confidence in her inviolable possession of herself: "this fair girl deemed herself conscious of a power—combined of beauty, high, unsullied purity, and the preservative force of womanhood—that could make her sphere impenetrable, unless betrayed by treachery within" (203). The language in which Alice expresses this claim attaches her sense of self-property to the way of thinking about womanhood characteristic of domestic ideology. Alice's claim, that is, brings together the two cultural positions—the Pyncheon emphasis on possession and the sentimental emphasis on womanly power—that have thus far seemed opposed. As in the image of Alice's power to induce the subjection of her male admirers, however, her gender role has been infiltrated by her Pyncheonesque belief in absolute rights of property. Maule's triumph over Alice, his ability to penetrate her "sphere," should not, given his plight at the end of the story, be taken as an assertion of the ultimate superiority of male force. Maule's achievement of a claim on Alice's interior demonstrates, rather, the need for a deeper understanding of the implications of the idea of "influence" that is at the center of the sentimental theory of selfhood. The self, then, is relational, established and shaped by the form of its connections with others. There is, short of the death-in-life made manifest in the character structure of Jaffrey Pyncheon, no such thing as absolute property in one's self.

Alice's loss of self-control clarifies the theory of human connection upon which the book's hopes for community are based. To the extent that the sentimental conception of self is infiltrated by the idea of absolute possession, it is subject to the appropriation it pretends to repudiate, just as Alice's "appreciation" of Maule and her absolutist sense of self subject her to the domination that her treatment of him has awakened. This interpretation is clinched, it seems to me, by the form Maule's punishment of Alice takes and by her understanding of it. After the unsuccessful search for the deed, Maule retains his power over Alice's person; by inducing a version of hysteria—sudden, inappropriate fits of laughter or tears and bouts of grotesque dancing—Maule both avenges her appropriation of him and provides a continual refutation of her claim to self-possession. Alice's lament—she "longed to change natures with some worm" (209)— and her refusal to marry imply a recognition that she is being punished for her initial violation of human interchange by being disqualified from its pleasures. The implication here is not that the self is utterly permeable or dizzyingly unstable; rather, community cannot, for Hawthorne, be founded on a static absolutism of the private self but emerges from the shared risks of transformative interchange.

Maule is finally the victim of his own revenge. His last punitive demonstration, Alice's enforced attendance at his wedding, leads to her death, and the tale ends with a glimpse of the repentant Maule at the end of the funeral procession, "gnashing his teeth, as if he would have bitten his own heart in twain" (210). He begins the tale as an ally of the domestic order, seeking to reclaim his familial home; even his mesmerical powers have interesting affinities with the "influence" that constitutes the cul-

tural power of the domestic. But when Maule uses his power to claim
Alice as his property—"Mine, by the right of the strongest spirit!"
(206)—he irrevocably enters the order of appropriation, and the closing
image of self-consumption makes a Pyncheon of him at last. Alice Pyncheon and Matthew Maule constitute a kind of "anticouple." They occupy a crucial cultural border, the boundary between love's self-risking
exchange and the desire for absolute possession. Their joint victimization
defines the lure of the appropriative—to which Maule is as susceptible as
Pyncheon—as the essential danger to the private and communal generation of meaning and demonstrates how mutually permeable are the economic and emotional spheres.[23]

Holgrave's tale, then, both helps us see the thematic shape of the book
as a whole and identifies romance as a genre with the clarification of a
culture's inner life. Moreover, Hawthorne makes Holgrave's act of story
telling a commentary on the cultural value of the kind of reading that
romance induces by establishing an unmistakeable analogy between his
ancestor's power over Alice and his effect on Phoebe. In the course of the
reading, Phoebe becomes mesmerized by Holgrave. The daguerreotypist
realizes his opportunity to "establish an influence" over his auditor; the
book pauses, as it were, on a threshold of its own, for Holgrave's next
action will either give another turn of the screw to this history of joint
victimization or break the appropriative pattern.

Holgrave's refusal to claim Phoebe as his erotic property or the object
of his dominion—"there is no temptation so great as the opportunity of
acquiring empire over the human spirit"—provokes an endorsement of
his character that carries the full authority of a narrator empowered to
speak for the community: "Let us, therefore—whatever his defects of nature and education, and in spite of his scorn for creeds and institutions—
concede to the Daguerreotypist the rare and high quality of reverence for
another's individuality. Let us allow him integrity, also, forever after to
be confided in; since he forbade himself to twine that one link more,
which might have rendered his spell over Phoebe indissoluble" (212).
Holgrave's decision moves the book toward thematic resolution in several ways. The narrator's acknowledgment of Holgrave's integrity, by
moving him from the margins of culture to its center, establishes "reverence for another's individuality"—the obverse of the Pyncheon habit of
treating people as property—as the ethical ground of community and the
basis for demarcating a legitimate form of democratic authority.
Holgrave's refusal to appropriate Phoebe breaks the relation between
Maule and Pyncheon out of the determinism of gothic legend and reveals
it to be part of a transformable history of human choices. And implicit in
Holgrave's act is an ethics of private relationship that understands the
violability of the self as the condition of human connection.

All these changes come about because Holgrave is able to interpret his own specimen of Hawthornian romance; grasping the logic of Maule's Pyncheonization, he resists the lure of appropriation. The cultural value of romance, then, lies not in the direct exercise of power—in its analogy, that is, to mesmerism—but in the room for interpretation and revision it makes available. Phoebe's fascination with Holgrave and his near-seduction by the lure of power are best understood, it seems to me, as representing the ease with which human desire assumes the configuration of appropriation. Holgrave's tale and his own response to it together establish that the cultural role of romance is the disciplining of the authoritarian and the consequent renovation of authority. Within the self and within the community, the romance perspective penetrates power's alluring representations to reveal the entrapment they conceal. A way of loving, of establishing a self, of constructing a community, of exercising authority that does not yield the domination of others and the moral death of the self depends upon the capacity for transformation liberated by the analytic force of romance. The marginal has become central.

Holgrave's revision of Pyncheon-Maule history is the cue for one of Hawthorne's moonlight serenades, his confirmations of the power of romance. The landscape becomes instinct with the possibility of transformation: "The common-place characteristics—which, at noontide, it seemed to have taken a century of sordid life to accumulate—were now transfigured by a charm of romance. A hundred mysterious years were whispering among the leaves . . ." (213). This evocation of a transformable world is answered by an inner transformation in Holgrave and Phoebe. The cynical Holgrave recovers a sense of his own youthfulness and with it a belief in political renewal: "after all, what a good world we live in! . . . How young it is, too, with nothing really rotten or age-worn in it!" His panicky vision of a present under the thumb of a monumental past has yielded to a romance theory of reform as an internal process that anticipates his decision to occupy the Pyncheon estate at the book's end: "Moonlight, and the sentiment in man's heart, responsive to it, is the greatest of renovators and reformers" (214). Phoebe, in response, feels herself suddenly grown older, and leaves behind the simplistic categories of domestic utopianism. Under the moonlight, "life does not look the same. . . . It seems as if I had looked at everything, hitherto, in broad daylight, or in the ruddy glow of a cheerful fire." With her realization that she has given to Hepzibah and Clifford much of her "sunshine," and that she "cannot both give and keep it" (214–15), Phoebe enters adulthood's world of irrevocable loss. When Holgrave leaves behind his Oedipally tinged determinism and Phoebe abandons her defenses against complexity, they together arrive at a cultural common ground upon which a new centrality might be founded. Holgrave calls this seasoned understanding of freedom and limitation a "second youth"; and in accord with the revisionary logic of romance, this moment of connection is the product, for both Holgrave and Phoebe, of a "second seeing."

In a characteristic act of self-scrutiny, Hawthorne is unwilling to leave this moment of affirmation unqualified. As if to mark the fragile status of Holgrave's achievement of the romance perspective, he suffers, on the heels of this moonlit moment, a particularly artistlike lapse into the appropriative. Phoebe responds to his dryly analytic character sketches of Hepzibah and Clifford by demanding to know the nature of his interest in her relatives. Holgrave's answer only makes her angrier: "It is not my impulse—as regards these two individuals—either to help or hinder; but to look on, to analyze, to explain matters to myself, and to comprehend the drama which, for almost two hundred years, has been dragging its slow length over the ground, where you and I now tread. If permitted to witness the close, I doubt not to derive a moral satisfaction from it, go matters how they may" (216). Phoebe's response, which has a new analytic bite, identifies Holgrave's high-toned moral spectatorship—an anticipation of Miles Coverdale—as a species of consumption: "You talk as if this old house were a theatre; and you seem to look at Hepzibah's and Clifford's misfortunes, and those of the generations before them, as a tragedy, such as I have seen acted in the hall of a country-hotel; only the present one appears to be played exclusively for your amusement! I do not like this. The play costs the performers too much—and the audience is too cold-hearted!" (217). That is, Phoebe's comment makes clear that an aesthetic practice that does not link analysis to a form of action—to sympathetic connection, say, or Holgrave's earlier refusal to victimize— conceals an appropriativeness of its own. The work of romance, we might say, is never done.

The "Alice Pyncheon" episode defines the role that personal transformation—the individual achievement of what I have called "cultural maturity"—plays in the drama of cultural renovation that *The House of the Seven Gables* enacts. And, simultaneously, it defines a role for fiction that, in opposition to the merely celebratory or decorative place it is assigned within the domestic world over which Phoebe presides, makes its very marginality, its analytic perspective, the source of its central importance in the life of the community. The "Governor Pyncheon" chapter— surely one of the most extraordinary acts of formal experimentation in the history of American fiction—represents the resolution of the book's action from an entirely different perspective. It is the culmination of Hawthorne's exploration of the cultural power of the communal voice.

"Governor Pyncheon" returns us, through the question of who speaks this chapter, to the book's drama of the narrative voice. The chapter's literal response to this question—"Would that we were not an attendant spirit, here!"—is just the beginning of an answer. This sentence's curious mix of persons, the plural "we" and the singular spirit, does suggest one of the speaker's most interesting characteristics: it is at once a collective voice, becoming more and more prominently a "we" as the chapter's emotional temperature rises; and it is also, in contrast to the wise self-control of realism's customary narrator, in possession of a distinct personality manifest in its raucous sense of humor, its moments of terror, its aggressive irony, and its general excessiveness. I wish to demonstrate that this chapter is spoken by the rebellious communal voice that has been driven underground by Pyncheon oppression, having heretofore emerged only intermittently, in the more proper narrator's citations from gossip and popular legend. This voice, we might surmise, has been freed into uninhibited expression by the very death it is engaged in celebrating—by the end, along with Jaffrey, of the line of appropriating Pyncheons.

This identification of the speaker of the chapter with a no-longer-suppressed communal voice is invited by several of its characteristics. First, its impropriety—its gleeful attention to Jaffrey's "breadth of beam"; its delight in the physical facts of his deadness ("what wholesome order in the gastric region" [268]); its enjoyment of a Rabelaisian joke at the Judge's expense ("that dog-day smile of elaborate benevolence, sultry enough to tempt flies to come and buzz in it" [282])—has the exhilaration typical of Hawthorne's depiction of the release of repression. (Think of Dimmesdale rampant in *The Scarlet Letter*.) In a time that took its mourning seriously, its mode of addressing the corpse is exuberantly irreverent. And, interestingly, its sole moment of identification with Jaffrey is based not on his individual identity but on the one way in which a man like him *can* be communally representative, as a sign of the terrifying disintegration that we fear in death: "There is no face! . . . Where is our universe? All crumbled away from us; and we, adrift in chaos, may hearken to the gusts of homeless wind, that go sighing and murmuring about, in quest of what was once a world!" (276–77). Finally, the connection between Jaffrey's death and the release of a suppressed voice is confirmed when, at the moment of Jaffrey's extinction as a distinct personality, the wind shifts and gives the house itself a voice; it becomes a "wonderful wind-instrument" and begins "to sing, and sigh, and sob, and shriek" (277). We hear in the exuberance of this voice both a communal celebration of the death of the authoritarian and, in the panicky edge Hawthorne gives to its exorcism of the Pyncheonesque, an acknowledgment of its former powerlessness.

There is, moreover, a thematic shape to the voice's celebration of Jaffrey's death that also marks it as belonging to the community. Its mock exhortation to the Judge to resume his busy schedule becomes an itinerary of the public relationships that constitute a community, and the voice records, in a vengeful mock-eulogy, Jaffrey's poisoning or undermining of each one of them. Thus, with the defunct Jaffrey "keeping house" (268)—a notation of the revenge of the domestic—this narrator recounts the Judge's sexual predatoriness, his domestic cruelty, his empty acts of charity, his financial stratagems. This indictment, all along celebrating the Judge's present impotence, culminates in the exposure of Jaffrey and his circle as mockers of democratic representation itself: "They are practiced politicians, every man of them, and skilled to adjust those preliminary measures, which steal from the people, without its knowledge, the power of choosing its own rulers" (274). This chapter's act of communal representation thus counters the misrepresentation that is Jaffrey's stock-in-trade. In its overall effect, this tirade by the communal voice does in the public sphere what "Alice Pyncheon" did in the private: it exposes and disciplines the will to power.

There is another significant parallel between this chapter and the "Alice Pyncheon" episode. In both cases, the chapter's crucial act—there Holgrave's refusal to victimize, here the casting out of Jaffrey Pyncheon— brings on the moonlight and with it an excursion into romance territory. Each chapter, that is, is engaged in establishing the cultural role of romance. The arrival of the moonlight summons to the narrator's mind one of the legends that popular tradition has preserved about the Pyncheons, and with it a sense of the history of communal story telling that has resisted the pressure of Pyncheon authority.[24] This will be one of "the stories which—in times when chimney-corners had benches in them, where old people sat poking into the ashes of the past, and raking out traditions, like live coals—used to be told about this very room" (278). The story itself has the kind of compressed, complex causal logic that we observed in "Alice Pyncheon." At midnight, all the generations of dead Pyncheons are summoned to pay their respects to the portrait of the original Colonel; while the wizardly Maule looks on, pointing and laughing, each Pyncheon repeats this action by their progenitor: "He looks up at the portrait; a thing of no substance, gazing at its own painted image!" (279). And each Pyncheon comes away frowning, thwarted by the mystery that the portrait never unravels. This phrasing and the image that it conjures up of an emptiness gazing into an abyss together capture the futile logic of appropriation that is the real Pyncheon legacy: one becomes the moral emptiness that one seeks. Finally, Maule's appearance as amused spectator within the Pyncheon scenario implicates him, as in "Alice Pyncheon," in the structure of domination he identifies.

The telling of this story confirms for the reader the crucial link we have already noticed between the practice of romance as we witness it in "Alice Pyncheon" and the tradition of communal story telling and gossip that has been criticizing Pyncheon authority throughout its history. "Analytic" romance, when properly understood, is not an irretrievably marginal or intellectual form. It originates in the kind of resistance to the authoritarian that animates the popular voice; it shares with popular tradition strategies of expression designed to penetrate authority's official representations; and it is thus capable of alliance with that voice in the reclamation of communal authority.

This chapter of exhilarating misrule ends with another exercise in and illustration of the communal force of romance. The voice's celebration of Jaffrey's demise finishes by imagining him as the hero of a narrative of repentance and conversion: "will he . . . go forth a humbled and repentant man, sorrowful, gentle, seeking no profit . . . ?" (282). The narrator's employment of one of the most significant of sentimental culture's narrative forms—think, for example, of the force of failed and successful conversions in *Uncle Tom's Cabin*—puts romance's obliquity at the service of the central. As he urges the corpse of Judge Pyncheon to "rise up," a transformed man, we recognize the fulfillment of our communal revenge: the grand misrepresenter, the emptier-out of the community's crucial forms of significance, both domestic and political, is sung to his rest in a mocking reminder of the kind of meaning that his way of life has threatened to destroy. The affinity between the narrative strategies of Hawthornian romance and those of the communal voice that this chapter reveals suggests, finally, a new way of understanding the causal logic of Judge Pyncheon's death. Rather than cite common sense's physiology or superstition's curse, we might surmise that Judge Pyncheon is done in by a joint act of romance: by the revision of Pyncheon history achieved by Holgrave and Phoebe, supplemented by the energies of communal anger, kept alive as stories, that find expression in this chapter's extraordinary drama of narrative voice.

In the events that unfold as a consequence of Jaffrey's death, Hawthorne explores the nature and implications of the alliance between the marginal and the central that he has been constructing. The chapter that follows "Governor Pyncheon" is full of signs that suggest that the Judge's death has produced a safe and playful public world. With the disappearance of Jaffrey's inhibiting authority, the whole representational atmosphere has altered. Images of disclosure are the order of the day ("Every object was agreeable, whether to be gazed at in the breadth, or examined more minutely" [284]), and the obliquity and compression that is the mark of the subversive gives way to a relaxed emblematics of the quotidian. Uncle Venner's pig, for example, who is fattened on the dinner scraps of the neighborhood and will, in turn, become the entrée at Venner's retirement dinner, comes to represent, if one is in the interpretive mood, the operation of a mutually beneficial marketplace safe from the predatory impulse—except from the porcine point of view. The blooming of Alice's posies and the appearance of a "mystic" golden bough on the Pyncheon elm signify, in the most direct way, the end of the covert, futile narrative of appropriation: "something within the house was consummated" (286). Most significantly, the Pyncheon mansion itself is transformed. It becomes readable not as the prison house that its actual history has made it but as an emblem of the history it might have had:

> The lines and tufts of green moss, here and there, seemed pledges of familiarity and sisterhood with Nature; as if this human dwelling-place, being of such old date, had established its prescriptive title among primeval oaks, and whatever other objects, by virtue of their long continuance, have acquired a gracious right to be. A person of imaginative temperament . . . would conceive the mansion to have been the residence of the stubborn old Puritan, Integrity, who, dying in some forgotten generation, had left a blessing in all its rooms and chambers, the efficacy of which was to be seen in the religion, honesty, moderate competence, or upright poverty, and solid happiness, of his descendants, to this day. (285–86)

The Pyncheon legacy of land grabbing and title disputes is erased by a grand condition contrary to fact, affirming our entry into romance's world of revision.

The most important effect of Jaffrey's death is the avowal of love that emerges as Holgrave and Phoebe confront the corpse—a union to be understood as the fulfillment of the alliance between marginal and central toward which Hawthorne has been working all along. As the proximity of the corpse suggests, their marriage is made possible by the transformations that attend the end of Jaffrey's cultural reign. When Phoebe crosses the threshold of the mansion, she finds that a shift toward disclosure has transformed the interior world as well as the communal landscape. The smile with which Holgrave greets her is "by far the most vivid expression that Phoebe had ever witnessed, shining out of the New England reserve with which Holgrave habitually masked whatever lay near his heart" (301). Jaffrey's death has made it safe for Holgrave to make himself legible, to abandon the guarded forms of self-representation and the guise of aesthetic distance that has protected him throughout the book. The mode of Jaffrey's death has also been revelatory, "making plain the innocence of Clifford" (304).

In a surprising postponement of the pleasures of novelistic closure, this marriage agreement takes considerable negotiation. Throughout the "Flower of Eden" chapter, the intimacy between Holgrave and Phoebe is worked out in terms whose cultural resonance the book has been teaching us to recognize. Through Phoebe, Jaffrey's corpse—and the perversion of

an ostensibly benign social order that it discloses—becomes a test of the
capacity of the domestic-centered system of values to engage, rather than
to repress, the difficult. Holgrave thus begins his disclosure of the corpse
by affirming his faith in her capacity to accommodate disturbing experience: "gentle as you are, and seeming to have your sphere among common things, you yet possess remarkable strength. You have a wonderful
poise, and a faculty which, when tested, will prove itself capable of dealing with matters that fall far out of the ordinary rule" (301). The language that Hawthorne gives Holgrave here and a little later in the chapter—"It was like dragging a hideous shape of death into the cleanly and
cheerful space before a household fire" (302) underscores Phoebe's ideological role. Holgrave's belief in her strength, in turn, becomes the ground
of the accommodation between the marginal and the central that Hawthorne is orchestrating. We should notice, too, that Holgrave first presents the Judge's death to Phoebe through the medium of a daguerreotype
of the corpse; Holgrave's art, the romance aspects of which we have already observed, mediates between the ideological positions that need
uniting if the authoritarian is to be resisted. Hawthorne is reminding us
that his version of romance aspires to be the medium of the alliance between the moral values that ground communal life and the analytic perspective that guarantees their public efficacy.

This first move toward alliance just begins the intricate process of personal and ideological rapprochement that their marriage ratifies. If Holgrave tests Phoebe's range of vision by confronting her with the meaning
of the Judge's death, she tests his skepticism by insisting that they disclose
the death immediately: "Let us throw open the doors, and call all the
neighborhood to see the truth!" (305). Phoebe insists that Holgrave at
last abandon the stratagems attuned to Jaffrey's world of power and trust
the community to recognize Clifford's innocence. Most striking, though,
is the way that Hawthorne's representation of the love that emerges between Holgrave and Phoebe and the doubts they express about that love
at once explores the nature of this alliance, celebrates its achievement,
and acknowledges the difficulty of sustaining it.

Holgrave and Phoebe pause on the threshold of public disclosure long
enough to avow their love. We begin with an interpretive puzzle: why
Hawthorne's odd, even grisly, emphasis on the role of the corpse in
strengthening their emotion and provoking its disclosure? Their shared
knowledge of the death and their deliberations over what to do about it
create for them a private world—"a remoteness as entire as that of an
island in mid-ocean" (305)—in which love can flower: "The image of
awful Death, which filled the house, held them united by his stiffened
grasp" (305). This moment has clear affinities with the logic of romance,
which takes reader or character to a territory from which what is poison-

ous about customary life can be perceived. The corpse's literal confirmation of Jaffrey's death-in-life moves each of the lovers from a defense
against experience to its engagement. If we remember the prominence of
the giant corpse of the past in Holgrave's deterministic fantasy, this me-
mento mori is even more resonant. The apparent implication of Clifford
in Jaffrey's death had returned him, he says, to a similarly despairing
vision of the world—a vision from which Phoebe has rescued him: "The
presence of yonder dead man threw a great black shadow over everything; he made the universe, so far as my perception could reach, a scene
of guilt, and of retribution more dreadful than the guilt. The sense of it
took away my youth. I never hoped to feel young again! The world
looked strange, wild, evil, hostile;—my past life, so lonesome and dreary;
my future, a shapeless gloom, which I must mould into gloomy shapes!
But, Phoebe, you crossed the threshold; and hope, warmth, and joy, came
in with you!" (306). This is, of course, a moment that carries great cultural authority. Phoebe's rescue of the despairing male from a morally
chaotic world is one of the high achievements of the domestic heroine.
But we should recognize as well the unorthodox spin that Hawthorne
gives this moment of rescue. For if Phoebe crosses a threshold, so does
Holgrave. This moment should not be dismissed as a regression to the
simplified or defensive sentimentality that the book has been discrediting;
the recurrence of the corpse identifies it, rather, as a move out of the trap
of Holgrave's adolescent absolutism—in which one is either utterly free
or fully imprisoned—into a cultural maturity that acknowledges that the
limitations on one's power to act within the community do not make
action futile. In this case, then, it is the marginal perspective, not the central, that needs expansion.

For both Phoebe and Holgrave, the love that guarantees meaning ("the
one miracle . . . without which every human existence is a blank" [307])
and transfigures the world is not a passport to a future of unproblematic
bliss but a step into a difficult present, rich in regret as well as in possibility, in risk as well as in pleasure. Both the lovers have a strikingly clear-
eyed sense of the difficulties that will attend their union. Holgrave's picture of the effect of Phoebe's influence upon him—"it will be my lot to set
out trees, to make fences—perhaps, even in due time, to build a house for
another generation—in a word, to conform myself to laws, and the peace-
ful practice of society" (307)—is delivered with "almost a sigh, and a
smile that was burthened with thought." Phoebe's admission of love is
accompanied by a forecast of the anxiety his iconoclastic habit of mind is
going to cost her, and by an intriguing desire not to be cast as the cause
of his reining in. Thus the reader has the interesting sense that the cultural
alliance this love achieves is at once of extraordinary significance and
likely, for its individual practitioners, not to deliver easy days. Still, the

love between Phoebe and Holgrave prepares them to cross the threshold of the house and enter the communal life that each, in some way, has been avoiding—Phoebe by suppressing its aspects of power and cruelty, Holgrave by regarding it as an occasion for analysis. Holgrave's "Now let us meet the world!" affirms the ambitions that animate the book: the kind of private transformation that reading Hawthornian romance works to provoke issues forth in a transformed relation to the community.

The coupling of Phoebe and Holgrave is not the only effect of Jaffrey's death; Hepzibah and Clifford also experience the changes it has wrought in the world. When they flee the corpse-ridden house, the antique siblings cross the threshold into a world that bears the unmistakable marks of the modern. It is as if Jaffrey's death has not only freed the immediate victims of his coercion but has ushered in an era in which no single figure of authority, no matter what his dominating energies, can hold the community in configuration; the authoritarian impulse is not dead, we might say, but, in analogy to the marketplace, it is becoming more widely distributed. Thus Hawthorne emphasizes, in his descriptions of the brave new world that the aged pair enters, the disorganized aspect of the urban social landscape. This effect is most spectacularly apparent when Clifford and Hepzibah take a ride on the railroad. The "strangely enfranchised prisoners" witness a world freed into flux: "The spires of meeting-houses seemed set adrift from their foundations; the broad-based hills glided away. Everything was unfixed from its age-long rest . . ." (256). The careening railroad car is seen not just as the means toward but an emblem of the new world of the extended market economy. Its fifty strangers, cast into "close relation," form a community on the new model, constructed by the accidents of trade and continually changing its membership. It condenses within its narrow space a kind of economy-in-motion: its denizens are reading the cheap, imported novels and penny papers made available by the newly national publishing industry, and at each stop merchandize-bearing boys work the car, doing business at top speed "lest the market should ravish them away with it." Their day on the railroad draws the siblings "into the great current of human life"; it represents, the narrator reminds us, "life itself" (256–57).

While this excursion into the modern merely unhinges the backward-looking Hepzibah, Clifford experiences not anxiety but exhilaration. The book has all along been suggesting that such an immersion might save Clifford from his fatigued aestheticism, and for most of his journey this promises to be true. But Clifford's cultural engagement ends abortively when they leave the train at a "solitary way-station": "The world had fled away from these two wanderers. They gazed drearily about them. At a little distance stood a wooden church, black with age, and in a dismal state of ruin and decay, with broken windows, a great rift through the main-body of the edifice, and a rafter dangling from the top of the square tower. Farther off was a farm-house in the old style, as venerably black as the church, with a roof sloping downward from the three-story peak to within a man's height of the ground. It seemed uninhabited" (266). Clifford's attempt at immersion in the present ends with a dismantled New England village, its spiritual and economic bases in decay—with a picture, that is, of the end of a once-coherent ideological structure. The deadness of the village that has turned out to be their destination not only discredits nostalgia for the old New England as a response to inevitable change; it makes us ask what has gone wrong with Clifford's attempt at cultural engagement, and thus clarifies the kind of participation in culture that Hawthorne has in mind.

Clifford's droll conversation with "a gimlet-eyed old gentleman" in the car helps us see both the nature of Clifford's exuberance and the logic of its failure to sustain him. His release from the inhibiting weight of Jaffrey's authority has given Clifford a transfusion of iconoclastic energy. He executes, with loony brio, the sacred cows of middle-class respectability—"those stale ideas of home and fireside" (259), the sacredness of real estate, the superiority of the pragmatic view, the clear boundary between the criminal and the businessman—exposing in the process the unattractive narrowness of this practical Yankee's cultural edifice. As with Dimmesdale, Clifford is at his most attractive when misbehaving; he seems at last to have a field of sufficient scope to put his imagination into action, and one delights in his casting out of the inhibitory: "I must talk, and I will!"

Without being unduly sober about this episode, we can nevertheless see the ways in which Clifford's cultural engagement goes awry. There is a brittle literalism about his strictures on the resources of middle-class life; his own entrapment in the Pyncheon mansion provokes an absolute repudiation of living in houses at all. Like Holgrave in the grips of his anxiety about the past, Clifford universalizes his own predicament. Holgrave's absolutism leads him to the protection of sophisticated observership; Clifford seizes on a vision of experience that must be read as a Hawthornian send-up of transcendentalist thinking. The railroad, he tells his interlocutor, will usher in the era of the higher nomadism: "all human progress is in a circle; or, to use a more accurate and beautiful figure, in an ascending spiral curve. While we fancy ourselves going straight forward, and attaining, at every step, an entirely new position of affairs, we do actually return to something long ago tried and abandoned, but which we now find etherealized, refined, and perfected to its ideal" (259). Despite the force of his criticisms of the complacency of middle-class life, Clifford takes refuge in a theory of universal etherealization that is a futile substitute for a cultural stance that might combine an imaginative criticism of the orthodox with the pragmatic force to produce a different way of living. Clifford's attempt to participate in the world delivers him to that burned-out village because he returns to an aestheticism that has no designs on the world it addresses. Between the Yankee pragmatist's sterile combination of common sense and an inert version of domestic sentimentality, Clifford's loony transcendentalism, and the agrarian nostalgia criticized by the chapter's closing image, Hawthorne offers a résumé of fruitless responses to—because they are merely defenses against—the flux of a marketplace world.

As we moved from the calm of history to the contested ground of the present when we entered the narrative at the beginning of the book, so we find ourselves back in the tranquil realm of finished stories as *The House*'s closing chapter begins. As if to assure us that Jaffrey's authoritarian reign has ended, the voice that greets us here belongs to the urbane historian we encountered in the opening chapter. He begins with a joke at Jaffrey's expense: "At his decease, there is only a vacancy, and a momentary eddy—very small, as compared with the apparent magnitude of the ingurgitated object" (309). His tone—relaxed, humorous, ranging freely from perspective to perspective—dramatizes the achievement of a new kind of authority, assured but not inhibitory. This narrator proceeds to put our story to rest, touching along the way the thematic bases that testify to the completion of the book's alliance-building work. Clifford's exoneration is recorded as the triumph of communal and romance story telling over the legal authority that had fixed his guilt: uninterested in the kind of "authority available in a court of justice," our historian cites as conclusive "a hidden stream of private talk" and a "theory" reportedly derived from Holgrave's interview with a "mesmerical seer"—distinctly a romance mode of information gathering. We are reminded that this new consensus must accommodate, not suppress, unsettling truths when the narrator refuses to swaddle Clifford in the robes of narrative closure, insisting instead that victimization cannot be erased: "After such wrong as he had suffered, there is no reparation" (313). Yet this acknowledgment of absolute loss does not prevent the sentimental from having its say when Phoebe rewards Uncle Venner with the "sweetest-looking" gingerbread cottage ever seen (317).

What are we to make of Holgrave's curious place in this newly ordered cultural center? The incipient conservatism suggested by his willingness to inhabit Jaffrey's country house has generated decades of critical controversy. The argument that Holgrave's changed view of houses constitutes a political self-betrayal on his part—and, by extension, a pandering to the orthodoxy of his audience on Hawthorne's—depends upon the odd notion that Holgrave's earlier, literal-minded fulminations on the dangers of living in houses constitute, from *any* point of view, a significant political position. As I have already argued, the book gives us every reason to see these positions as transcriptions of anxiety rather than genuine political ideas. What Holgrave actually envisions in his notion of a house with a permanent exterior and an interior revisable by each succeeding generation is an allegory of reform that acknowledges the life of the past within the present and is attuned to the kind of personal transformation that romance reading might aspire to bring about.[25] The "half-melancholy laugh" with which he acknowledges Phoebe's amazement at his new ideas about houses should be read, it seems to me, not as an admission of bad faith but as the consequence of Holgrave's move out of the coherence of a finished story and back into the uncomfortable flux of the present, where choices must carry the baggage of ambivalence. The up-in-the-air effect of Holgrave's enigmatic smile is echoed in our narrator's playfulness about the customary maneuvers of narrative closure; he has two literal-minded passers-by wonder whether the ending's liberally scattered financial rewards constitute luck, Providence, or just "pretty good business," and he leaves us with a vision of Maule's well pumping out prophecies about our characters that he does not bother to specify. The emergent inconclusiveness with which the book comes to a close leaves us at the threshold between romance territory and the interesting flux of the present, at which the alliance the book has sought to call into being will find its work.

· · ·

I have been arguing that *The House of the Seven Gables* must be understood as a work of extraordinary sophistication in its account of the culture it addresses and of extraordinary ambition in its attempt to reshape that culture. Out of Hawthorne's invention of a narrative form capable of representing a cultural system in action emerge some striking principles for communal renovation. The book identifies a marriage between—rather than a bifurcation of—domestic values and action in the world at large as the key to both resisting the authoritarian and constructing a community that can sustain its inevitable encounter with the economic and social forces that will unmoor it. Sentimental ideology, that is, must use the resources of the marginal perspective to see the world it faces and to grasp itself as a form of power within that world rather than as a refuge from it. In the same way, a rigorously thought-out art must give up the éclat of marginality or the prestige of ethereality and understand the culture it addresses as contested ground, where different representations of value and meaning compete for the authority that only an audience can confer. By distinguishing between escape and action, between diagnosis and cure, between refuge and risk, *The House of the Seven Gables* is all along illustrating and enacting a theory of the cultural centrality of fiction.

The account I have offered of the revisionary work that this romance seeks to do within its culture helps us see, finally, how Hawthorne sought to position himself in relation to his community and how we, as analysts of his work, might ourselves place him ideologically. If I am right about the cultural drama implicit in the exchange between writer and reader that the book constructs, then Hawthorne occupies a position within the ideology of antebellum America that is more complicated, acute, and interesting than we have yet imagined. From this perspective, we are able to see the book not as an attempt to evade, erase, or condemn the world of the marketplace but as an attempt to discipline it, to make it a place of fair exchange rather than predation, of joint risk rather than coercion, of mutual benefit rather than victimization—just as Hawthorne sets out to discipline the authoritarian within the psyche in much of his other work. We see, too, that what is most strikingly political about this romance is not its attack upon Jaffrey Pyncheon's version of authority but its remarkable attempt to make culture visible as a system. For when a culture loses its invisibility—when it ceases to be conceived of as an atmosphere, an environment, a "given"—and becomes visible as a set of roles and actions that one might choose, the act of communal revision that the book envisions becomes possible. We see, then, that in *The House of the Seven Gables* Hawthorne is providing American middle-class culture with the means and the occasion for its own reimagining—a form of power that the book's attention to representation has been teaching us to value.

Chapter Six

ROMANCE AS ATTACK:
THE BLITHEDALE ROMANCE

Nothing else; nothing but self, self, self!
—Zenobia on Hollingsworth

But what, after all, have I to tell? Nothing, nothing,
nothing!
—Coverdale on himself

AT THE CENTER of Hawthorne's depiction of character and culture in *The Blithedale Romance* is the suspicion that existence within the middle-class culture that the novel depicts and addresses has been reduced to the self's absorbing effort to disguise its own emptiness. This personal and communal anxiety finds continual expression in forms of uneasiness about the authenticity of the self and in the fantasies of power and acts of domination that assuage that uneasiness: in Coverdale's fear of exposure, in the attraction of veiling and masquerading, in the fascination of occult access to the secrets—and thus to the selves—of others. The book's combination of interests—in the elaborately defended psyches of its characters; in the forms of cultural expression that manifest the shared anxieties of the community; and in the new emotions and experiences that belong to life in the city—reveals that Hawthorne is engaged in this romance in a striking act of cultural diagnosis. He is identifying what Raymond Williams calls a "structure of feeling": the presence of a specific historical moment—here, the emergence of a careening market economy in the middle years of the nineteenth century—as it expresses itself in private feeling and in the cultural forms that a community produces.[1]

Because these anxieties and fantasies belong by implication to the culture that Hawthorne addresses as well as the one he depicts—and because of their extraordinary power to entrap character and stultify experience within the world of the novel—*The Blithedale Romance* calls into being a new version of romance to match its diagnosis, a more aggressive narrative practice designed to break the confining circle of anxiety, fantasy, and cruelty the book describes. In a sustained and specific way, *The Blithedale Romance* is a counternovel to *The House of the Seven Gables*. The forms of feeling and behavior that had seemed the resources of middle-class culture in the earlier book—sympathetic attachment, one person's capacity to "influence" another, the vision of reform, the shared stories that hold a community together—all become in *Blithedale* either masks for acts of self-aggrandizement and predation or defenses against awareness. It is as though Hawthorne had seen the undercurrent of anxiety beneath the surface of the middle-class culture that he seeks to celebrate and renovate in *The House* and set out to administer, in *The Blithedale Romance*, the shock treatment that might cure it. This chapter explores Hawthorne's enterprise by describing the complex connections between the book's depiction of the logic of identity, its account of social psychology, and its way of engaging its reader.[2]

CHARACTER AS SYMPTOM

The invention of Miles Coverdale is Hawthorne's most complex investigation of the vicissitudes of identity; Coverdale's composition of the novel is in essence his attempt to compose a self, to locate in retrospect the traces of an authenticity that continues to elude him. Coverdale discovers, as he writes, a self built upon a principle of displacement, structured by "that quality of the intellect and the heart, which impelled me (often against my own will, and to the detriment of my comfort) to live in other lives, and to endeavor—by generous sympathies, by delicate intuitions, by taking note of things too slight for record, and by bringing my human spirit into manifold accordance with the companions whom God assigned me—to learn the secret which was hidden even from themselves" (160). Apparent in this passage is Coverdale's characteristic combination of perspicacity and the ability to ignore the implications of what he notices. He identifies the logic of vicariousness upon which he constructs a self with precision: a sustained act of observation will yield him not an inner life of his own, but something he finds more compelling—possession of the "secret" that constitutes the selfhood of another. Coverdale's ceaseless attempts to penetrate the mysteries that experience presents him—Zenobia's sexual history, Priscilla's "maidenly mystery," Hollingsworth's romantic transactions with each of them—constitute his way of "living," of having a self. Coverdale's hypocrisy lies in the rhetoric that sets out to erect this vicariousness into an appointment as novelist to God. Yet Coverdale's attempts to beguile the reader are always attempts to deceive himself; what needs to be uncovered in *The Blithedale Romance* is not simply the logic of Coverdale's voyeurism but a full description of the nature of the need that induces it.[3]

We might begin such a description by looking at the language Coverdale chooses to depict the dynamics of mind. As an apology for the intensity of his speculations about Zenobia's sexual past, he offers this description of the physics of fever: "Vapors then rise up to the brain, and take shapes that often image falsehood, but sometimes truth. The spheres of our companions have, at such periods, a vastly greater influence upon our own than when robust health gives us a repellent and self-defensive energy. Zenobia's sphere, I imagine, impressed itself powerfully on mine, and transformed me, during this period of my weakness, into something like a mesmerical clairvoyant" (46–47). The passage suggests that Coverdale feels the usual interactions between people as a state of perpetual warfare, each self at risk of being penetrated and controlled by the "sphere" of another unless it summons a charge of "repellent" energy sufficient for self-defense. This interpsychic warfare implies a self doomed by its vulnerability to constant, anxious vigilance and a sense of others as always on the attack. His portrayal of himself as entrapped by his relation to Zenobia, Hollingsworth, and Priscilla employs a similarly revealing range of metaphor:

> There seemed something fatal in the coincidence that had borne me to this one spot, of all others in a great city, and transfixed me there, and compelled me again to waste my already wearied sympathies on affairs which were none of mine, and persons who cared little for me. It irritated my nerves; it affected me with a kind of heart-sickness. After the effort which it cost me to fling them off—after consummating my escape, as I thought, from these goblins of flesh and blood, and pausing to revive myself with a breath or two of an atmosphere in which they should have no share—it was a positive despair, to find the same figures arraying themselves before me, and presenting their old problem in a shape that made it more insoluble than ever. . . . As for me, I would look on, as it seemed my part to do, understandingly, if my intellect could fathom the meaning and the moral, and, at all events, reverently and sadly. The curtain fallen, I would pass onward with my poor individual life, which was now attenuated of much of its proper substance, and diffused among many alien interests. (157)

Coverdale's use of the language of enchantment—he has been "transfixed," "compelled"—registers, like the fever passage, his frustration at his own passivity and his sense of the power latent in others. Allied to this fear of being controlled is a deeper anxiety: a fear of being consumed. He is forced to "waste" his store of sympathies; the "goblins" infect the atmosphere he sought to preserve as his own; he envisions his connection to them, even as an observer, leaving his life "attenuated" of "substance," and "diffused." Coverdale's refuge in vicariousness—a refuge that itself threatens in this passage to entrap him—is provoked, his science of mind suggests, by a sense of the self as at once dangerously permeable and frighteningly depletable, and of the other as at once voracious and in possession of a power that Coverdale knows only by its absence in himself.

The world of *The Blithedale Romance* is full of what might be called icons of vicariousness. An examination of one of them, Coverdale's hermitage, will help us understand further the fragility that lurks beneath his observatory aggression. What sends Coverdale to the woods is a self-protective impulse, a worry that his self has been dissipated by too much communality: "Unless renewed by a yet farther withdrawal towards the inner circle of self-communion, I lost the better part of my individuality" (89). A curious principle, however, governs his choice of the place of rescue: "I . . . looked about me for some side-aisle, that should admit me into the innermost sanctuary of this green cathedral; just as, in human acquaintanceship, a casual opening sometimes lets us, all of a sudden, into the long-sought intimacy of a mysterious heart" (89–90). Coverdale's hunger for authenticity is fierce; he sees even the physical world in the shape of his wish to penetrate the reality that he assumes to be possessed by other selves. But even more crucial is the way in which Coverdale's fear and desire are linked together: his hunger for access to the mystery of another is revealed as the form taken by his flight from the danger to which actual contact with others exposes his tenuous self.

The iconography of the hermitage itself reflects the intricate logic of the usurpation of desire by anxiety. Here are some moments from Coverdale's description of it:

> It was a kind of leafy cave, high upward into the air, among the midmost branches of a white-pine tree. A wild grapevine, of unusual size and luxuriance, had twined and twisted itself up into the tree, and, after wreathing the entanglement of its tendrils almost around every bough, had caught hold of three or four neighboring trees, and married the whole clump with a perfectly inextricable knot of polygamy. . . . A hollow chamber, of rare seclusion, had been formed by the decay of some of the pine-branches, which the vine had lovingly strangled with its embrace, burying them from the light of day in an aerial sepulchre of its own leaves. It cost me but little ingenuity to enlarge the interior, and open loop-holes through the verdant walls. Had it ever been my fortune to spend a honey-moon, I should have thought seriously of inviting my bride up thither, where our next neighbors would have been two orioles in another part of the clump. . . . This hermitage was my one exclusive possession, while I counted myself a brother of the socialists. It symbolized my individuality, and aided me in keeping it inviolate. (98–99)

Miles Coverdale has marriage on his mind. He finds in his hermitage a representation of what he fears about the customary route to the intimacy he so desires. The marriage of grapevine and pine tree yields not possession of another but loss of self definition in a "perfectly inextricable knot of polygamy." Sexuality appears as a form of murder; the pine branches become the victims of the vine's loving strangulation, present only as the absent possessors of the "aerial sepulchre" their depletion leaves behind. Coverdale finds himself quite at home in this emptiness excavated by the dangers of love; the creation of some loopholes—the transformation of the bower from a place of love to a place of watching—redeems it for him. Coverdale goes to the hermitage literally to watch out for himself; his looking is not simply a perversion of desire but an act of self-defense. His musing on the suitability of the hermitage for his honeymoon seems to me to acknowledge the displacement of desire by a more compelling anxiety: the fear that the self is not simply malleable and depletable but utterly fugitive. This place of refuge, where an emptiness, an "aerial sepulchre," is securely protected by sustained watching is all the honeymoon Coverdale's psyche can manage to covet.[4]

It is in this sense, then, that Coverdale's hermitage "symbolizes" his individuality: selfhood is paradoxically conceived as both empty and endangered. The hermitage "aids" in keeping that fragile self "inviolate" by representing the danger of intimacy and inviting the compensations of fantasy. Worth noticing as well is the habit of mind that induces the discovery of this iconic refuge: as striking as the *way* that the hermitage symbolizes Coverdale's selfhood is his sense that the self *needs* symbolizing in order to maintain its wholeness. To be so on the lookout for external representations of the self is to testify to its internal attenuation. All of Coverdale's symbols, all the details of setting that most fascinate him, seem to function as externalizations of the drama of endangered selfhood that I have been describing. Thus, to take a single example, the silk purses that Priscilla manufactures, whose "peculiar excellence . . . lay in the almost impossibility that any uninitiated person should discover the aperture" (35), capture Coverdale's desire to penetrate and possess her mystery, his sense that he in particular lacks the sexual initiation to do so, and his interest in the hermetically sealable purse as an ideal image of the adequately guarded self.

If Coverdale's vicariousness is, most deeply, a form of flight from himself, what unspoken knowledge does he seek to evade? I think an answer to this question can be inferred from Coverdale's reaction to Professor Westervelt, to whom, as a number of readers have noticed, he responds with the kind of incommensurate repulsion that indicates self-recognition. Two aspects of Westervelt's character engender particular loathing in Coverdale. The first is apparent in this portrait.

> He was still young, seemingly a little under thirty, of a tall and well-developed figure, and as handsome a man as ever I beheld. The style of his beauty,

however, though a masculine style, did not at all commend itself to my taste. His countenance—I hardly know how to describe the peculiarity—had an indecorum in it, a kind of rudeness, a hard, coarse, forth-putting freedom of expression, which no degree of external polish could have abated, one single jot. Not that it was vulgar. But he had no fineness of nature; there was in his eyes (although they might have artifice enough of another sort) the naked exposure of something that ought not to be left prominent. With these vague allusions to what I have seen in other faces, as well as his, I leave the quality to be comprehended best—because with an intuitive repugnance—by those who possess least of it. (91–92)

Coverdale criticizes a sin of expression rather than commission, a failure of concealment: "the naked exposure of something that ought not to be left prominent." We all seem to share—even if we recognize it only by the repugnance it induces—this quality that Westervelt so rudely, hardly, and coarsely puts forth and that Coverdale will not name. Lurking in the language of erection that Coverdale chooses here is not simply a recognition of the aggressiveness he shares with Westervelt but the suspicion that for him, as in the murderous embrace of the grapevine in his hermitage, sexuality and aggression are disturbingly linked.[5]

Coverdale finds Westervelt loathsome, then, for mirroring an aspect of selfhood that might need suppressing, the permeation of desire by aggression. But the moment of identification that follows this one is deeper and more unsettling.

Here the stranger seemed to be so much amused with his sketch of Hollingsworth's character and purposes, that he burst into a fit of merriment, of the same nature as the brief, metallic laugh already alluded to, but immensely prolonged and enlarged. In the excess of his delight, he opened his mouth wide, and disclosed a gold band around the upper part of his teeth; thereby making it apparent that every one of his brilliant grinders and incisors was a sham. This discovery affected me very oddly. I felt as if the whole man were a moral and physical humbug; his wonderful beauty of face, for aught I knew, might be removeable like a mask; and, tall and comely as his figure looked, he was perhaps but a wizened little elf, gray and decrepit, with nothing genuine about him, save the wicked expression of his grin. The fantasy of his spectral character so wrought upon me, together with the contagion of his strange mirth on my sympathies, that I soon began to laugh as loudly as himself. (94–95)

Westervelt presents Coverdale with a vision of the self as mere mechanism. Selfhood is the most tenuous kind of representation, "removeable like a mask," genuineness attenuated in Coverdale's speculation to the merest flicker, "the wicked expression" of the elf's grin. This "discovery," as Coverdale notes, affects him strangely. Coverdale's laughter answers Westervelt's revelation of the inauthenticity of the self with an appropriately automatic acknowledgment, an act of "sympathy" reduced to "contagion," a moment of unconscious mimicry. This intense, unconscious recognition of his affiliation with Westervelt's embodiment of the falseness of the self suggests that, for Coverdale, the self-loathing provoked by what he does—by his predatory, voyeuristic form of love—is less extreme than that engendered by his sense of what he lacks. He evades the guilt that attaches to his voyeuristic raids on the secrets of others so easily because that guilt assuages a deeper one, the guilt of the absence of a self to generate even so oblique a form of desire.[6]

Westervelt continues to serve Coverdale as a mirror, enabling him to articulate, as character analysis, what is essentially self-portraiture. Westervelt becomes the occasion for this meditation on men who cannot love.

> Externally, they bear a close resemblance to other men, and have perhaps all save the finest grace; but when a woman wrecks herself on such a being, she ultimately finds that the real womanhood within her has no corresponding part in him. Her deepest voice lacks a response; the deeper her cry, the more dead his silence. The fault may be none of his; he cannot give her what never lived within his soul. But the wretchedness on her side, and the moral deterioration attendant on a false and shallow life, without strength enough to keep itself sweet, are among the most pitiable wrongs that mortals suffer. (103)

The acuity and poignance of this description give us Coverdale at his best. His anxious vision of selfhood as the absence left when one has gone dead from within here expands into an act of mourning that is cultural as well as private. Coverdale is particularly prone to moments, like this one, of sudden perception of the deadness of things. On his first evening at Blithedale, he records this vision: "Starting up in bed, at length, I saw that the storm was past, and the moon was shining on the snowy landscape, which looked like a lifeless copy of the world in marble" (38). What so horrifies Coverdale about Zenobia's body when they pull it from the water is its rigidity, its "terrible inflexibility" (235). A principle of recognition seems to govern moments like these; Coverdale's horror of rigidity, his sense of the ease with which the animate becomes empty, the authentic a copy, all testify to the fear for his own actuality that is manifest in the passages I have been discussing.

The double self-loathing implicit in Coverdale's reaction to Westervelt—the sense that a shamefully aggressive sexuality covertly organizes his behavior, the suspicion that even that manifestation of selfhood is illusory—accounts for some of Coverdale's most interesting traits. His affinity for embarrassing situations and enjoyment of moments of abasement—he finds Priscilla's imperious dismissal of him after one of his attacks upon her, for example, "bewitching" (126)—seem to offer the relief of simultaneously punishing and demonstrating the sexual aggression that he both repudiates and treasures as a sign of selfhood. His tribute to the beauty of Priscilla's absolute, passive adoration of Zenobia suggests his hunger for so safe and self-guaranteeing a form of love. More crucially, his attachment to the Blithedale project is generated by the fantasy (which he shares with his fellow utopians) that the self is utterly reformable—exactly the wish that would most appeal to someone convinced of its present inauthenticity: "My fit of illness had been an avenue between two existences; the low-arched and darksome doorway, through which I crept out of a life of old conventionalisms, on my hands and knees, as it were, and gained admittance to the freer region that lay beyond. . . . In literal and physical truth I was quite another man" (61). Above all, and as I will argue later, the telling that constitutes the novel becomes for Coverdale an attempt to incarnate the self that eludes him.

Hawthorne makes understanding a character in *The Blithedale Romance* a matter of understanding a particular strategy of self-construction; what constitutes character, that is, is one's share of and response to the anxiety about selfhood that Coverdale so complexly exemplifies. The most economical summation of the connection between the logic of identity and the relations between the four central characters occurs in one of Coverdale's dreams.

> It was not till I had quitted my three friends that they first began to encroach upon my dreams. In those of the last night, Hollingsworth and Zenobia, standing on either side of my bed, had bent across it to exchange a kiss of passion. Priscilla, beholding this—for she seemed to be peeping in at the chamber-window—had melted gradually away, and left only the sadness of her expression in my heart. There it still lingered, after I awoke; one of those unreasonable sadnesses that you know not how to deal with, because it involves nothing for common-sense to clutch. (153)

The parts the characters play in Coverdale's dream correspond precisely to the logic of selfhood that each of them embodies. He and Priscilla are miniature, infantile, while Hollingsworth and Zenobia loom over them, sexual and substantial.

Coverdale's identification of himself with Priscilla is made on the basis of a shared tenuousness of identity; both are elided from the central action of the scene. Throughout the novel as well Priscilla manifests an insubstantiality analogous to his own. Priscilla lives out what Coverdale experiences as one of his chief anxieties: the self's permeability to others. Thus she begins to resemble Margaret Fuller as she hands Coverdale a letter from her (52). The origins of the clairvoyance that makes her marketable as the Veiled Lady lie in her near absence of personality: "There was a lack of human substance in her; it seemed as if, were she to stand up in a sunbeam, it would pass right through her figure, and trace out the cracked and dusty window-panes upon the naked floor" (185–86). While Coverdale feels his interest in his friends as the threat of their consumption of him, Priscilla experiences her relations with others passively, as a form of weather: "I am blown about like a leaf . . . I never have any free-will" (171). Coverdale possesses as a manifestation of selfhood only a pallid hybrid of aggression and desire. Priscilla is more fortunate, inheriting "a profound and still capacity of affection" (186). Priscilla uses this capacity to love, however, the way Coverdale uses his powers of observation: as a defense against disappearance. Her unshakeable love for Hollingsworth successfully provides her with what she lacks, a presence, a gravitational force that will hold her translucent selfhood in configuration. Thus Coverdale is struck by the ease with which she sheds her attachment to Zenobia: "Her engrossing love made it all clear. Hollingsworth could have no fault. That was the one principle at the centre of the universe" (220). Like Coverdale, Priscilla sets out to achieve an identity by displacing herself, by colonizing the selfhood of another.

As Hollingsworth's final collapse into regression indicates—"the powerfully built man showed a self-distrustful weakness, and a childlike, or childish, tendency to press close, and closer still, to the side of the slender woman whose arm was within his" (242)—his place as a figure of substance in Coverdale's dream and throughout the novel is the result of a kind of intrapsychic con game. Hollingsworth generates the magnetism that enables Priscilla to build a selfhood upon him and attracts the love of Coverdale and Zenobia by an elaborate act of self-containment. Zenobia charges that Hollingsworth is a "self-beginning and self-ending piece of mechanism," that he is Blithedale's best masquerader because his "disguise is a self-deception" (218). The logic of her accusation, which claims that Hollingsworth's apparent generosity is merely the manifestation of his self-enclosure, is unfolded in Coverdale's sermon on the philanthropist.

> They have an idol to which they consecrate themselves high-priest, and deem it holy work to offer sacrifices of whatever is most precious, and never once seem to suspect—so cunning has the Devil been with them—that this false deity, in whose iron features, immitigable to all the rest of mankind, they see only benignity and love, is but a spectrum of the very priest himself, projected upon the surrounding darkness. And the higher and purer the original

object, and the more unselfishly it may have been taken up, the slighter is the probability that they can be led to recognize the process, by which godlike benevolence has been debased into all-devouring egotism. (70–71)

Hollingsworth's particular brand of identity is exposed as a form of un-recognized self-worship, of pure self-reference. An apparently compel-ling, substantial self is generated by mere duplication: it consists of two images of self, one worshiping the other. That this sustained self-mirror-ing passes so compellingly for selfhood, taking in, for a time, even Zeno-bia, seems to testify to an endemic thinness of identity in the world of *The Blithedale Romance.* Indeed, the attenuated form that Hollingsworth's love takes—the recruitment of adjuncts to his project of self-adoration—unintentionally invites the tactic of achieving identity by substitution that Priscilla and Coverdale both practice. Thus he describes for Priscilla a vision of womanhood as idealized vicariousness: "Her place is at man's side. Her office, that of Sympathizer; the unreserved, unquestioning Be-liever" (122). And the offer of discipleship that so tempts Coverdale sug-gests a dark version of the Oedipal bargain, the paternal Hollingsworth conferring substantiality and potency in return for complete submission: "Strike hands with me; and, from this moment you shall never again feel the languor and vague wretchedness of an indolent or half-occupied man! . . . there shall be strength, courage, immitigable will—everything that a manly and generous nature should desire!" (133).

It is a measure of the bitterness of *The Blithedale Romance* that the only character who possesses an identity not constructed as a defense against selflessness commits suicide. Zenobia simply has what the other characters lack; because her selfhood is *there* it becomes impossible to describe the strategy of its manufacture, and Coverdale's language finds a different metaphoric register when he describes her. Unlike the translu-cent Priscilla, the artificial Westervelt, the self-inflated Hollingsworth, and the embarrassed Coverdale, Zenobia is in full possession of her body. Coverdale's interesting reaction to this "womanliness incarnated" is to wish for its "multiplication" all over the earth in the form of painted and sculpted images, which seems to reflect both a hope that such unique substantiality might be possessed by replication and a desire to defuse her power by returning her to the realm of the inauthentic. He notes that she possesses the rare gift of "natural movement," exclusively "the result and expression of the whole being" (155); so substantial is her presence that, when she leaves him after her final display of grief, "it was as if the vivid coloring of her character had left a brilliant stain upon the air" (228). In his invention of the passionately theatrical Zenobia, Hawthorne antici-pates the ethical discovery that informs the late novels of Henry James: there is a form of self-conscious performance that leads not to inauthenticity but to existence. In *The Blithedale Romance* the measure of morality and the measure of authenticity are one. Zenobia is the only character that deserves ethical evaluation because she is the only one who has an adequately established identity, the only character whose way of loving is not, in essence, a defense. Zenobia's substantiality, the "stain" she leaves upon the novel, suggests that the ethical standard implicit in *The Blithedale Romance* is, quite desperately, this: morality consists not in displacing emotions but in feeling them. So ridden is the world of the novel by inauthenticity, so empty are its forms of expression, that suicide—the sacrifice of the self—becomes the only guarantee of the genuineness of love, and hence the sole indisputable sign of the authenticity of the self.

Coverdale's dream, then, replicates the novel's essential distinction between characters who seem endowed with selfhood and those who experience identity as an inner absence. We still need to articulate the logic of the dream's action, the relation Coverdale unconsciously proposes between the realized and the fugitive self. In order to interpret this dream, we need first to notice how completely Coverdale identifies himself with Priscilla. In the chameleon logic of dreams, Coverdale is both himself and Priscilla; he *sees* the kiss of passion directly but feels it by observing its effect on her. Thus the dream elides the distinction between their reactions: when she melts away, he finds the sadness of her expression in his heart. This identification reveals the theory of causality that informs the dream; the passionate kiss exchanged by Hollingsworth and Zenobia does not simply exclude Coverdale but causes his dissolution. Already marginal and merely observatory in his relation to the others—lying ignored in bed, and, as Priscilla, "peeping in at the chamber window"—he sees himself in the act of disappearing. Implicit in the dream's causality is the chief emotion of the attenuated self: the reality of others, expressed here as sexual passion, is felt as a form of attack. Coverdale's dream possesses the obvious lineaments of a primal scene, but it is a primal scene performed under the aspect of anxiety about the very existence of the self. The "unreasonable sadness" that Coverdale feels in the wake of the dream is not simply grief for the wound of sexual exclusion but a moment of mourning for a selfhood that will not take shape.[7]

Condensed in Coverdale's dream is the dominant logic of identity in *The Blithedale Romance*. At the center of identity is a suspicion of the absence of the self. This sense of emptiness, which flickers at the edge of consciousness, engenders an anxiety strong enough to twist desire to its own shape; in every case but Zenobia's, both love and aggression are reducible either to defenses against the suspicion of emptiness or to fantasies of self-possession. The self is a fugitive, seeking protection, by acts of stealth and watching, from the dissolution that exposure to others threatens.[8]

American Anxiousness

Coverdale is at once a character and a symptom. Hawthorne's complex articulation of the anxiety that produces Coverdale's oblique strategies of identity alerts us to an answering unease in the urbanizing culture he depicts.[9] *The Blithedale Romance*'s extensive and wide-ranging cultural portraiture constitutes Hawthorne's attempt to illustrate, with an intricacy that matches his characterization of Coverdale, the behavior of a culture governed by an unacknowledged anxiousness. Let me begin with some moments, characteristic of the novel, that seem to inhabit a kind of shared space between private and public perception, moments at which Coverdale elevates what I have been describing as the condition of self into the condition of life. I will give several of them in series because their effect on our reading is cumulative.

> The storm, in its evening aspect, was decidedly dreary. It seemed to have arisen for our especial behoof; a symbol of the cold, desolate, distrustful phantoms that invariably haunt the mind, on the eve of adventurous enterprises, to warn us back within the boundaries of ordinary life. (18)

> The fantasy occurred to me, that she was some desolate kind of a creature, doomed to wander about in snow storms, and that, though the ruddiness of our window-panes had tempted her into a human dwelling, she would not remain long enough to melt the icicles out of her hair. (27)

> The sense of vast, undefined space, pressing from the outside against the black panes of our uncurtained windows, was fearful to the poor girl, heretofore accustomed to the narrowness of human limits, with the lamps of neighboring tenements glimmering across the street. The house probably seemed to her adrift on the great ocean of the night. A little parallelogram of sky was all that she had hitherto known of nature; so that she felt the awfulness that really exists in its limitless extent. Once, while the blast was bellowing, she caught hold of Zenobia's robe, with precisely the air of one who hears her own name spoken, at a distance, but is unutterably reluctant to obey the call. (36)

> The evening wore on, and the outer solitude looked in upon us through the windows, gloomy, wild, and vague, like another state of existence, close beside the littler sphere of warmth and light in which we were the prattlers and bustlers of a moment. (37)

Each of these passages, which together create a kind of recognizable *Blithedale* "moment" or place of mind, emphasizes the significance of boundary, the fragility of the division between the miniaturized community and the environment that seems on the verge of penetrating and en-

gulfing it. Just as Coverdale feels his connection to his three friends as a
dangerously depleting form of attack, so the world here is imagined as
frighteningly other: a presence that "haunts" the mind, trapping us
within accepted limits; a vastness that seems to shrink us to nothingness,
that calls us to dissolution; a seer whose gaze informs us of the alienness
that awaits the slightest breach in the fragile boundary that defines us. All
of these moments belong to Coverdale and might simply be considered a
product of his anxious way of perceiving. But they come, I think, to characterize the way the world feels to the characters that we encounter in *The
Blithedale Romance*. To read this novel, as to exist within its world as a
character, is to find everywhere manifest the fragility of the self and of the
communities we build around it.[10]

The extension of anxiety about the security of identity from the private
to the communal sphere, implicit in the passages I have just cited, helps us
understand the impulses that animate the Blithedale project itself. The
flight from the marketplace and established culture that the utopians attempt to engineer suggests that social and economic life, like the physical
world, is felt by its inhabitants as dangerously invasive: it threatens—
through the internalization of its structures of habit and restriction,
through its instability and competitiveness, through the anonymity city
life confers—the solidity of the self. Blithedale farm attempts to rescue a
small community from the meaninglessness of the marketplace: to replace
self-defense with self-discovery, competition with "familiar love." But the
admirable generosity of its conception gradually reveals itself to be subverted by defensiveness. Like the romantic attachments it fosters, the project suffers from the logic of infatuation: what had looked like love turns
out to be need. Coverdale comes to conceive of the experiment less as a
form of creation than an attempt at definition, at boundary building.
Joined by a collective act of refusal, a bond "not affirmative but negative"
(63), the brethren hope to locate and preserve some authentic form of
relation by keeping out anything else. Just as Coverdale's voyeurism is
exposed as a form of love shaped by a deeper aggression, so their self-
sequestration conceals the "latent hostility, which is sure to animate peculiar sects, and those who, with however generous a purpose, have se-
questered themselves from the crowd" (90). And just as Coverdale's
aggression is employed as a defense against an inescapable emptiness of
self, so the Blithedale project is a magnified version of his hermitage, an
effort to sequester the self against what threatens to reveal its inauthenticity. The members of the community set out to represent the significance
of their new-made selves in their labor, which they expect to become
"spiritualized," "symbolic" (65–66). Yet when the work of the farm
stubbornly refuses to yield the anticipated transcendence, they turn to the
empty arts of vicariousness; performing masquerades, allegorical tab-

leaux, scenes from plays, they give up the attempt to represent themselves and counterfeit the characters of others. These experimenters in communality, as the most attentive readings of the novel have noted, manage only to replicate the inner and outer emptiness that they flee.[11]

Hawthorne enfolds his fullest account of the psychology of this culture of anxiousness in the stories told within the world of the novel, particularly as they find expression as forms of popular legend. A set of symptomatic ghost stories haunts the middle-class culture that Hawthorne depicts. The most prominent of these is the legend of the Veiled Lady, which Zenobia dramatizes in "The Silvery Veil." The ability of the Veiled Lady to attract so much attention derives, I suggest, from her representation of the kind of speculations about selfhood that obsess the inhabitants of *The Blithedale Romance*. On the one hand the access that her veiling offers to the occult, and in particular to the secrets of other selves, confirms the hope that power is latent in the self, capable of being generated by an act of sequestration. On the other hand, however, her power is accompanied by all the trappings of subordination; the Veiled Lady is enslaved by a magician whose own power is rumored to derive from the sale of his soul to the devil. As in the passages that envision the vulnerability of the self to an engulfing outer world, power is imagined to reside outside of the self, available only at the cost of the identity that such power is sought to guarantee. The speculations that Zenobia cites about what lies beneath the veil amount to a catalog of anxieties and fantasies about the nature of one's own inner life and the hidden selves of others:

> Some upheld, that the veil covered the most beautiful countenance in the world; others—and certainly with more reason, considering the sex of the Veiled Lady—that the face was the most hideous and horrible, and that this was her sole motive for hiding it. It was the face of a corpse; it was the head of a skeleton; it was a monstrous visage, with snaky locks, like Medusa's, and one great red eye in the centre of the forehead. Again, it was affirmed, that there was no single and unchangeable set of features, beneath the veil, but that whosoever should be bold enough to lift it, would behold the features of that person, in all the world, who was destined to be his fate. (110)

The popular imagination oscillates between images of the deadness of the unveiled self (or the Medusa-like power of the other to confer such rigidity by gazing) and this anxiety's obverse, the notion that identity is fluid, literally unidentifiable.

Its significance unattended, like a myth that everyone has forgotten how to read, the story of Theodore's encounter with the Veiled Lady describes the etiology of this disease of selfhood. The skeptical Theodore, on a dare, sets out to solve the mystery of the Veiled Lady's identity. His errand brings him more than he bargained for; the lady agrees to the lifting of the veil but with a condition. He must kiss her before he lifts the veil, an act of faith that, she informs him, will confer this blissful reward: "thou shalt be mine, and I thine, with never more a veil between us! And all the felicity of earth and of the future world shall be thine and mine together." The other option: to lift the veil "in scornful scepticism and idle curiosity," which will transform her into his "evil fate," destroying his future happiness (113). Theodore, a wary consumer, decides to inspect before kissing; he gets a glimpse of her beautiful face as the lady disappears, dooming him "to pine, forever and ever, for another sight of that dim, mournful face . . . to desire, and waste life in a feverish quest, and never meet it more" (114). What the Veiled Lady offers Theodore is the self-risking interchange that Hawthorne—implicitly in his fiction, explicitly in his letters to his wife—defines as love. This mutual lifting of the veil of selfhood, we should notice, is precisely the act that the novel's logic of attenuated identity establishes as most threatening (and most necessary). Theodore's refusal to risk himself paradoxically robs him of the chance for the self-completion that love, for Hawthorne, promises. The punishment Theodore earns—"to desire, and waste life in a feverish quest"—is appropriately insidious. The refusal to risk the self engenders a form of desire that effects the depletion of the self, the "waste" of life. To refuse love is to condemn oneself to desire what is necessarily absent, the disappearing image that mirrors the self one lacks. The phrase that describes Theodore's punishment also captures the logic of Coverdale's quest for love; and the momentary glimpse of what has been lost describes the shape of Coverdale's experience: the pursuit of a significance that is always slipping out of sight.

The auditors of this cautionary tale elude its meaning by treating it as an amusement. The successful forms of art that we encounter in *The Blithedale Romance* offer gratifications more immediate than those of interpretation.[12] In "The Village Hall" chapter, which records Hollingsworth's rescue of Priscilla from the lecture circuit, Coverdale delivers an anatomy of the kinds of popular entertainment that his culture makes available. His catalog culminates in the following performance by a member of the audience.

> I heard, from a pale man in blue spectacles, some stranger stories than ever were written in a romance; told, too, with a simple, unimaginative steadfastness, which was terribly efficacious in compelling the auditor to receive them into the category of established facts. He cited instances of the miraculous power of one human being over the will and passions of another; insomuch that settled grief was but a shadow, beneath the influence of a man possessing this potency, and the strong love of years melted away like a vapor. At the bidding of one of these wizards, the maiden, with her lover's kiss still

burning on her lips, would turn from him with icy indifference; the newly made widow would dig up her buried heart out of her young husband's grave, before the sods had taken root upon it; a mother, with her babe's milk in her bosom, would thrust away her child. Human character was but soft wax in his hands; and guilt, or virtue, only the forms into which he should see fit to mould it. The religious sentiment was a flame which he could blow up with his breath, or a spark that he could utterly extinguish. It is unutterable, the horror and disgust with which I listened, and saw, that, if these things were to be believed, the individual soul was virtually annihilated, and all that is sweet and pure, in our present life, debased, and that the idea of man's eternal responsibility was made ridiculous, and immortality rendered, at once, impossible, and not worth acceptance. But I would have perished on the spot sooner than believe it. (198)

Coverdale's reaction, though intriguingly overheated, seems logically correct. The claim made in this narrative for the magical power over "the will and passions of another" available to the mysterious initiate denies the essentiality of all the emotions that are thought to guarantee the existence of a unique, sustainable, consistent self. Still, the nature of the gratification that makes these stories so compelling to their hearers needs to be deciphered.

For one thing, these tales, unlike the novel that contains them, offer the pleasures of identification: there is obviously one very good part in these vignettes, that of the "man possessing . . . potency." His mysterious powers place this figure in the position that Coverdale's yearnings identify as ideal: he has complete access to the inner lives of others while himself remaining invulnerable. The uses the teller finds for this potency, moreover, bear a high libidinal charge, involving primarily the adjustment of women's affections, presumably to the benefit of the enchanter. This potent male figure can also be seen as engaged, more covertly, in an act of revenge against women for their apparently privileged access to the kinds of deep emotional ties—love, grief, mothering—that verify the existence of a self to do the feeling. But in the notion that "human character was but soft wax in his hands; and guilt, or virtue, only the forms into which he should see fit to mould it" whispers a different, deeper order of wish, a wish for confirmation of what is already felt or feared to be true: the insubstantiality of the self and its emotions. These tales of the violation of the self contain the oblique cry of a psyche overburdened by the responsibilities that have customarily belonged to a degree of being, of substantiality, that it finds itself unable to sustain. Love and grief, guilt and virtue *have* become merely "forms" in the world of the novel, and the storyteller's attribution of power to a figure external to the self conceals an offer of forgiveness of the burden of feeling. Coverdale's horrified reaction to these tales seems to me a submerged acknowledgment of their accuracy; hearing them raises for him not a question of truth but a problem of volition: will he have the strength *not* to believe this transcription of his own anxieties?

The stories of the man with the blue spectacles, pieces of the mythology of his cultural moment, work like the horror movies of our own: they locate widely shared anxieties and turn them into a source of pleasure, offering fantasies of inordinate potency or the comforting illusion that what they are portraying is alien to the self. We need to notice, too, how Hawthorne is using this tale to forecast or warn against the disintegration, under the pressure of the anxiousness he diagnoses, of the cultural consensus that he had celebrated in *The House of the Seven Gables*. For the character-erasing power of the mesmerist-magus is a sustained inversion of the idea of "influence" that is customarily celebrated as the key to the formation of a stable, moral character when exercised by a properly domestic "magician" like Phoebe Pyncheon or by the figure of the mother so widely invoked in antebellum writing about the middle-class home. The notion of the self's permeability to others—the central hope of sentimental ideology—is simply becoming too frightening for the vulnerable, defensive inhabitants of the novel's world to accommodate.

In the last of these spectral legends, "Fauntleroy," Hawthorne explores the relation between the marketplace and the economy of self construction. "Fauntleroy" chronicles the earlier career of Old Moodie, the progenitor of both Priscilla and Zenobia. In his present incarnation, Moodie represents the insubstantial self in pantomime: "His very gait demonstrated that he would gladly have faded out of view, and have crept about invisibly, for the sake of sheltering himself from the irksomeness of a human glance" (184–85). He practices an urban variation on the strategy of self-preservation that Coverdale relies on in his trips to his hermitage; his near removal from view ensures that the absence that constitutes his identity will elude discovery. Fauntleroy's personal history links this inner emptiness, quite specifically, to the experience of economic life in a developing market economy.[13] We first encounter Fauntleroy as a financial success, his form of selfhood the product of his wealth: "His whole being seemed to have crystallized itself into an external splendor . . . and had no other life than upon this gaudy surface" (182). For Fauntleroy, "conscious of no innate worth to fall back on," to lose his money is utterly to lose himself. He thus defends himself against economic ruin "with the instinct of a soul shrinking from annihilation" (183), committing a crime in the process. The disgraced and impoverished Fauntleroy, "being a mere image, an optical delusion, created by the sunshine of prosperity" (183), fades from sight and memory, eventually reappearing in Boston as Old Moodie. As Coverdale notes in his narration of the tale, both these identities are "alike impalpable," the manifestation in the realm of personality of the cycle of boom and bust.

This legend adds to our understanding of the anxious culture of *The Blithedale Romance* a sustained analogy between the condition of character and economic activity. Identity for Fauntleroy/Moodie is not a stable quantity but a kind of fluctuation; like an inflated currency or a stock under speculation, the self possesses negligible intrinsic value, its worth instead determined by the vagaries of the market. The tale describes Fauntleroy's offense in this way: "it was just the sort of crime, growing out of its artificial state, which society (unless it should change its entire constitution for this man's unworthy sake) neither could nor ought to pardon. More safely might it pardon murder." This crime, apparently forgery, bespeaks an economy in which the authenticity of financial documents is paramount while persons are quite expendable. Fauntleroy's association with sudden, unpredictable fluctuations in value; with the paper instruments that newly, mysteriously, and not necessarily reliably represented wealth; and with secretive forms of transaction conducted in the seamier interstices of urban life reveal him to be an embodiment of the manifold queasiness of antebellum economic life.[14] Even the product by which Moodie earns his living, Priscilla's hermetic purses, links monetary value to the strategies of concealment and mystification that produce identity in the world of the novel. Taken together, these analogies between Fauntleroy's economic behavior and the evacuated condition of his character hint at an economic cause for the anxiety that permeates the novel. In Fauntleroy, the marketplace itself seems to generate, as a kind of emanation, the liminality that constitutes selfhood in *The Blithedale Romance*.[15]

"The Silvery Veil" and "Fauntleroy" are linked within the book by their status as freestanding tales, and this distinctive mode of presentation insists that we think about the relation between them. The two stories operate as explanatory legends, each proposing a theory of cause to account for the anxiousness that pervades character and culture in *Blithedale*. In the legend of the Veiled Lady the etiology proposed is psychological: an inner lack—an inherent or characteristic fragility in the constitution of the human self—generates a private defensiveness that unfolds in this culture's predatory fantasies and forms of behavior. In "Fauntleroy" an inexplicable, unstable market world infects the self, making it feel continually at risk and putting it constantly on guard. The book does not equip us to choose between or rank these diagnoses. Their equal authority within the text suggests, rather, that it is the mutual permeation of the economic and the psychological that makes the anxiety that the book depicts so powerful: private emotion and communal connection are alike endangered by a peculiar, unhappy synergy between the constitution of the self and the experiences that belong to a new economic and social life.[16]

Hawthorne is making about his historical moment the kind of analytic point we might make about our own in noticing, say, that our cultural atmosphere is shaped by a similarly powerful affinity between the psychological and the economic: between the objectifying quality of male desire and the commodity form. Such an access of awareness, in which we locate a purchase that lets us penetrate the plausible surface of an entrapping ideology is, it seems to me, the animating purpose of the book. As we have seen, all the forms of exchange that we witness in *The Blithedale Romance*, whether emotional or economic, legendary or lived out, are revealed to be defenses against an unspoken emptiness at the center of the self and of the culture that enfolds it. The diagnosis of the way this anxiety misshapes experience that emerges from the book's portraits of character and its renditions of communal fantasy constitutes a different kind of interchange, one that offers its readers not the comforts of defense or the allure of fantasy but an uncomfortable, freeing awareness of ideology itself. To interpret *The Blithedale Romance*, to perform its version of the work of romance, is to become an analyst, not a creature, of this culture of anxiousness.

ROMANCE AND ANGER

"I agree with you in your detestation of Hawthorne," wrote Sarah Hale to her son, Edward Everett Hale, upon completing *The Blithedale Romance*; "the more I think of his book the more the disagreeable preponderated." Hale seems to have felt *Blithedale* as excessively unpleasant in its depiction of contemporary life, and, her anger indicates, as an act of aggression against its audience. Her response provides a useful starting point for a fuller discussion of the way the book constructs its interchange with the reader, its way of performing the work of romance, for in several ways anger and aggression are at the center of the book's engagement with its culture.[17] For one thing, this is a novel of exposure, the literary equivalent of exploratory surgery. As we have seen, it defines the task of reading as itself aggressive, the penetration of the self-deceiving psychology of the teller of this story and the unveiling of the predatory emptiness of an anxious culture that kills off, in Zenobia, its sole possessor of the capacity to love. Yet the resistance to transformation characteristic of this culture of anxiety insists that we complicate our question. Does the novel do more than diagnose an incurable illness? What happens in *The Blithedale Romance* to romance's ambition to cure? How might the novel open, on behalf of its readers, the circle of anxiety and compensatory fantasy that entraps its characters? As in *The Scarlet Letter*, our best access to the book's designs upon us comes by examining its depictions of interpretation.

Let us begin with the novel's most curious and controversial moment, Coverdale's confession. This is *The Blithedale Romance*'s moment of interpretive demand, where Hawthorne leaves us on our own, submitting his work most radically to the risk of reading. This brief chapter, containing his attempt to "say a few words about myself," records Coverdale's interpretation of his own memoir. He begins the chapter with the statement of the problem that has troubled him throughout the novel: how does one go about having a self? Even in the telling of his own story, an act seemingly susceptible to his control, he has failed to establish his presence: "I have made but a poor and dim figure in my own narrative, establishing no separate interest, and suffering my colorless life to take its hue from other lives. . . . But what, after all, have I to tell? Nothing, nothing, nothing!" (245). The confession is Coverdale's solution to the problem of his absence, and he is quite particular about its reception; he informs us that it is "essential to the full understanding of my story" and gives us the visual accompaniment: "As I write it, [the reader] will charitably suppose me to blush, and turn away my face:—I—I myself—was in love—with—Priscilla!" (247). What Coverdale's act of writing—and his consequent reading of his own life—has given him to understand is this: to have nothing, nothing, nothing to tell is to be nothing. Throughout the novel, the secrets that Coverdale assumes other selves to possess are what elude him; to have a secret in a world largely emptied of significance is, at least, to have something. Coverdale's confession is an attempt to claim a secret and hence to invent, retrospectively, the selfhood he now understands to be missing.

More significant than the question of the truth or falsehood of this statement—Coverdale is in love with everybody and able to love no one—is the *way* he makes it. This moment of revelation, which claims that his behavior has all along been governed by an occult principle known only to him, is itself tinged by his customarily oblique aggression: he seeks to put the reader in his own accustomed position—adrift in the wake of mystery—and to place himself among those who possess selves and secrets. But there is a more deeply revealing logic at work here as well. Our understanding of Coverdale's anxiety suggests that the success of this confession is vital; it is his last, best hope for selfhood. But, as all the apparatus of the bogus that accompanies it—the blush, the melodramatic punctuation—makes clear, Coverdale can only make such a confession in a way that announces its own inauthenticity, that declares him not guilty of any genuine emotion. Yet this incapacity *not* to despoil his own confession at last acknowledges the depth of his anxiousness and the guilt of having nothing to confess, nothing to say, because he has succeeded in being nothing. The failure of his confession announces as well the failure of his artistic project; his act of telling succeeds not in enacting the self-hood that has eluded him in the original experiencing but only in representing, through an act of aggression directed against both the reader and himself, the guilt and anxiety generated by his sense of his own inauthenticity. In Coverdale's art as in his life, nothing will come of nothing.

What Coverdale has missed, as the reader of his own tale, is the possibility that defines Hawthornian romance: the chance to recognize and revise the self. This private failure of reading is extended, via the book's recurrent interest in acts of reading and responses to communal spectacle, to the culture more largely. Coverdale is not only this culture's representative man; he is its representative reader. He habitually justifies his voyeurism by presenting himself as a model interpreter, an adept at the detection of "the final fitness of incident to character" and the distillation of "the whole morality of the performance" (97). The problem with Coverdale's reading of his experience, which Hawthorne has him demonstrate again and again, is not a lack of acuity or even sympathy; Coverdale offers a number of striking essays in the analysis of character and culture. Coverdale possesses, however, an impenetrable defense against applying anything he notices about the latent motivations of others to his own case; he thus imagines one of his periodic attacks on Priscilla's happiness as a form of education—"beneficiently seeking to overshadow her with my own sombre humor" (75). More subtly, he displays an ability to describe his own failures of intimacy with a meticulousness that seems to dissipate any impulse to change. His frequent comments on the dangers of an analytic relation to others—"It is not, I apprehend, a healthy kind of mental occupation, to devote ourselves too exclusively to the study of individual men and women" (69)—never yield an attempt to change the form that his friendship takes. Analysis, for Coverdale, is not a prologue to action but a completely adequate substitute for it.

Coverdale, then, can read everything but himself. When he literally does some reading, he does so as a refuge from troubling thoughts, and significantly alternates reading with looking out the window (147); reading is a safe activity because it protects him from his own experience. Moreover, Coverdale is not alone in his ability to elude the implications of the experience, whether explicitly artistic or not, that he encounters. Every audience we witness in *The Blithedale Romance* is either escapist in its choice of art—like those who attend the Veiled Lady's performance at the Village Hall, hungry for fantasies of power or guiltlessness—or dysfunctional in its reception of it. The Blithedale brethren, for example, witness Zenobia's rendition of "The Silvery Veil" without noticing that it performs the same kind of attack on Priscilla's fragile selfhood that it depicts as evil; Priscilla's agitation at this forecast of her betrayal to

Westervelt is dismissed as a small price to pay for so effective a piece of theater. Hawthorne, then, gives us, within the work, a reader insulated by defenses against self-recognition made impenetrable by anxiety.

Such an unreachable reader, if encountered in the world at large, threatens to destroy the exchange at the center of romance, turning Hawthorne, despite himself, into a version of Coverdale, condemned to write out a covert testimony to his own isolation and impotence. How does the *figure* of the defensive reader called into being by the book's manifold failures of response effect our own act of interpretation? The exhortation implicit in Hawthorne's attack on the self-protective reader forges, it seems to me, a curious form of alliance with the actual reader that paradoxically transforms our hostile relation to the book's narrator into a form of connection with its author. By defining the personal and cultural costs of failing to read the self so compellingly, Hawthorne in effect dares one to risk being part of the portrait. Encoded in *The Blithedale Romance* is a relation between writer and reader based on shared anger: anger against Coverdale's evasions and self-evasions, against the constricting culture that endorses them—against what the book represents and the defensive form that representation takes. We feel Coverdale's narration, I am suggesting, as alienating both us and the Hawthorne that he has displaced. The reader imagined by this novel is not, as in *The House of the Seven Gables*, on the threshold of community, a voice to be transformed, with like-minded others, into a "we." *The Blithedale Romance* seems to aim, rather, at a kind of joint apostasy, a salutary mutual rage.

But if this achievement of shared anger is indeed the form of relation with the reader that Hawthorne establishes in *The Blithedale Romance*, what saves his project from merely replicating the entrapping logic of Coverdale's memoir and the Blithedale experiment? Is not this attacking novel itself an act of aggressive withdrawal, designed to elude the dangers of full participation in a community? Is not the bond forged between writer and reader "not affirmative, but negative"? The moral logic of the novel leads us, it seems to me, to a crucial distinction. Cruelty is generated in *The Blithedale Romance* when anxiety displaces emotion: thus love appears in the novel only as infiltrated by aggression or deployed by narcissism or greed. Unlike Coverdale's voyeurism or the fantasies that emerge as popular entertainment, the anger shared by writer and reader is not a defense against emotion but an expression of it, not a displacement of selfhood but its exercise. To belong to the community described in *The Blithedale Romance* is not to share an ethical vision but to acquiesce in the structure of anxiety and fantasy that the novel exposes. Only the anger we earn by reading this novel can break writer and reader out of the empty circle in which *The Blithedale Romance*'s culture of anxiety confines us. Our angry reading of the novel implicates us, along with

Hawthorne, in the guilt of an aggressive relation to communal life, of speaking what the community cannot bear to hear. But our anger, our guiltiness, might save us from the deeper guilt of Coverdale's perennial observership, his empty relation to himself and others. This, then, is the hope implicit in the way *The Blithedale Romance* engages its audience: that the anger that Hawthorne risks calling forth in his reader—an anger easily directed against the writer, as the responses I have cited indicate— might induce the clarity of mind and generosity of purpose needed to break the hold of the culture of anxiousness that he depicts. He sets out, in his own chastened version of reform, to renovate his community of readers from the inside out.

Yet some of the uneasiness created by the paradox of a regenerative hostility remains intractable, the consequence of the novel's own account of the culture of anxiousness arrayed against it. The failure of the Blithe-dale community suggests that there exists no safe margin of culture, no "outside" from which to work the needed transformation. Even the cura-tive "neutral territory" of romance—the place of freeing revision of mind called into being in Hawthorne's writings—may, in the face of our elabo-rate defenses against self-recognition, be only a wish, a compensatory fantasy. The residual uneasiness of *The Blithedale Romance* is Haw-thorne's acknowledgment of the problematic nature of a writer's cultural power, a statement, as it were, of the long odds against romance. If it is to do more than replicate the pattern of attack and withdrawal it reveals, the book must free the anxious reader it describes. But Hawthorne must rest his hopes for cure on a support undermined by his own analysis: the unverifiable capacity of fiction to change its readers' minds. Haunted by the specter of the unreachable reader, Hawthorne engages and resists in *The Blithedale Romance* his own version of the anxiety he discovers in the world of the novel: an anxiety induced by the suspicion of one's pow-erlessness, by an intuition of the emptiness of one's form.

Chapter Seven

THE DEFEAT OF ROMANCE:
THE MARBLE FAUN

Whether one has killed one's father or has abstained
from doing so is not really the decisive thing. One is
bound to feel guilty in either case, for the sense of guilt
is an expression of the conflict due to ambivalence, of
the eternal struggle between Eros and the instinct of
destruction or death.
—Sigmund Freud

THE MARBLE FAUN is a novel of farewell and a novel of return. It begins
with a eulogy for the "Gentle Reader" who had welcomed Hawthorne's
previous work into existence: "If I find him at all, it will probably be
under some mossy grave-stone, inscribed with a half-obliterated name,
which I shall never recognize" (2). Hawthorne builds his book upon this
all-but-certain loss of the connection that has called romance into being.
He makes a novel, full of echoes, out of a review of his career, thus raising, with disturbing force, the questions that have all along provoked his
work. What kind of cultural role does fiction perform? Is there a way of
telling stories that can tame or subvert the authoritarian impulse within
the psyche and within the community? Or is a constricting culture the
strongest storyteller, its rigid stories—the propitiatory or punitive tales
that too often structure our behavior—at last defeating the curative possibility of freedom of mind made animate by the practice of romance?

I want to use the remarkable sentence from *Civilization and its Discontents* that I have chosen as this chapter's epigraph to forecast those elements of *The Marble Faun* that will most concern us: its psychological
excavations, its understanding of the condition and history of contemporary culture, its implicit stance toward experience. This last romance returns us to territory familiar from "Roger Malvin's Burial" and *The Scarlet Letter*: we explore once more the imperium of conscience. The characters in *The Marble Faun* confront an understanding of moral psychology
like that proposed by Freud: guilt is not the simple result of what we do
but the inevitable expression of what we are. Within the book, Hawthorne juxtaposes two opposite responses to this condition. In the story
of Miriam and Donatello, one has killed the father, in his distorted in-

carnation as the Model, and confronts the consequences of that liberating and confining act; in the story of Hilda and Kenyon, one simply abstains. Hawthorne is less occupied here with analyzing the inner experience of guilt than with demonstrating the kind of experience that each response entails: what kind of love, art, community does each tale sponsor? Like Freud in *Civilization and its Discontents*, Hawthorne asks what happens when the excessive conscientiousness that misshapes inner life becomes the informing principle of culture itself. Finally, I want to propose that the act of mind performed in Freud's sentence, the clear-seeing of an unhappy complexity and the willing engagement of its consequences—as opposed to the evasion, erasure, or suppression of it that the book will identify as characteristically American—is the effect sought by this version of romance.

The interpretive task this romance sets for us is to locate, if we can, the meaning of the book's daunting pattern of unresolvable opposition. To read *The Marble Faun* is to witness two quite different books engaged in frustrating one another's smooth progress toward their appointed ends. In the territory that constitutes *The Marble Faun*, a plot of redemption confronts a plot of condemnation; maturation confronts regression; freedom confronts restriction; a cynical, cosmopolitan narrator confronts a pious, sentimental one; plot confronts travelogue; an aesthetic of originality confronts an aesthetic of imitation; moral complexity confronts moral absolutism. As one might expect, even interpretations of this novel tend to divide into two camps. One strategy of reading takes these proliferating oppositions as a symptom of the author's confusion or exhaustion and attributes them to neurosis or a decline in imaginative power. The other brackets the uneasy experience of reading the novel and finds coherence in the intricacies of the novel's plot, its thematic recurrences, its meditations on art or history.[1]

I will argue that the "confusion" of *The Marble Faun* is the product of Hawthorne's riskiest experiment in narrative form, his most insistent subversion of orthodox literary authority. He has chosen to explore the fate of his kind of fiction by embodying the struggle between romance—the fiction of transgression—and the genteel novel—the culturally ascendant fiction of suppression—in what might be called a "double novel." A compendium of Hawthornian romance, the story of Miriam and Donatello and their guilt-tainted love, opposes a fictive flight from complexity, the uplifting tale of Kenyon's pious quest to make Hilda his "household saint." *The Marble Faun* is composed of a struggle for hegemony between these two precisely opposed novels. In this last enactment of romance, Hawthorne defines his artistic project by describing the conditions of its failure. Or, to put this another way, he sets out to bring the Gentle Reader back to life by showing us what it is like—as an individual and as a culture—to become dead to romance.

THE DOUBLE NOVEL

As I have suggested, the crucial distinction between these two novels—the distinction from which the other oppositions derive—is that between the response to guilt that each describes. In the story of Miriam and Donatello, guilt is confronted by way of transgression, while the story of Hilda and Kenyon is generated by the defenses against guilt that the characters employ: by a logic of denial. Each novel links its way of responding to guilt to attendant forms of behavior, to a particular notion of love, and to a specific artistic practice and the aesthetic theory that underlies it. The willed difficulty of *The Marble Faun* derives, it seems to me, from the extraordinary range of implication that Hawthorne now attaches to the problem of conscience.

All of the crucial moments of the novel inhabited by Miriam and Donatello take place under the sign of romance. The stagy lighting of Miriam's studio; the recovery of the present moment, with its sudden access of pleasure, during the sylvan dance at the Villa Borghese; the murder by moonlight; the uncanny moment of the bronze pontiff's benediction: these allusions to the characteristic atmosphere and effects of Hawthornian romance urge us to think of the Miriam novel as an exemplar of the tactics and possibilities of that form. The most striking romance element in the book is the Model, a characteristically overdetermined allegorical emanation of the psychological knot that Hawthorne is examining. Conscience is embodied in *The Marble Faun* by the figure of the Model, whose persecution of Miriam drives Donatello to murder. The origin of the Model's power over Miriam is made hazy, as befits so complex a psychic institution. He is her inheritance, his hold upon her the consequence of an obscure familial wrong, in which Miriam somehow shares. As in Freud's account of the inevitability of the sense of guilt, her literal innocence is irrelevant; she behaves *as if* guilty, whatever her actual case. The causality of the Model's materialization within the novel is especially revealing; Miriam herself "evokes" him by descending into the subterranean, subconscious territory of the catacombs: "She came to me when I sought her not. She has called me forth, and must abide the consequences of my re-appearance in the world" (31). The Model is the figure of patriarchal authority that resides within, reappearing simply as the consequence of an emblematic moment of introspection. He represents guilt as a necessity of the psyche, and the gestures of propitiation that he extorts from Miriam before the murder reveal that in her case, as in Reuben Bourne's, the sense of guilt precedes any actual transgression.

The Model exemplifies, in a particularly focused form, other familiar characteristics of the Hawthornian conscience. "Nothing was stranger in his dark career," the narrator tells us, "than the penitence which often seemed to go hand in hand with crime" (432). The Model's oscillation between acts of persecution and rituals of penance—his handwashing in the Trevi fountain, his circuit of the Coliseum's shrines—establishes the kind of link between guilt and obsession that we recognized in Dimmesdale. His compulsive penitence is revealed to be a system designed not to escape the sense of guilt but to perpetuate it in ineffectual pantomimes of remorse. Moreover, the monk/Model's dual career reflects Hawthorne's sense that the authority of conscience is not reliably based in any coherent moral system but derives simply from its power to punish, its "formal" position in the hierarchy of the psyche. Thus the Model earns his living by his form rather than by his content, providing a figure whom artists turn into a saint or an assassin at will (19); thus he switches, with mysterious ease, from model to monk.

To kill the Model—Donatello literally overthrows him—is to attempt to overturn the authority of conscience, a kind of transgression in the abstract. The joint crime Miriam and Donatello commit has two immediate results, the "ecstatic sense of freedom" that attends the breaking of a law (176) and the beginning of a love that is reciprocated, sexual, and grounded in a shared sense of guilt—which is to say, adult. Yet the passing of this moment of freedom reveals the true power of conscience, for the Model is not dead but internalized: Miriam and Donatello themselves begin to carry out his characteristic patterns of behavior. Hence Donatello's fixation in his guilt; hence Miriam's compulsive returns to view the corpse and her modellike shadowing of Donatello. To rebel against the authority of conscience, to risk transgression, is to give up the simple comforts of projection—the notion that evil is external to the self—and to experience one's intimate connection to the Model, to claim one's share of guilt.

The love that Miriam and Donatello build upon their crime is endangered by the internalization of the Model, by the authority of conscience within the psyche. Donatello's penetential obsession threatens to become permanent; the expression of his love for Miriam becomes, as Kenyon notes, an ideal form of self-torture. Miriam's notion of love veers toward the ideal of self-sacrifice. The central action of the novel shared by Miriam and Donatello is the second subversion of the power of conscience, their escape from the impasse of self-enclosure generated by their guilt. Their defeat of the authoritarian within is brought about by the curative process we have come to recognize as romance.

Their rescue must be a dual one: like the Hawthorne of the prefaces, Miriam needs deliverance from the purposelessness that balks her creativity ("It is my too redundant energy that is slowly—or perhaps rapidly—wearing me away, because I can apply it to no use" [280]); Donatello needs deliverance from his isolating obsession ("He has struggled long enough with one idea" [284]). Like the joint rescue of reader and writer that romance institutes, this cure depends upon interchange: "Who else, save only me—a woman, a sharer in the same dread secret, a partaker in one identical guilt—could meet him on such terms of intimate equality as the case demands" (282–83). It depends upon entering new mental terrain, here enacted in the course of travel that Kenyon prescribes for Donatello: "he will re-create the world by the new eyes with which he will regard it. He will escape, I hope, out of a morbid life, and find his way into a healthy one" (284). It depends, finally, on the free choice of the receiver of the cure, and on the refusal of coercion by Miriam, its artist-arranger: "But—do you not see?—his heart must be left freely to its own decision whether to recognize me, because on his voluntary choice, depends the whole question whether my devotion will do him good or harm" (317).

This experiment in romance that Miriam and Kenyon conduct yields a moment of success. Donatello, by speaking Miriam's name, finds his way out of self-entrapment and into love. Kenyon, on vacation from Hilda and her world of constraint, vindicates his observership by providing the moral justification that brings the hesitating lovers together—the theory of the "fortunate fall," that transgression is the necessary beginning of moral education. The narrator celebrates the beauty that attends this recovery of love and gently suggests the possibility that a fugitive happiness might attach even to so guilty a union. The completion of this curative project is marked by a moment out of romance's vocabulary of the uncanny, the blessing of the lovers by the bronze statue of Pope Julian. The authority of conscience, this scene suggests, has been tamed; in the place of the Model we have an "educated" figure of authority, not a punisher but a forgiver. Romance has done its work, then; it has subverted the tyranny of conscience and recovered—though in a chastened form—the possibility of love.

The rest of *The Marble Faun*, however, records the blocking of this moment of possibility, of pleasure. The novel that belongs to Hilda and Kenyon seizes control of the book and reveals that the success of their pious love depends upon the punishment of Miriam and Donatello—depends, that is, upon the defeat of romance. In contrast to the confrontation with conscience that composes the Miriam novel, the response to guilt that the Hilda novel enacts is a strategy of denial and projection. Hilda and Kenyon seek above all to maintain the illusion of guiltlessness, and the power of conscience is expressed in their hysterical attempts to defend themselves against it.

The actions that constitute Hilda and Kenyon's novel can all be seen as attempts to deflect the kind of complex awareness that transgression makes available in Miriam's romance: in effect, to deny that romance a hearing. Thus both Kenyon and Hilda refuse Miriam the opportunity to tell her story out of a kind of moral squeamishness, a fear of guilt by association, of being tainted even by what they might hear. These acts of censorship are significant, for, as Kenyon himself implies late in the novel (with telling obtuseness), it is the lost opportunity to speak her story that leads to Miriam's victimization by it. Even Kenyon's contribution to Miriam and Donatello's moment of rescue is tainted by an influx of the punitive. The sculptor, "anxious not to violate the integrity of his own conscience," issues a warning to the lovers: their union, he instructs them, "is for effort, for sacrifice, but not for earthly happiness" (322). What is an act of scrupulosity by the moral measure of the Hilda novel is an act of suppression and a culpable failure of sympathy in the light of Miriam's romance.[2]

The story of Hilda and Kenyon's progress toward marriage, in describing a very different relation between love and guilt, corresponds precisely to the pattern established by Miriam and Donatello. There is a confrontation with sin (Hilda's witnessing of the murder of the Model), a trial by guilt (the anguish that leads Hilda to the confessional), a period of painful separation (Kenyon's search for Hilda during her imprisonment), a moment of mutual rescue, complete with benediction (the proposal at the Pantheon, under Miriam's protection.) In every case, however, the relation between the sentimental fiction engaged in by Hilda and Kenyon and the romance enacted by Miriam and Donatello is governed by a logic of defense or denial. The events of the Miriam novel can only be admitted into the Hilda novel in attenuated, parodic, or immature form.

Hilda's brush with sin is conducted by proxy; like a child viewing a primal scene, she witnesses a transgression but commits none. The particular shape that guilt assumes in Hilda's psyche can be inferred from the extremity of her reaction to this scene. Here are two moments from the encounter with Miriam that follows the murder.

> If I were one of God's angels, with a nature incapable of stain, and garments that never could be spotted, I would keep ever at your side, and try to lead you upward. But I am a poor, lonely girl, whom God has set here in an evil world, and given her only a white robe, and bid her to wear it back to Him, as white as when she put it on. Your powerful magnetism would be too much for me. The pure, white atmosphere, in which I try to discern what things are good and true, would be discolored. And, therefore, Miriam, before it is too late, I mean to put faith in this awful heart-quake, which warns me henceforth to avoid you! (208)

> It seems a crime to know of such a thing, and to keep it to myself. It knocks within my heart continually, threatening, imploring, insisting to be let out! Oh, my mother! My mother! Were she yet living, I would travel over land and sea to tell her this dark secret, as I told all the little troubles of my infancy. (210–11)

In the magical thinking that Hilda displays in the first of these passages—in her sense that mere exposure to Miriam would somehow amount to a kind of sin—we might discover a symptom of a repressed sense of connection to or imaginative participation in Miriam's transgression. (It seems suggestive that Hilda emphasizes an aspect of Miriam's act—her kneeling to the Model—that mirrors Hilda's own authority-worshipping turn of mind.) In any case, Hilda clearly takes mere proximity to transgression for the real thing, and launches into a strategy of avoidance and projection designed to identify guilt as completely other. Hilda's urge toward projection—the strategy that Miriam and Donatello forego by transgressing—is accompanied by a regressive impulse: she imagines depositing her dark secret with her mother. While Miriam and Donatello's act yields a direct experience of guilt and an attendant maturation, Hilda's defense against guilt, itself seemingly induced by a prior sense of guiltiness, places her in the confining safety of psychological childhood.

Hilda's desperate urge to jettison her sense of guilt leads her, by way of a search for the perfect Madonna, to the confessional at St. Peter's, which is one of this pious novel's analogues to the scene of the statue's benediction (the closing scene in the Pantheon is the other). The release from guilt that Hilda feels after successfully expelling her difficult knowledge in the confessional, in contrast to Donatello's escape from his analogous obsession, takes the form not of a transformation but of a restoration: "It was all gone; her bosom was as pure now as in her childhood. She was a girl again" (358). This "confession" is an attenuated form of the kind of self-revealing interchange at the center of Hawthorne's concept of romance; Hilda tells the sin of another, and receives release without self-risk. The experience confirms rather than challenges the authority of Hilda's overactive conscience. With its appeal for forgiveness to a patriarchal authority (Miriam, we remember, attempts to "confess" to her friends), the confession replicates in its outward form the internal authority of conscience. Note, too, the formal analogy to Miriam's kneeling before the Model. The confession erases Hilda's vision of the linked complexity of love and aggression, returning her to a child's relation to her experience and to the authority of conscience.[3] Guilt operates in Hilda's psyche as a fear of punishment so extreme that it tends toward an ideal of experiencelessness; no event or emotion that does not in some way reinforce the principle of authority is permitted to enter the psyche unpunished.

Hilda and Kenyon's quest for marriage is governed by an analogously defensive logic: they successfully evade the temptation of complexity. This triumph of conscience can be traced in the career of the notion of the "fortunate fall" within the text. Kenyon is the originator of the idea, using it to welcome the spiritual growth that results from Donatello's sin and to justify his marriage to Miriam. The concept, which understands the existence of sin as fortunate because it makes human goodness a freely

chosen achievement rather than an act of divine fiat, demands the recon-
ciling of the opposed concepts of good and evil. This "double" idea seems
to represent, in an abstract way, moral complexity in the novel, just as the
murder of the Model represents transgression. The idea has an unimpeachable lineage—St. Augustine by way of Milton—and Kenyon confi-
dently proposes it to Hilda. Hilda, shocked, repudiates the idea precisely
on the grounds of its rudimentary complexity: "there is, I believe, only
one right and one wrong; and I do not understand (and may God keep me
from ever understanding) how two things so totally unlike can be mistaken for one another" (384).

Even so brief an exposure to the complex, however, profoundly dis-
turbs Hilda, calling into question her unsympathetic rejection of Miriam
("must a selfish care for the spotlessness of our own garments keep us
from pressing the guilty one close to our hearts"?). The narrator describes
this reassertion of Hilda's connection to Miriam in language that suggests
the loosening of a repression: Kenyon's speech "had set, as it were, a
prison-door ajar, and allowed a throng of torturing recollections to escape from their dungeons." And the result of Hilda's self-questioning is to
place her temporarily in the condition of ambivalence that belongs to an
undefended relation to conscience: "It was a sad thing for Hilda to find
this moral enigma propounded to her conscience, and to feel that, whichever way she might settle it, there would be a cry of wrong on the other
side" (385–86). This, then, is Hilda's trial by complexity, her brush with
adulthood. It leads, by way of her delivery of Miriam's packet, to Hilda's
imprisonment—which emblematically enacts the resuppression of her affinity to Miriam and reestablishes the sovereignty of conscience.

Kenyon, because of Hilda's imprisonment, suffers a parallel trial.
Hilda's absence deprives him of the comfort of the moral simplicity she
enforces: "The idea of this girl had been like a taper of virgin wax, burning with a pure and steady flame, and chasing away the evil spirits out of
the magic circle of its beams" (409). It produces an attendant crisis of
faith: Kenyon can find "no star of Hope—he was ready to say, as he
turned his eyes almost reproachfully upward—in Heaven itself!" (408).
This exposure to the problematic engenders in Kenyon a fever of orthodoxy. When, hoping for news of Hilda, he meets with Miriam and Donatello in the campagna, we have the curious experience of hearing him
repudiate the theory that he himself has introduced. Miriam suggests,
virtually quoting Kenyon, that Donatello's crime has been "a means of
education, bringing a simple and imperfect nature to a point of feeling
and intelligence, which it could have reached under no other discipline."
Kenyon reacts hysterically: "I dare not follow you into the unfathomable
abysses, whither you are tending. . . . It is too dangerous, Miriam! I cannot follow you. . . . Mortal man has no right to tread on the ground

where you now set your feet" (434–35). Implicit in Kenyon's anxiety is an attempt to propitiate the punishing authority that has spirited Hilda away, to disclaim, in Hilda's fashion, all knowledge of punishable complexities. The final trial in Kenyon's quest for Hilda's hand takes the appropriate form of an immersion in ambiguity per se. Kenyon enters the world of the carnival, where identity is itself in flux and sexual innuendo, with its double meaning, seems to have come to life.[4]

Kenyon's endurance is rewarded by Hilda's materialization, and their pious plot achieves its moralistic fulfillment at the Pantheon with the final repudiation of the fortunate fall idea and the complex relation to experience that it represents. Here is the conversation—which I quote at length because it illustrates so well the panicky, joyless, inhibitory feel of life within the novel of earnestness—that records the dismissal of Kenyon's theory and the marriage proposal that dismissal makes possible. Kenyon trots out the fortunate fall notion one more time:

"Here comes my perplexity," continued Kenyon. "Sin has educated Donatello, and elevated him. Is Sin, then—which we deem such a dreadful blackness in the Universe—is it, like Sorrow, merely an element of human education, through which we struggle to a higher and purer state than we could otherwise have attained? Did Adam fall, that we might ultimately rise to a far loftier Paradise than his?"

"Oh, hush!" cried Hilda, shrinking from him with an expression of horror which wounded the poor, speculative sculptor to the soul. "This is terrible; and I could weep for you, if you indeed believe it. Do not you perceive what a mockery your creed makes, not only of all religious sentiment, but of moral law, and how it annuls and obliterates whatever precepts of Heaven are written deepest within us? You have shocked me beyond words!"

"Forgive me, Hilda!" exclaimed the sculptor, startled by her agitation; "I never did believe it! But the mind wanders wild and wide; and, so lonely as I live and work, I have neither pole-star above, nor light of cottage-windows here below to bring me home. Were you my guide, my counsellor, my inmost friend, with that white wisdom which clothes you as with a celestial garment, all would go well. Oh, Hilda, guide me home!"

"We are both lonely; both far from home!" said Hilda, her eyes filling with tears. "I am a poor, weak girl, and have no such wisdom as you fancy in me." (460–61)

This passage at once records the triumph of conscience and reveals the scope of its cultural authority. Hilda reacts to Kenyon's mildly complex speculation with the excessive anxiety that characterizes her response to moral complication throughout the novel. Her language suggests that what drives that anxiety is the fear of the inner discomfort that authentic moral difficulty produces, for what Hilda cannot bear is the obliteration of the absolutes that conscience inscribes upon the psyche—"whatever precepts of Heaven are written deepest within us." Hilda's metaphor of inscription suggests a battle between two forms of writing, two opposed stories. The price of Hilda's freedom from the direct experience of guilt—of the preservation of the precepts that protect her from ambivalence—is the erasure of Miriam's romance—which enacts as its plot the theory of the fortunate fall.

As striking as the linguistic form that this struggle between the absolute and the complex takes for Hilda is the curious consequence of her authoritative censoring of Kenyon's idea. The sculptor's abject surrender of his theory turns suddenly into what must be one of the least romantic proposals of marriage in all of literature. Neither Kenyon's proposal nor Hilda's response has anything to do with love. The sculptor seeks protection from his own complexity of mind and erects Hilda into an icon of moral simplicity, a charm against ambivalence. Hilda's acceptance takes the form of an acknowledgment of her own need for protection, her permanent girlhood. Their joint yearning for home suggests an abdication of adulthood, a marriage built not upon transgression but upon regression, and along with that the allure of an American culture that successfully disguises the history of complex experience too visibly inscribed upon the Roman setting. Implicit in this sudden transition from censorship to espousal is the guiding hand of the overactive conscience. The regressive form of love that Hilda and Kenyon achieve is clearly the consequence of and reward for their joint rejection of the kind of demanding morality that might challenge the absolutist logic that protects them from experience. The marriage of Hilda and Kenyon converts love to the service of conscience, translating it from the shared experience of pleasure and suffering claimed by Miriam and Donatello into a mutual defense against guilt. We witness in Hilda's successful transformation into Kenyon's "household Saint" (461) the narrowing of love into worship, the attenuation of the interchange upon which romance is built.

Miriam presides over this triumph of mere conscientiousness, this defeat of romance which ends *The Marble Faun*, in a manner reminiscent of the bronze pontiff's supervision of her reunion with Donatello. But while the statue's uncanny blessing of the lovers seemed to confirm the power of romance, Miriam's benediction acknowledges its necessary exile from the fiefdom of conscience that Hilda and Kenyon have chosen to inhabit. No words can be exchanged between Miriam and the happy couple, and her gesture is at once benediction and warning: "those extended hands, even while they blessed, seemed to repel, as if Miriam stood on the other side of a fathomless abyss, and warned them from its verge" (461). The abyss that Miriam warns the lovers away from is, it seems to me, the kind of complex experience that the culture of earnestness can no longer accommodate except at a cost in anxiety that it refuses to pay: the abyss of ambivalence, the abyss of adulthood, the territory of romance.[5]

ART AS IDEOLOGY

Miriam's silenced presence in the book's closing scene—her enacted exile—typifies what we might think of as the power relations between the two novels that *The Marble Faun* contains. As the book moves toward its close, Miriam and Donatello are permitted to enter it only in ways that emphasize their removal from the field of experience that the Hilda novel is willing to recognize as real. Thus they appear masked, or disguised as peasant and contadina, or tricked out in the trappings of fantasy fiction as when a bejeweled Miriam materializes in a fancy carriage. It is as if the Hilda novel contains the threatening complexity of their experience by reducing it to a kind of artiness. The act that leads to the final triumph of the forces of conscience in *The Marble Faun* is Hilda's delivery of the "packet" of writing that Miriam has entrusted to her to the authorities; the emblematic logic of this moment suggests that the successful completion of Hilda's novel depends upon the censorship of Miriam's romance. And it is strongly hinted that Hilda's release from her imprisonment is bought with Donatello's internment. The kind of merely defensive freedom that Hilda and Kenyon finally arrange for themselves depends upon the suppression, trivialization, or erasure of the emotions, forms of expression, and points of view that threaten the brittle moralism they have come to espouse.

The progressive defeat of Miriam and Donatello's romance and all it represents by the sentimental fiction constructed by Hilda and Kenyon becomes the occasion for the implicit meditation that Hawthorne conducts in the book upon the nature of cultural authority and upon the connection between artistic practice and ideology. Hawthorne is exploring in *The Marble Faun* both the psychological and the cultural meaning of the flight from complexity; the internal triumph of conscience in Hilda and Kenyon is writ large in the genteel culture that enfolds them. Just as we could measure the development of Kenyon's moral anxiety by tracing his changing relation to the idea of the fortunate fall, so the shock that Hilda feels at that notion is a sign that the earnest culture she represents is itself governed by an analogous momentum of orthodoxy. Hawthorne's choice of so recently hallowed a concept as his scandal seems designed to demonstrate that the moral authority of a community, like the psychological authority of conscience, is impelled by an appetite for its own augmentation. Just as Hilda's conscience moves toward an ideal of experiencelessness, so communal authority—the collective expression of conscience—seeks a condition of utter restriction.

Hawthorne offers in *The Marble Faun* the vision of a culture progressively dominated by conscience, a culture that has begun to prefer the tranquility of guiltlessness to pleasure. This momentum of restriction seems most insidiously at work in the conversion of love into a form of worship that we witness in Kenyon's attachment to Hilda. As we have seen, in terms of private psychology Kenyon surrenders the difficult pleasure of an adult relationship for the refuge from guilt that his connection with Hilda confers. In terms of cultural psychology, the domination of love by conscience seems to be an equally bad bargain. The version of love that conscience is willing to accommodate can be inferred by juxtaposing two moments from Kenyon's search for Hilda. One records Kenyon's first glimpse of Hilda's bedroom; in the second, Kenyon imagines what might be happening to Hilda on the loose in the nasty atmosphere of Rome.

> Thence, the sturdy Roman matron led the sculptor across a narrow passage, and threw open the door of a small chamber, on the threshold of which he reverently paused. Within, there was a bed, covered with white drapery, enclosed within snowy curtains, like a tent, and of barely width enough for a slender figure to repose upon it. The sight of this cool, airy, and secluded bower caused the lover's heart to stir, as if enough of Hilda's gentle dreams were lingering there to make him happy for a single instant. But then came the closer consciousness of her loss, bringing along with it a sharp sting of anguish. (404–5)

> For here was a priesthood, pampered, sensual, with red and bloated cheeks, and carnal eyes. With apparently a grosser development of animal life than most men, they were placed in an unnatural relation with woman, and thereby lost the healthy, human conscience that pertains to other human beings, who own the sweet household ties connecting them with wife and daughter. And here was an indolent nobility, with no high aims or opportunities, but cultivating a vicious way of life, as if it were an art, and the only one which they cared to learn. Here was a population, high and low, that had no genuine belief in virtue; and if they recognized any act as criminal, they might throw off all care, remorse, and memory of it, by kneeling a little while at the confessional, and rising unburdened, active, elastic, and incited by fresh appetite for the next ensuing sin. Here was a soldiery who felt Rome to be their conquered city, and doubtless considered themselves the legal inheritors of the foul license which Gaul, Goth, and Vandal have here exercised in days gone by. (411–12)

The first of these passages, rich in sentimental iconography, reveals the logic by which love is narrowed into worship. The moment bears a palpable voyeuristic charge—Hilda's bed!—but what seems to be alluring here is the utter banishment of sexuality. That is, Hilda is desirable to Kenyon, this scene suggests, precisely because of her independence from desire, her self-enshrinement in purity's solo boudoir. This is sexuality as conducted under the gaze of conscience, and we see its cultural costs reflected in Hilda and Kenyon's relationship. Marriage becomes a form of joint entrapment: Hilda is frozen into an icon of purity; Kenyon purchases a share in that purity by a willing self-censorship, an escape from his sexuality via their mutual denial of hers. Inherent in this relationship is the infantilization of Hilda that consistently accompanies Kenyon's romantic piety.

The second passage, when linked to its predecessor, exposes the underside of this hunger for purity. The sleazy prudery of Kenyon's vision of carnal Rome ineffectually conceals a fantasy of rape. The flavor of Kenyon's fantasy suggests that the consequence of the desexualization of love that gentility sponsors is the eroticization of aggression. Moreover, what links the fantasy of purity to the fantasy of rape is the control of female sexuality and freedom that each yields. For all his abjectness, Kenyon wants to domesticate Hilda's piety, to make her his "*household* Saint." Yet Hilda's acquiescence in the fantasy of purity suggests that the deepest desire the couple shares, along with the culture they represent, is the desire for self-control, for freedom from guilt. We witness in the reduction of love in *The Marble Faun* the progressive domination of people by the worshipful emotions, even as the culture becomes more secular; it appears that conscience has rescued the idiom of religion so ideal to the exercise of its authority and used it to manage the threatening emotion of love.[6]

The Marble Faun yields, along with this portrait of the spoiling of intimacy within a culture progressively under the sway of guilt, an exploration of the relation between different kinds of artistic practice and the maintenance of the culture of conscience. Hawthorne juxtaposes, throughout the novel, the ideas about art that cluster around Hilda's story to those that accompany the experience of Miriam and Donatello. The pattern of Hilda's and Kenyon's artistic careers, like that of their relationship, is one of attenuation. Art, like love, is reduced from a form of self-expression to a form of worship. This infiltration of art by the principle of authority is most apparent in Hilda's self-transformation from a promisingly original artist into a supreme copyist of the works of the old masters. The honorific rhetoric that the narrator attaches to Hilda's facility is all borrowed from the register of religion. She possesses "the gift of discerning and worshipping excellence in a most unusual measure. . . . Reverencing these wonderful men so deeply, she was too grateful for all they bestowed upon her—too loyal—too humble, in their awful presence—to think of enrolling herself in their society. . . . All that she would henceforth attempt—and that, most reverently, not to say, religiously—was to catch and reflect some of the glory which had been shed upon canvas from the immortal pencils of old" (56–57). This sacrifice of her own work to the propagation of established masterpieces amounts to an artistic martyrdom, which seems to yield Hilda a kind of sanctification by association.

The affinities between the aesthetic of imitation that Hilda comes to practice and the principles of authority so dear to conscience are several. Hilda's enterprise is governed by an ideal of fidelity to works—all, of course, by male artists—whose authority is established by tradition. Hilda's interest in art lies exclusively in its "spiritual" qualities, and during the course of the novel she becomes progressively stricter about what works sufficiently evade the taint of the earthly or the ambiguous to meet her standard of piety; in genteel aesthetics as in genteel ethics a momentum of restriction operates. Hilda's copying displays a logic that is doubly childish: not only does it sacrifice self-expression in order to earn the imaginary approval of aesthetic authority figures but it attempts to deny the necessity of loss by producing a perfect repetition. Hilda, by substituting a process of reverent replication for the invention of content, locates an utterly safe, guilt-free form of art.

The cultural stakes of Hilda's regressive aesthetic are most apparent in her effect as a critic. As Nina Baym argues, Hilda's influence transforms Kenyon into a merely genteel artist; he moves from the erotic power and originality of his statue of Cleopatra—a work that both expresses his sexuality and calls into being the full presence of another—to his "beautiful little statue of Maidenhood gathering a Snow-drop" (375)—a work borrowed from the safely presexual idiom of sentimental love.[7] (Note its emotional affinity to the scene of Kenyon's visit to Hilda's bedroom.) Unlike Kenyon's statue of Cleopatra, which deserves to be called a creation, the maidenhood miniature is essentially a reproduction: a version of an already authorized icon of female purity. Kenyon's art in turn reinforces the myth of womanhood that sponsors it, assisting in the denial of sexuality that operates as a powerful control over experience within the culture of restriction that Hawthorne is describing.

Hilda's art worship, then, puts art at the service of the anxious authoritarianism of genteel culture. Even her ability, by means of self-suppression, to recover utterly the intention of the artist whose work she copies, which might seem to be an ideal response to art, conceals an inhibiting principle. "There is a class of spectators," she tells Kenyon, "whose sympathy will help them to see the Perfect, through a mist of imperfection.

Nobody, I think, ought to read poetry, or look at pictures or statues, who cannot find a great deal more in them than the poet or artist has actually expressed. Their highest merit is suggestiveness" (379). Hilda's theory that the project of art is the recovery of "the Perfect" and its corollary, that the artist is himself the imperfect medium of a higher power, subordinate both artist and audience to some extrahuman and quite constricting ideal; no wonder she has given up doing paintings of her own. Her notion of art thus incorporates the habit of obeisance to an imagined figure of authority that is the essential story of the Hilda novel. This perfectionist theory of art is countered immediately—but obliquely—by a discussion of the power of Kenyon's bust of Donatello, which has been left in an unfinished state, as though emerging from the marble. Its highest merit is its "suggestiveness"—but not its suggestion of "the Perfect." The power of the statue, the contemplation of which, the narrator tells us, was the origin of *The Marble Faun*, is shown to be the consequence of its very imperfection, its analogy to the incomplete state of Donatello's moral growth.

Hilda and Kenyon share this curious characteristic: they can both occasionally accommodate—and even produce—as art what they cannot compass in experience. Thus Kenyon can create the fiercely erotic statue of Cleopatra but is too squeamish to listen to Miriam's life story; thus Hilda can capture the ambiguous essence of Guido's portrait of Beatrice Cenci but banishes Miriam for participating in an analogous crime. Hawthorne's portrayal of Hilda's theory of art implies that Hilda and Kenyon can maintain this split between the complexity of their art and the simplicity of their experience precisely because they come to define art as other than experience: as ideal, perfect, spiritual. Art worship, like woman worship, deprives its object of a real—and hence potentially powerful—relation to experience. Hilda's reverent aesthetic transforms art into a kind of vaccine against experience: a small dose of complexity in a work of art seems to confer immunity against its disturbing effect on everyday life.

Hawthorne's depiction of Hilda's artistic theory and practice identifies art as unavoidably in relation to the exercise of authority within the culture it reflects and helps create. While art in the Hilda novel reinforces the principle of authority, the artistic practice of the Miriam novel tends to subvert it. Yet the relation between these two aesthetics is not a simple opposition between freedom and restriction, for art in Miriam's romance is not playful or exuberant. Rather, the relation between Miriam's art and Hilda's resembles the relation between adulthood and childhood. Art in the Miriam novel encounters rather than evades guilt; it suffers the condition of ambivalence.

While Hilda seeks the safety of a form of art that completely defends the self from exposure, Miriam's work reveals as its deepest impulse a yearning for self-expression.[8] Yet the presentation of self that Miriam's art achieves is complicated by the sense of guilt induced by the impulses that her work reveals. I have already suggested the affinity between Miriam's story and the curative project of Hawthornian romance; we should also notice how precisely Miriam's problem of self-presentation conforms to Hawthorne's dramatization of his own. Here is the novel's description of the isolation induced by Miriam's sense of guilt.

> Yet it was to little purpose that she approached the edge of the voiceless gulf between herself and them. Standing on the utmost verge of that dark chasm, she might stretch out her hand, and never clasp a hand of theirs; she might strive to call out—"Help, friends! Help!"—but, as with dreamers when they shout, her voice would perish inaudibly in the remoteness that seemed such a little way. This perception of an infinite, shivering solitude, amid which we cannot come close enough to human beings to be warmed by them, and where they turn to cold, chilly shapes of mist, is one of the most forlorn results of any accident, misfortune, crime, or peculiarity of character that puts an individual ajar with the world. Very often, as in Miriam's case, there is an insatiable instinct that demands friendship, love, and intimate communion, but is forced to pine in empty forms; a hunger of the heart, which finds only shadows to feed upon. (113–14)

This figure of estrangement, made insubstantial by isolation from a progressively shadowy world, we recognize as the Hawthorne of the prefaces, imprisoned by the "entangling depths of his obscurity," and despite his hunger for "intimate communion" forced to pine in the "empty forms" of unread fiction. Miriam's sense of guilt places her in the position Hawthorne identifies as his own before the establishment of "some true relation" to the reader, before the invention of romance.[9]

Like Hawthorne's fiction, Miriam's work betrays an ambivalent relation to her culture. The sketches that Donatello examines during his visit to Miriam's studio reveal that her art moves in two apparently opposed directions: toward transgression in her sketches of female revenge, and toward a celebration of domestic emotions in her scenes of family life. The drawings of transgression—Jael driving the nail through the temples of Sisera, Judith decapitating Holofernes—are at once visions and revisions. They begin as passionate representations of women murdering their oppressors, only to be trivialized by later, "wayward quirks" of Miriam's pencil. Jael is turned into a "vulgar murderess," and the head of Holofernes grins at a befuddled Judith (43–44). The sketches begin as rebellious acts of identification but are reduced, via the grotesque, into self-punishments. Miriam's sketches place her in the impasse that Hawthorne continually identifies as his own: she is caught, like Hester in the Puritan community, between a perception that makes her marginal and the longing to be central.

Miriam's other genre of sketches displays a similarly divided content. The subjects of these sketches of "domestic and common scenes"—budding romance, the stages of wedded affection, the baby's shoe—aim right at the heart of the sentimental audience that Hawthorne simultaneously courts and flouts throughout his career. These sketches, the narrator tells us, are sincere, "but in each a figure was portrayed apart." The excluded figure, always "depicted with an expression of deep sadness," is Miriam herself (46). The double focus of these sketches, which portray both the emotional strengths of a culture and the condition of exclusion from them, dramatizes the danger of the artist's self-conscious relation to his community. For these drawings inherently ask whether there is a causal relation between the apparently benign values celebrated in these sentimental vignettes and the simultaneous exclusion of the figure of Miriam that they record.

Miriam's art is condemned, in both its subversive and celebratory moments, to an unhappy relation both to the community it addresses and to its own antiauthoritarian generating impulse. Her investment in her pictures is many-sided: she rebels and punishes, sympathizes and withdraws. Miriam's troubled relation to her own art implies an analogy between the psychological experience of guilt and the position of an artist exiled by his vision from the stock of moral stories that define his culture. In Miriam's paintings, art's transgression is specified. Like Hawthorne's fiction, her work uncovers disturbing connections between what a culture claims to value and what it claims to repudiate—the urge to dominate that lurks within moral authority, the way communal values can turn into forms of restriction or cruelty. Miriam's self-betraying art, unlike Hilda's contentless copying or Kenyon's authorized reproduction, portrays the condition of lived ambivalence that results from an unacquiescent relation to the authority of conscience and to the culture of earnestness that is its communal expression.

The adulthood of art within the Miriam novel is implicit not only in its ambivalence but in its intimate relation to the idea of loss, the necessity of which both Hilda's copying and her aesthetic of the perfect attempt to deny. Just as Kenyon's statuette of Maidenhood exemplifies a willfully innocent art, so the battered statue of the nymph that Donatello shows Kenyon at Monte Beni captures the condition of art under the taint of guilt.

A fountain had its birth here, and fell into a marble basin, which was all covered with moss and shaggy with water-weeds. Over the gush of the small

stream, with an urn in her arms, stood a marble nymph, whose nakedness
the moss had kindly clothed as with a garment; and the long trails and tresses
of the maiden-hair had done what they could in the poor thing's behalf, by
hanging themselves about her waist. In former days, (it might be a remote
antiquity,) this lady of the fountain had first received the infant tide into her
urn, and poured it thence into the marble basin. But, now, the sculptured urn
had a great crack, from top to bottom; and the discontented nymph was
compelled to see the basin fill itself through a channel which she could not
control, although with water long ago consecrated to her. (243)

The statue, we learn, is intended as an act of reparation. The water
nymph, in an earlier version of the Miriam-Donatello story, had died
when her human lover had washed off a bloodstain in her stream, and he
had the statue erected as a sign of penance. Since it was established as an
acknowledgment of guilt, the statue has fallen on hard times; it suffers its
entry into a world where its nakedness is an embarrassment that needs
covering over, and it becomes worn and cracked. Art as portrayed here
inhabits human history rather than the realm of the perfect; it is subject to
obscuring, vulnerable to damage. For me, the most intriguing characteristic of the statue is the nymph's loss of control over the fountain's flow of
water, for art in the Hilda novel is both technically and thematically an
exercise in self-control. The nymph, compelled to witness the partial nature of her direction of the fountain, acknowledges art's share in the volatile energies of a psyche that is itself resistant to channeling.

Yet the beauty of this scene is said to depend upon the statue's representation of these losses, and throughout the Miriam novel the power of
art is understood to be grounded in its fidelity to loss. Thus Miriam's
remarkable song, which Donatello and Kenyon overhear, derives its force
from its origin in her anguish: "It was as the murmur of a soul, bewil-
dered amid the sinful gloom of earth, and retaining only enough memory
of a better state to make sad music of the wail, which would else have
been a despairing shriek" (269). And the beauty of Monte Beni, clearly an
evocation of the romance place, is discovered to be the consequence of its
remembrance of loss, its accumulated history: "The sculptor strayed
amid its vineyards and orchards, its dells and tangled shrubberies, with
somewhat the sensations of an adventurer who should find his way to the
site of ancient Eden, and behold its loveliness through the transparency of
that gloom which has been brooding over those haunts of innocence, ever
since the fall. Adam saw it in a brighter sunshine, but never knew the
shade of pensive beauty which Eden won from his expulsion" (276).

The crime that Miriam commits in *The Marble Faun* is an act of representation: she gives Donatello a "look" that expresses her desire for the
murder of the Model. It is simultaneously a crime of self-revelation; as

Hilda tells her, that look "revealed all your heart" (210). Miriam incarnates, then, the romance's difficult relation to its own power. The freeing of impulse that enables romance to renovate a stifling culture necessarily endangers that culture, for the emotions that romance reveals are not necessarily benign or fully subject to control. Insofar as romance succeeds, it is condemned to guiltiness, for its form of cure endangers the patient—at least, as the joint hysteria of Hilda and Kenyon indicates, in the judgment of the patient. But the overpowering of Miriam and her romance by Hilda's genteel, censorious novel suggests that, as the culture moves toward the increasingly constricting moralism that assuages its fears of complexity, it may succeed in extinguishing the forms of expression that unsettle it. The guiltiness of romance is in danger of becoming a distressingly minor issue.[10]

Narrative Combat

So far in this essay I have been guilty of what I suggested at the outset is the besetting sin of arguments for the coherence of *The Marble Faun*: I have written as though reading this book were just about like reading any other. This critical strategy evades the sense of ongoing conflict—of two mutually exclusive sensibilities struggling for authority over the same story—that characterizes the moment-by-moment experience of reading this work. If I were to identify a scene that epitomized the narrative practice of *The Marble Faun*, it would be the moment, late in the book, when Kenyon is hit simultaneously by the rosebud that signals Hilda's restoration and by a cauliflower thrown by a passer-by. This brief episode occupies what might be thought of as the seam that joins the two novels, and it inhabits both of them at once. Kenyon is hero or buffoon, depending on whether this scene is viewed from Hilda's sentimental novel or Miriam's romance. Why does Hawthorne employ the tactics of doubleness that this scene exemplifies? Why risk the confusion that this narration-as-conflict engenders? Where is the Hawthorne who presides over this strange novel, and where does he place us in relation to him? Let me begin by looking at this strategy of double narration at work.

The Marble Faun does not simply oppose two sets of characters and their allied ideas; it unleashes two distinct narrative voices, each of which produces a chorus of mutually antagonistic moral pronouncements, observations, witticisms, and explanations; it becomes impossible to say authoritatively at any given moment whose side the novel as a whole is on. That is, both Hilda's innocence and Miriam's complexity are wholeheartedly espoused during the course of the book—each by the narrator that belongs to her own particular novel. The variations in narrative voice that we encounter seem to be governed by both character and context. Thus Hilda is worshipped by a pious hagiographer and Miriam is appreciated by an acute psychologist with a sense of the erotic; Kenyon's moralizing seems to induce an analogous sententiousness in the narrator, while Donatello's presence invites passages of freer speculation. Scenes from Hilda's and Kenyon's courtship that pull at the "heart-strings" are greeted by a gushing narrator too fond of exclamation points; moments from the Miriam novel, like the murder of the Model, are rendered by a careful analyst, interested in the range of complex, contradictory emotions that their crime engenders. The reader experiences the conflict between the two novels that compose *The Marble Faun* in the disorienting form of a narrative civil war.

Because this argument that two versions of literary authority simultaneously inhabit the terrain of the book may not be immediately plausible—though *The House of the Seven Gables*'s play of narrative voices clearly lays the theoretical groundwork for *The Marble Faun*'s narrative combat—it will take me a fair amount of quotation to demonstrate its validity. The disjunction between the two sensibilities that alternatively occupy the formal position of narrator is simply too great and too pointed, it seems to me, to be thought of as one voice—even as an extremely confused, ambivalent, or ironic voice. Consider the sensibility responsible for the following vignette (an ironic version of which appears in *The Blithedale Romance*):

> What a sweet reverence is that, when a young man deems his mistress a little more than mortal, and almost chides himself for longing to bring her close to his heart! A trifling circumstance, but such as lovers make much of, gave him hope. One of the doves, which had been resting on Hilda's shoulder, suddenly flew downward, (as if recognizing him as its mistress's dear friend, and perhaps commissioned with an errand of regard,) brushed his upturned face with its wings, and again soared aloft. The sculptor watched the bird's return, and saw Hilda greet it with a smile. (372)

Could it possibly produce this jaded mock piety?

> What better use could be made of life (after middle-age, when the accumulated sins are many, and the remaining temptations few) than to spend it all in kissing the black cross of the Coliseum! (154)

Or this urbane lament—which anticipates the argument of *Civilization and its Discontents*—for the despoilation of pleasure by duty?

> It is the iron rule in our days, to require an object and a purpose in life. It makes us all parts of a complicated scheme of progress, which can only result in our arrival at a colder and drearier region than we were born in. It insists

upon everybody's adding somewhat (a mite, perhaps, but earned by incessant effort) to an accumulated pile of usefulness, of which the only use will be, to burden our posterity with even heavier thoughts and more inordinate labor than our own. No life now wanders like an unfettered stream; there is a mill-wheel for the tiniest rivulet to turn. We go all wrong, by too strenuous a resolution to go all right. (239)

While most of the book's scenes are dominated by one of these voices or the other, Hawthorne occasionally juxtaposes narrators in a way that insists that we puzzle over the meaning of the conflict between them. Here is Kenyon daydreaming of Hilda atop Donatello's tower:

Then rose tumultuously into his consciousness that strong love for Hilda, which it was his habit to confine in one of the heart's inner chambers, because he had found no encouragement to bring it forward. But, now, he felt a strange pull at his heart-strings. It could not have been more perceptible, if, all the way between those battlements and Hilda's dove-cote, had stretched an exquisitely sensitive cord, which, at the hither end, was knotted with his aforesaid heart-strings, and at the remoter one, was grasped by a gentle hand. His breath grew tremulous. He put his hand to his breast; so distinctly did he seem to feel that cord drawn once, and again, and again, as if—though still it was bashfully intimated—there were an importunate demand for his presence. Oh, for the white wings of Hilda's doves, that he might have flown thither, and alighted at the Virgin's shrine!

But lovers (and Kenyon knew it well) project so lifelike a copy of their mistresses out of their own imaginations, that it can pull at the heart-strings almost as perceptibly as the genuine original. No airy intimations are to be trusted; no evidences of responsive affection less positive than whispered and broken words, or tender pressures of the hand, allowed and half returned, or glances, that distil many passionate avowals into one gleam of richly colored light. Even these should be weighted rigorously, at the instant; for, in another instant, the imagination seizes on them as its property, and stamps them with its own arbitrary value. But Hilda's maidenly reserve had given her lover no such tokens, to be interpreted either by his hopes or fears. (263–64)

This sequence gives us the same event—a moment of intuitive connection with the beloved—as it might be rendered by the narrators of two quite distinct novels. Two essentially opposed understandings of romantic emotion are at work. The first narrator is an evangelist for the religion of love that is one of the hallmarks of sentimental fiction. His view of the operation of love is at once exquisitely spiritual and strangely mechanistic. Kenyon's connection with Hilda produces specific physical manifestations, and thus claims some of the supernatural authority of a minor miracle or a conversion experience. The narrator proceeds, like a high-flown Rube Goldberg, to give us a detailed diagram of the actual operation of the heartstrings metaphor ("Tie exquisitely sensitive cord [A] to heartstrings [B–F]"), as though love obeyed a perfectly explicable, rather rudimentary physics. This simpleminded passage ends in the familiar gush of pious sentiment: by his exclamation point shall ye know him.

The paragraph that follows reflects a much more disturbing understanding of the psychology of love. Experiences of mystic connection like Kenyon's are unreliable, likely the consequence of a projection of one's own desire. Love is dangerously susceptible to infiltration by the urge to dominate or control another, expressed in the passage's metaphors of ownership and coinage. The experience of love, for this narrator, is not a supernaturally endorsed certainty but a most crucial case of the problematic nature of all our relationships to others: our liability, by means of projection, to connecting primarily with ourselves. The warning against solipsism that this narrator issues invokes the uncomfortable notion that morality depends upon enlightened self-distrust, upon resisting the seemingly authoritative inner conviction—an idea that belongs, say, to the moral world of a Jane Austen novel or to that of Hawthorne's own stories, not to the divinely arranged moral landscape of the preceding conceptual locale. Love here has fallen into the morally ambiguous place of interpretation.

The strategic juxtaposition of these two moral perspectives enacts within the narrative the conflict that is simultaneously occurring within Kenyon. For Kenyon is engaged through most of *The Marble Faun* in choosing which novel he will finally inhabit, which narrative voice will define the range of his experience. His willful frustration of the potential for complex vision that he displays here—he "knows well" what the second narrator has to say—is rewarded when the idealizing fantasy of the heartstrings turns out, once the Hilda novel takes over, to be unambiguously true: Hilda, in her despair, *had* been engaged in longing for the sculptor's comforting presence at the very moment that Kenyon felt the tug (343).

The tactic of doubleness at work in this passage—the oscillation between opposed narrators—takes over whole chapters of the book. Chapter 48, for example, which introduces us to the Roman carnival, consists of alternating condemnations and celebrations of the same event. One strain of commentary laments the defilement of the carnival's once-innocent antics. The bouquets, once tossed by would-be lovers to each other with modest seriousness, now "symbolize, more aptly than was intended, the poor, battered, wilted hearts of those who fling them; hearts which—crumpled and crushed by former possessors, and stained by various mishap—have been passed from hand to hand, along the muddy street-way of life, instead of being treasured in one faithful bosom!" (440–41). Note the fear of the instability of desire and the consequent urge toward its control that animate this passage and ally it with the Hilda novel. The competing commentary, alive to paradox, praises the carnival as a healthy communal release: "there was a sympathy of nonsense; a true and genial brotherhood and sisterhood, based on the honest purpose—and a wise one, too—of being foolish, all together" (439). A nearly paranoid voice of enforcement confronts an indulgent voice of toleration, producing a stalemate of narrative authority.

This technique of opposition also operates at the level of the sentence; each voice makes occasional forays into the territory of its competitor, rendering an apparent espousal problematic. This is a sentence from the Miriam novel, recording her reaction to the Model's corpse: "This form of clay had held the evil spirit which blasted her sweet youth, and compelled her, as it were, to stain her womanhood with crime" (190). Here is a moment from the Hilda novel, in which the narrator accounts for Hilda's resemblance to the Beatrice Cenci portrait after she witnesses the murder: "But, as regards Beatrice's picture, the incident suggests a theory which may account for its unutterable grief and mysterious shadow of guilt, without detracting from the purity which we love to attribute to that ill-fated girl" (205). In the former sentence, the impulse to understand Miriam's crime—if that is what it is—as "compelled" and thus only complicatedly culpable, gets sabotaged by the suspicious "as it were" injected into the sentence, I suggest, by the condemnatory voice of the sentimental narrator. The attempt to exonerate both Hilda and Beatrice Cenci from anything but the knowledge of another's guilt is disrupted by the subversive hint in the phrasing that the purity—"which we love to attribute"—to Beatrice may only be the consequence of our need to find it there. Both these sentences find their authority made doubtful by doubleness, by the injection of the exiled perspective.

As the Hilda novel comes progressively to dominate *The Marble Faun*, the complex narrator gets fewer opportunities to speak, and seems able to smuggle his perspective into the book only under the veil of irony. Thus Hilda can be attacked—but only in the guise of praise:

> With respect to whatever was evil, foul, and ugly, in this populous and corrupt city, she had trodden as if invisible, and not only so, but blind. (387)

> . . . a pair of [doves] (who were probably their mistress's especial pets, and the confidants of her bosom-secrets, if Hilda had any) came shooting down, and made a feint of alighting on his shoulder. (402)

In both these sentences, the signs of Hilda's innocence—her blindness to evil, her secretless bosom—have too much in common with stupidity.

Kenyon is exposed as a buffoon from time to time, but only by indirection. With Donatello's guilt-induced maturity comes a fall into aphorism—"I am not a boy, now. Time flies over us, but leaves its shadow behind"—which Kenyon greets with condescension: "The sculptor could not but smile at the triteness of the remark" (218). After a protective interval of several pages, though, Kenyon produces this fatigued moralism in appreciation of the wine of Monte Beni: "The flavour must be rare indeed, if it fulfil the promise of this fragrance, which is like the airy sweetness of youthful hopes, that no realities will ever satisfy!" (223). Kenyon is revealed never to have read *The House of the Seven Gables* (he tells Donatello that in America "each generation has only its own sins and sorrows to bear" [302]), while Hilda asks the question—"Was Donatello really a Faun?" (459)—that Hawthorne tells us in the postscript indicates that the book has been, for the reader who asks it, a failure. These potshots at Hilda and Kenyon, which by virtue of their obliqueness have the air of having been smuggled past the censor, dramatize the fate of a complex perspective within the genteel culture that sponsors Hilda's novel: criticism, deprived of the hope of a hearing, can surface only as nastiness.

The experience of encountering this narrative warfare while trying to put together an interpretation of *The Marble Faun* is quite disorienting. One's allegiance to the novel's characters and to either of the moral perspectives I have been describing is subject to continual encouragement and frustration—both conducted by what orthodox novel reading accustoms us to regard as a single voice in command of the moral meaning of the events it depicts. I have been arguing that the experience of being morally unmoored that the book induces is the product of an extremely unorthodox experiment in narrative strategy: two independent structures of narrative authority, two utterly convinced narrators, are engaged in combat. While I am convinced that this theory accurately describes what is going on in the *The Marble Faun*, we still need to ask why Hawthorne might have risked the chaos of readings that such a narrative-in-conflict has produced.

The effect of this double form of narration is to take what I have been calling the moment of interpretive demand characteristic of Hawthorne's fiction—the moment when the reader is left alone to interpret without or in opposition to the confirmation of narrative authority—and to extend it to occupy an entire novel. The coexistence of two contradictory but irrefutable forms of narrative authority creates an interpretive problem even more troubling than the authorial reticence or ironic deployment of narrative authority that romance has taught us to accommodate. Interpretation ceases to be a process of locating the inclusive form of wisdom that seems to govern the work—even if that wise perspective is inferred from its literal exile from the text, as in "Roger Malvin's Burial" or *The*

Blithedale Romance—and forging an alliance with it. We are forced instead to choose one of two opposed moral perspectives over the irreconcilable but equally authoritative objections of its opposite. Thus a pro-Hilda reading of *The Marble Faun* must confront the silencing of Miriam, despite her embodiment of the perspective of Hawthorne's previous work; thus a pro-Miriam reading must account for the way the book awards itself to Hilda. We are condemned to an ambivalent relation to our own interpretation, and thus to a subversive relation to whichever of the two novels we repudiate.

The Marble Faun, then, demands that its reader sacrifice the comforts of intellectual reconciliation and choose. This is not to say that there is not a right choice; I think that a careful account of the novel will, as I have been arguing, make the reader a partisan of Miriam. But the choice remains a most uncomfortable one, for it demands that we reconceive the figure of the author, producing, implausibly enough, a writer who designs a book engaged in dramatizing its own defeat. The presence of Hawthorne that we infer from this novel, the authority to which we finally appeal, is more intently elusive than ever. His evasiveness creates, as the requests for clarification Hawthorne addresses in the postscript testify, a proportionate hunger for certainty in the reader—a hunger ("What was Miriam's real name?") that Hawthorne proceeds to mock, even more cruelly than in the novel proper, under the guise of satisfying it. *The Marble Faun*'s book-length attack on our desire for interpretive confirmation reveals the extent to which novel reading is itself permeated by the habit of allegiance. The uncomfortable interpretive independence that Hawthorne confers in this book, at the risk of confusing us completely, is designed to overturn that habit, to attach to our interpretation of this novel all the distress that ought to accompany difficult ethical choice. *The Marble Faun* reveals, in comparison with Hawthorne's previous work, an even wider apprehension of the permeation of experience by anxiety and by the moral authoritarianism and emotional attenuation that attend it. It is this augmented sense of the fruitless aggrandizement of authority within the psyche and within his culture that necessitates, it seems to me, the extraordinary unmooring of authority that composes the narrative strategy of *The Marble Faun*. The difficulty of the act of interpretation that this novel asks of its readers is proportioned to the resilience of the habits of mind that our response must overcome.

To choose the Miriam novel over the Hilda novel is not to choose one form of certainty over another, but to sacrifice the comforts of certainty that Hilda's way offers and enter the condition of ambivalence that the espousal of Miriam's romance—an espousal earned at the cost of choice—confers. It seems to me that Hawthorne, during the course of the book, makes an analogous sacrifice. He acknowledges a deepened ambivalence about his own artistic practice even as he obliquely reestablishes his commitment to it. To understand the significance of this sacrifice we must return to the figure of the Model, through whom Hawthorne considers the relation between the power of conscience and the energies of the romance he arrays against it. I have already suggested that the Model exemplifies through his behavior the operation of a self-poisoning authority within the psyche; we must also notice that all his appearances in the book are heralded by an invocation of the moonlit or shadowy territory of romance. Thus the Model appears at the dance in the Villa Borghese, the novel's most sustained excursion into romance's untrammeled place of mind, "footing it" as merrily as "rustic Pan" (88). Just as he is evoked by Miriam, the Model is called into being by romance itself. A second surprising feature of the Model is his relation to Donatello, a relation that seems to be simply an opposition but turns out also to be an analogy. The Model, the "last survivor" of the "vanished race of satyrs" (30), has origins as antique as Donatello's. More significant is the way Donatello's avowal of his love for Miriam ("Shroud yourself in what gloom you will, I must needs follow you" [50]) echoes the Model's proclamation of his obsession ("Henceforth, I am nothing but a shadow behind her footsteps" [31]). The Model's consistent association with romance and the affinity of form between his persecution and Donatello's adoration together not only acknowledge a disturbing affinity between aggression and love; their connection hints as well that to evoke one may be to evoke the other.[11]

The Marble Faun, then, seems to reconceive the nature of the psychic freedom effected by romance. Throughout his career, Hawthorne has connected romance with an ethic of liberation and the allied notion of cure. What is dangerous in Hawthorne's fictive world is the urge to dominate; the self is entrapped by its efforts to master an elusive world by mastering others and by its efforts to master itself by denying the mixed nature of its own desires. The territory of romance, though always endangered by the authoritarian, whether cultural or psychological, is itself quite a safe place. The loosening of the strictures of conscience that romance brings about reveals that the danger of our impulses has largely derived from the very fact of their repression; the therapeutic awareness conferred by romance seems able to lift the taint of fixation, compulsion, and aggression from our desires and to make possible saner forms of feeling and moral action. In *The Marble Faun* Hawthorne elides the clear opposition between romance and repression that his art, for all its risky complexity, had preserved. The Model, as simultaneously a figure of romance and an embodiment of the punitive, represents Hawthorne's developing sense that the authoritarianism against which romance struggles is not simply the reverse of the impulses it sets out to free but also an aspect of them. Hawthorne's invention of the Model parallels, it seems to me, Freud's disturbing discovery of the death instinct in *Beyond the Pleasure Principle*. The untrammeled scrutiny of mind that promises a cure simultaneously reveals the formidable powers of repetition and entrapment that resist it.

The Marble Faun acknowledges more fully than ever before the dangers of Hawthorne's artistic project. In accomplishing the release that romance envisions, one risks unleashing in another form the disease one had set out to cure. The book, we might say, at least entertains the notion that Hilda and Kenyon might be right. To those fragile selves and to the anxious culture they represent, romance *is* dangerous, it *is* guilty; for to enter romance territory is to lose the simple opposition as a conceptual, emotional, and cultural support. What writer and reader come to share during the course of *The Marble Faun*—what this last romance's version of interchange is built upon—is the experience of ambivalence, the unevaded discomfort that turns out to be the only form of freedom the book envisions.

We still have to account for the most curious aspect of Hawthorne's implicit relation to this work and to his reader: the novel's quality of unhappiness. This quality is obliquely dramatized by the expressions of reluctance, fatigue, and restlessness that appear at lulls in the narrative combat—as though a third, disaffected voice were speaking from the margins of the novel, wondering aloud whether the whole project were worth the effort. This sense of authorial disaffection is present from the start of our reading. The preface to *The Marble Faun* is in effect an anti-preface; it dismantles the interchange between writer and reader that Hawthorne's other prefatory pieces set out to invoke. As I noted at the start of this chapter, Hawthorne begins the book by recording the probable death of the "Gentle Reader" who had given him the confidence to bring his work—and himself—before the public. The consequence of his demise is the absence of the essay in self-presentation that has customarily opened his books: "I stand upon ceremony, now, and, after stating a few particulars about the work which is here offered to the Public, must make my most reverential bow, and retire behind the curtain" (2). There is, of course, a presentation of self taking place here, but it is a dramatization of the author's loss of faith in the receptivity of his audience, of the chilling into formality of the relationship that makes romance work.

A thread of impatience with the work of novel writing runs throughout *The Marble Faun*, starting in this detached preface and culminating in the labored goodwill of the postscript. The book is full of careful echoes of moments and phrases from Hawthorne's earlier work (I count more than twenty of these reminiscences). While I think they primarily connect to the summation of his career that he is conducting, these repetitions also begin to convey a sense that the writer is suffering from diminished enthusiasm for the invention of phrases. Such a moment of writer's fatigue is, in fact, acted out late in the book, when the narrator finds himself repeating the same simile within a couple of pages, and calls our attention to his lapse (380).

The figure of the reluctant novelist most often surfaces to bemoan the tiresomeness of writing with a moral purpose. Hence this expression of distaste for a pictorial version of Hawthorne's own allegorical method: "Donatello made no answer, but sat awhile, appearing to follow with his eyes one of the figures, which was repeated many times over in the groups upon the walls and ceiling. It formed the principal link of an allegory, by which (as is often the case, in such pictorial designs) the whole series of frescoes were bound together, but which it would be impossible, or, at least, very wearisome, to unravel" (227). This yearning for freedom from moral suasion is accompanied by an impatience with narrative itself. In the preface Hawthorne identifies the descriptive passages of the novel as those written "freely, and with self-enjoyment" (3). The reader comes to feel the pull toward travelogue in the book as an urge for a vacation from the insistent teleology of plot—a notion that is encouraged by the book's several encomiums to aimless travel: "This sunny, shadowy, breezy, wandering life, in which he seeks for beauty as his treasure, and gathers for his winter's honey what is but a passing fragrance to all other men, is worth living for, come afterwards what may" (214). I think we also see an enactment of this aversion to purpose in the "wandering" quality of those passages of philosophizing in the book that seem neutral with respect to the thematic conflict between Hilda's perspective and Miriam's. Passages of meditation—on the force of the past, the nature of Rome, Catholicism, exile, America—tend to meander from notion to notion when traced through the course of the novel, evading the conclusiveness they seem to promise.

The Marble Faun also contains a prominent strain of what we might call "Golden Ageism"—the notion, associated with Donatello's ancestral estate, that there existed a culture of pleasure before our culture of guilt, a communal life untainted by psychic conflict. This nostalgic myth, itself a manifestation of the unhappiness of maturity as we know it, also has a writerly analogue: the sense that language is a fallen, inadequate form of communication and that interpretation ruins what it analyzes. Note, for example, this lament for the extinction of gesture, "the language of the natural man . . . laid aside and forgotten by other men, now that words have been feebly substituted in the place of signs and symbols" (77–78), and Kenyon's refusal to analyze the pathos of Donatello's preverbal call to the animals "lest . . . it should at once perish in his grasp" (248).

Taken together, these signs of intramural resistance to the book's composition produce a portrait of the artist in flight from his own work. The expression of a particular distaste for the requirement that novels assume a moral shape acts out, I think, the romancer's intuition of the powerlessness that will be his fate as conscience's culture of earnestness progresses toward ever more stringent restriction. It is as though even to enter the realm of plot—of inescapable moral consequence—were to play into authority's earnest hands, to be defeated in one's project of liberation even before one begins to write. We witness, in this dramatization of the author's weariness of his own book, yet another victory for conscience: the divorce of art from pleasure—though we might hear whispering, beneath the weariness, the covert brio of this maniacally ingenious counterattack on the reverential.

The dauntingly complex narrative strategy at work in *The Marble Faun* seems designed with a double purpose. It reproduces as its experience of reading the unhappy experience of inhabiting a fruitlessly defensive, needlessly constricting culture, thus teaching us where we are. And it engages us in the practice of thwarting, by an unsponsored act of interpretation, the defeat of Miriam's romance by Hilda's conscientious fiction, thus teaching us how and why to resist the narrow version of experience that such a culture produces. *The Marble Faun* might be thought of as depicting what happens to a community that has, in its hunger for stability or in the unexamined momentum of its own conscientiousness, erased from its experience the energies and pleasures that make it worth inhabiting. In quite a specific way, the world of *The Marble Faun* is the world of *The House of the Seven Gables* with the hope of consensus removed; and the interplay of cultural voices and resources that the earlier book had sought, through the power of romance, to form into an inclusive and generous community has been reduced to the cultural stalemate of which this last romance is the record and to which—slenderest of hopes—it might become the antidote.

· · ·

The Marble Faun is at once an exercise in romance and a bleak prediction of the cultural fate of that demanding form. It becomes Hawthorne's meditation on the significance of his career, incorporating, in the Miriam novel, a compendium of his previous work, and simultaneously recording, in the Hilda novel, the psychology of its rejection or sequestration by the culture that receives it. Does its ongoing account of the defeat of his curative project—its extraordinary experiment in narrative strategy—make Hawthorne's last completed fiction a work of despair? There is a moment, during Donatello's farewell appearance in the novel, in which Miriam reports his determination to turn himself in. "When a wrong has been done," he reasons, "the doer is bound to submit himself to whatever tribunal takes cognizance of such things, and abide its judgment" (433). *The Marble Faun* might at last be understood as Hawthorne's account of his relation to the cultural tribunal that will judge his literary "wrongs," and his admission, in analogy to Donatello, of the unavoidable fact of its jurisdiction over him. Though there is little likelihood that justice will be done, Hawthorne persists—despite the dramatized weariness of its delivery—in offering his antiauthoritarian testimony. *The Marble Faun* enacts, both within its plot and on behalf of its author, a return to America—an America that has come to represent, supremely in the world, the triumph of the culture of reverence. We might hear, in this rhythm of return, the book's final echo. Hawthorne engages, in this account of his own career, the difficult task that brings Hester back to Boston: he will address a culture too anxious to grant him a hearing. He calculates the wages of romance: to love and hate the community that defeats his attempts to make it happy.

NOTES

INTRODUCTION

1. For a sustained exploration of these worries about the cultural role and private psychology of the artist as they manifest themselves in Hawthorne's fiction, see Millicent Bell, *Hawthorne's View of the Artist* (Albany: State University of New York Press, 1962), especially chaps. 1 and 9. My own interest is in the way this problem of authority transforms itself into the subjects and strategies of Hawthornian romance.

2. I will have more to say about Hawthorne's thinking about the problems of representation in chaps. 2 and 3. For the letter on mesmerism, see *Letters 1*, 588–90. On views of reading, see G. Harrison Orians, "Censure of Fiction in American Romances and Magazines, 1789–1810," in *PMLA* 52 (1937): 195–214, for the earlier, panicky view of novel reading; and Nina Baym, *Novels, Readers and Reviewers: Responses to Fiction in Antebellum America* (Ithaca: Cornell University Press, 1984), chaps. 2, 3, and 9, for the emphasis on novelistic power and the logic of moral influence in reviewers' accounts of reading. And for an interesting instance of the incursion of this point of view into Hawthorne's life, see the letter to Hawthorne from the British novelist G.P.R. James, reproaching him for inducing too much sympathy for a prideful Hester: "You have tremendous power. Use it wisely—use it thoughtfully; for the responsibility is awful." *Letters 2*, 451 n. 6. My comment on "interesting" is based primarily on readings in antebellum family correspondence in the Sophia Smith Collection, Smith College; this usage is frequently evident in the reviews that Baym cites. I will be suggesting in my chapters on *The House of the Seven Gables* and *The Blithedale Romance* that Hawthorne is our most acute analyst of this conception of self.

3. Stephen Nissenbaum's tracing of the relation between Hawthorne's fictive output and his financial situation—the better he was doing the less he wrote—leads him to the interesting speculation that Hawthorne simply did not like to write very much. The account of writerly anxiousness I am offering might suggest a reason: writing for Hawthorne may have had more to do with the experience of conflict and the removal of obstacles than with excursions on the wings of art. An extremely interesting, historically specific account of Hawthorne's earlier career is emerging in Nissenbaum's work. The speculation I cite is from an unpublished essay, "Nature's Priest: Hawthorne in the Marketplace."

4. *Reading for the Plot: Design and Intention in Narrative* (New York: Knopf, 1984), 236.

5. I am referring here to work by Burton J. Bledstein, George Forgie, R. Jackson Wilson, and Michael Paul Rogin. A fuller account of this historical work appears in chap. 2.

6. My sense of the way in which Hawthorne's works are "political" in purpose thus differs, in its focus on the terrain of character and community forma-

tion, from the emphasis on his political conservatism or quietism found in the work of Jonathan Arac, Sacvan Bercovitch, and Larry J. Reynolds. My differences with Arac and Bercovitch are specified in chap. 4. For Reynolds's account of the way Hawthorne's attitude toward the French revolutions shape *The Scarlet Letter*, see *European Revolutions and the American Literary Renaissance* (New Haven: Yale University Press, 1988), chap. 5. For a lucid discussion of the kind of political action that American novels might be said to perform, see Susan L. Mizruchi, *The Power of Historical Knowledge: Narrating the Past in Hawthorne, James, and Dreiser* (Princeton: Princeton University Press, 1988), xv–xvii.

7. For a strong argument on behalf of the kind of reading-centered account of Hawthorne's fiction that I am proposing here—and for an exemplary reading of "Rappaccini's Daughter"—see Steven Mailloux, *Interpretive Conventions: The Reader in the Study of American Fiction* (Ithaca: Cornell University Press, 1982), 72–91.

8. For an account of Hawthorne's relationship to Una, the part played by his own emotions about gender roles in her illness, and the cultural knot that mutually entangled them, see a remarkable essay by T. Walter Herbert, Jr., "Nathaniel Hawthorne, Una Hawthorne, and *The Scarlet Letter*: Interactive Selfhoods and the Cultural Construction of Gender," in *PMLA* 103 (1988): 285–97.

9. "Ideology as a Cultural System," in *The Interpretation of Cultures* (New York: Basic Books, 1973), 217–20. For a lucid account of the value of Geertz's work for students of American literature and culture, see Giles Gunn, *The Culture of Criticism and the Criticism of Culture* (New York: Oxford University Press, 1987), chap. 5.

10. As I have noted, Hawthorne burned most of what was to be his earliest collection, "Seven Tales of My Native Land," after a prolonged delay in their publication. "The Story-Teller" itself was never published as a collection, a victim of the vicissitudes of magazine publication. For an account of this manuscript burning and a description of the possible contents and arrangement of "The Story-Teller," see Arlin Turner, *Nathaniel Hawthorne: A Biography* (New York: Oxford University Press, 1980), 49–51, 71–79. For a bolder speculation about the probable contents of this collection and a valuable argument about the importance of "Passages" as a dramatization of Hawthorne's career, see Michael J. Colacurcio, *The Province of Piety: Moral History in Hawthorne's Early Tales* (Cambridge: Harvard University Press, 1984), 496–515.

11. For an important account of the significance of the problem of authority in American culture at present, see Richard Sennet, *Authority* (New York: Vintage, 1981).

CHAPTER ONE

1. *The Sins of the Fathers: Hawthorne's Psychological Themes* (New York: Oxford University Press, 1966), chap. 5, esp. 85.

2. See Sigmund Freud, *The Ego and the Id*, trans. Joan Riviere, rev. and ed. James Strachey (New York: Norton, 1960), 39–44.

3. T. C. Upham, *Elements of Mental Philosophy* (Portland, Maine, 1839), 402–3. The appraisal of the influence of Upham's text is that of A. A. Roback in

The History of American Psychology (New York: Library Publishers, 1952), 50. For an account of the cultural significance of Common Sense philosophy, see David Brion Davis, *Homicide in American Fiction* (Ithaca: Cornell University Press, 1957), chaps. 1 and 2.

4. See R. Jackson Wilson, *In Quest of Community: Social Philosophy in the United States, 1860–1920* (New York: John Wiley and Sons, 1968), 22.

5. *Uncle Tom's Cabin* (1852; reprint New York: Penguin Books, 1985), chap. 35, 528–29.

6. I do not mean to suggest that Stowe's depiction of the revenge of conscience is merely orthodox while Hawthorne's is interestingly subversive. Rather, Stowe uses her culturally central tribute to conscience, imaged as the revenge of the mother on the love-spurning male, in support of the book's attack on the moral authority of willful (or ineffectual) men, in thrall to the inhumane values of the marketplace. This passage thus supports Jane P. Tompkin's influential thesis that Stowe's novel, like other popular nineteenth-century domestic novels, "represents a monumental effort to reorganize culture from the woman's point of view." See *Sensational Designs: The Cultural Work of American Fiction, 1790–1860* (New York: Oxford University Press, 1985), 124.

7. Here is a passage—less confident than Upham or Stowe in the outcome of moral struggle, but just as intense in its fidelity to conscience—from an 1838 lecture by Horace Mann: "The same Almighty Power which implants in our nature the germs of these terrible propensities, has endowed us also with reason and conscience and a sense of responsibility to Him; and, in his providence, he has opened a way by which these nobler faculties can be elevated into dominion and supremacy over the appetites and passions. But if this is ever done, it must be mainly done during the docile and teachable years of childhood. I repeat it, my friends, *if this is ever done, it must be done in the docile and teachable years of childhood.* Wretched, incorrigible, demoniac, as any human being may ever have become, there was a time when he took the first step in error and in crime; when, for the first time, he just nodded to his fall, on the brink of ruin. Then, ere he was irrecoverably lost, ere he plunged into the abyss of infamy and guilt, he might have been recalled, as it were by the waving of the hand. Fathers, mothers, patriots, Christians! it is this very hour of peril through which our children are now passing." Quoted in Edwin C. Rozwenc, ed., *Ideology and Power in the Age of Jackson* (New York: New York University Press, 1964), 150–51. Mann was to become Hawthorne's brother-in-law.

8. *Cradle of the Middle Class: The Family in Oneida County, New York, 1790–1865* (Cambridge: Cambridge University Press, 1981), 159–62. Compare the outcome of Roger Malvin's exercise of parental influence.

9. Our sense of the tale's subversive reach has been expanded in another direction by readings that follow up Hawthorne's references to Lovewell's Fight, the ostensibly heroic battle—in reality a squalid scalp-hunting expedition by white settlers—from which Reuben Bourne and Roger Malvin are returning. Michael Colacurcio argues that the tale ironically attacks the tendency to simplify and heroicize the past prevalent in post-Revolutionary America and insistently points to the brutality of the policy of "supplanting" Native Americans who stood in the way of western expansion. *The Province of Piety*, 120–30.

CHAPTER TWO

1. Compare Jeffrey Steele's valuable account of Hawthorne's portrayal of the "psychology of victimization" in *The Representation of the Self in the American Renaissance* (Chapel Hill: University of North Carolina Press, 1987), 151–59.

2. Hyatt Waggoner sees a connection between ambition and a guilty order of wish in Hawthorne's notebook entry on the publication of *Twice-told Tales*: "In this dismal and squalid chamber, *fame* was won." Waggoner argues that "squalid," which Sophia Hawthorne excised from her edition of the notebooks, at this cultural moment would have carried the meaning of "impure, morally polluted, . . . shameful." *Hawthorne's Lost Notebook 1835–1841*, transcript by Barbara S. Mouffe, introduction by Hyatt H. Waggoner (University Park: Pennsylvania State University Press, 1978), introduction, 25. The entry is dated 25 October 1836.

3. Burton J. Bledstein, *The Culture of Professionalism* (New York: Norton, 1976), chap. 1. R. Jackson Wilson identifies this cultural moment as "that disconcerting time in American history when a progressive atrophy in social institutions coincided with an almost violent expansion in territory, economy, and population," in *In Quest of Community*, 10. On the financial conditions of the publishing industry and their effect on Hawthorne, see William Charvat, *The Profession of Authorship in America, 1800–1870* (Columbus: Ohio State University Press, 1968); and Richard H. Brodhead, *The School of Hawthorne* (New York: Oxford University Press, 1986), 53–57.

4. George Forgie, *Patricide in the House Divided: A Psychological Interpretation of Lincoln and His Age* (New York: Norton, 1979), chaps. 2 and 3. Michael Paul Rogin, *Subversive Genealogy: The Politics and Art of Herman Melville* (Berkeley and Los Angeles: University of California Press, 1985), 19. See also Rogin's complex account of the psychology of the post-Revolutionary generation, especially as it found expression in the Indian removals of Jackson's presidency, in *Fathers and Children: Andrew Jackson and the Subjugation of the American Indian* (New York: Knopf, 1975).

5. The connection Hawthorne implies between an intolerance for uncertainty and the shape taken by the work lives of his careerists is especially interesting in light of Bledstein's argument that what would become "professional" authority is based on a claim to master an uncertain world, too complex for the layman. Bledstein writes: "The jurisdictional claim of [professional] authority derived from a special power over worldly experience, a command over the profundities of a discipline. Such a masterful command was designed to establish confidence in the mind of the helpless client. The professional person possessed esoteric knowledge about the universe which if withheld from society would cause positive harm." *The Culture of Professionalism*, 20, 89–90.

In an important new study of the relation of antebellum writers to their culture's constricting ideals of male character, David Leverenz offers a much fuller exploration of the cultural terrain I am sketching here. Leverenz provides a valuable account of the historical conditions that combined to make "a striving, anxious manly ego based on ownership, work, competition, and social position" the dominant version of maleness, and strikingly reads the work of classic male writers as complex, strategic attacks on this self-poisoning cultural ideal. My argument that Hawthorne's tales of the careerist work to question male ambition and disrupt the patterns of experience it sponsors thus accords with Leverenz's view. Readers will discover that our converging interests produce quite different specific readings and, ultimately, different versions of Hawthorne. In general, I think Hawthorne is more in control of his relation to this aggressive model of maleness and his attacks upon it are more therapeutic in their purpose than Leverenz suggests. For him, a covert resurgence of the "fascination with malice and humiliation" that Hawthorne attacks in his characters significantly shapes and destabilizes his narratives. See *Manhood and the American Renaissance* (Ithaca: Cornell University Press, 1989), 18, 227–29.

6. My view of the ethics of Hooper's veiling accords with that proposed by Michael J. Colacurcio in *The Province of Piety*, chap. 6. For Colacurcio these ethical questions are located in the specific history of New England Puritanism; I am arguing their bearing on the contemporary question of ambition and authority.

7. This punning reading of "figure" is suggested by Hawthorne's use of "figuratively"—as a synonym for "metaphorically"—earlier in the same paragraph.

8. *Letters 1*, 462 (19 May 1840). I first came across this passage in Newton Arvin, *The Heart of Hawthorne's Journals* (1929; reprint Ann Arbor: University Microfilms, 1962), 62.

9. Margaret Ferguson, in an analysis of the rhetorical strategies characteristic of defenses of poetry, identifies a tactic she calls a "defense against defense" that resembles the strategy of "acknowledgment" I have described here. In the course of defending their work against hostile critics, writers like Boccacio, Sidney, Shelley, and Freud confront their own anxiety about the validity of their representation of experience. They defend themselves against "the guilt engendered by the tropological nature of writing itself" by admitting the crime of "interpretive distortion" they must necessarily commit. Thus "Freud's interpretation of the bible [in *Moses and Monotheism*] does commit a kind of murder, but it defends against the murderer's guilt by *not* hiding the traces." In its affection for prefaces and its self-conscious interest in artist surrogates, Hawthorne's whole body of fiction can be seen as a simultaneous defense of and experiment in the ethics of the poetic career. "Border Territories of Defense: Freud and Defenses of Poetry," in *The Literary Freud: Mechanisms of Defense and the Poetic Will*, ed. Joseph H. Smith, M.D., Psychiatry and the Humanities, vol. 4 (New Haven: Yale University Press, 1980), 177–79.

10. For a history of the interpretation of the tale, see Lea B. V. Newman, *A Reader's Guide to the Short Stories of Nathaniel Hawthorne* (Boston: G. K. Hall, 1979), 6–8. There have been a number of recent attempts to demonstrate its importance and internal coherence, most interestingly that of Michael Colacurcio in *Province of Piety*, 78–93. I join Colacurcio (and a number of previous readers) in seeing projection as the habit of mind under analysis in this work.

11. Crews, 51. Compare Hawthorne's account of the role of projection in "abnormally intense" jealousy with Freud's. Freud describes "projected" jealousy this way: if a person's impulses toward unfaithfulness are denied or repressed—rather than admitted and innocuously played out in the "safety-valve"

of flirtation—he is likely to seek relief from importunate desires by using an "unconscious mechanism": projection. "This relief—more, absolution by his conscience—he achieves when he projects his own impulses to infidelity on to the partner to whom he owes faith." The jealous person, moreover, becomes adept at reading the sexually omniverous impulses covertly expressed in his partner's actions, and thus receives confirmation of his suspicions and the comfort that his guilt is shared. Compare Leonard's sense of Alice's "undefinable, but powerful interest" in Brome. "Certain Neurotic Mechanisms in Jealousy, Paranoia, and Homosexuality" (1922), in *Sexuality and the Psychology of Love*, ed. Philip Rieff, trans. Joan Riviere (New York: Collier Books, 1963), 161.

12. *Hawthorne and the Historical Romance of New England* (Princeton: Princeton University Press, 1971), 75–76.

13. In "The Devil in Manuscript," a sketch that depicts this book-burning episode, Oberon, the disenchanted author, remarks, "Oh, I have a horror of what was created in my own brain, and shudder at the manuscripts in which I gave that dark idea a sort of material existence! Would they were out of my sight!" (*SI* 171).

14. Mark M. Hennelly, Jr. points out a number of these links in "Alice Doane's Appeal: Hawthorne's Case Against the Artist," in *Studies in American Fiction* 6 (1978): 125–40. Hennelly, though, sees the narrator as the guilty embodiment of the artist as victimizer.

15. See George Forgie's valuable reading of the tale in *Patricide and the House Divided*, 110–15. Forgie argues convincingly that the story addresses the predicament of Hawthorne's own generation; he sees Robin as acting out a fantasy-rebellion against paternal authority that has the effect merely of initiating Robin into the more dispersed but quite stable authority structure of the democratic city.

CHAPTER THREE

1. One of the many valuable things about Nina Baym's *Novels, Readers, and Reviewers* is its demonstration that "romance" was a critical term so broadly and inconsistently used when Hawthorne was writing that its meaning, in every instance, was being established on the spot and tailored to the idiosyncratic needs of the writer or critic using it. See 225–35. Two valuably sophisticated recent attempts to establish romance, retrospectively, as a genre with a distinctive cultural force are Michael Davitt Bell's *The Development of American Romance: The Sacrifice of Relation* (Chicago: University of Chicago Press, 1980), which includes a lucid account of the preceding critical tradition; and Evan Carton's *The Rhetoric of American Romance* (Baltimore: Johns Hopkins University Press, 1985). Accounts of Hawthorne's particular way of defining and practicing "romance" that I have found especially useful include Richard H. Brodhead on Hawthorne's deployment of narrative elements characteristic of romance within his work in *Hawthorne, Melville, and the Novel* (Chicago: University of Chicago Press, 1976) and Brook Thomas on the political force of the kind of reading that Hawthorne's work induces, in *"The House of the Seven Gables*: Reading the Romance of America," in *PMLA* 97 (1982): 195–211.

2. My account of the relationship to his reader that Hawthorne establishes should be compared to several discussions of the same subject, which is taking its

place as a central issue in Hawthorne criticism. One is Kenneth Dauber's argument, in *Rediscovering Hawthorne* (Princeton: Princeton University Press, 1977), that an attempt to establish intimacy with the reader is the animating purpose of Hawthorne's writing. He writes that Hawthorne "desired, ultimately, not to mediate between story and reader, but that the story mediate between the reader and him" (52–53). He thus suggests that romance is "a form generated by the mutual possession of writer and reader" (101). Dauber's emphasis on Hawthorne's effort to establish "intimacy" with the reader seems exactly right, but he establishes the centrality of Hawthorne's relation to the reader by discounting the interest of Hawthorne's themes. That is, he never identifies what gives psychological, intellectual, or cultural urgency to Hawthorne's project. A second work, Edgar Dryden's chapter "The Enchantment of Reading," in *Nathaniel Hawthorne: The Poetics of Enchantment* (Ithaca: Cornell University Press, 1977), offers an intriguing account of Hawthorne's strategy of self-presentation. Dryden sees Hawthorne's veiling as an effort to communicate by keeping something always "in reserve." The prefaces describe "a mode of communication that maintains a tension between the hidden and the shown, thereby ensuring that neither reader nor writer can ever be completely caught by the other." Such mutual reserve makes it possible "for the writer to speak to a potentially hostile audience about matters of which silence is the safest form of expression, and for the reader to respond to his words without the fear of becoming his mystified victim"(134–35). Most recently, Gordon Hutner has identified a complex dynamic of incomplete self-revelation as the animating principle of Hawthorne's work. See *Secrets and Sympathy: Forms of Disclosure in Hawthorne's Novels* (Athens: University of Georgia Press, 1988), chap. 1.

3. Hawthorne's sense of the dangers of too deep a penetration into the "cavern" of another psyche is suggested by this passage from his notebooks: "The human Heart to be allegorized as a cavern; at the entrance there is sunshine, and flowers growing about it. You step within, but a short distance, and begin to find yourself surrounded with a terrible gloom, and monsters of divers kinds; it seems like Hell itself" (*AN* 237).

4. "I. A. Richards and the Dream of Communication," in *The Fate of Reading and Other Essays* (Chicago: University of Chicago Press, 1975), 35. See Eric J. Sundquist's extremely interesting expansion and application of Hartman's remarks in his discussion of the psychology of representation in Hawthorne's work in *Home as Found* (Baltimore: Johns Hopkins University Press, 1979), chap. 3.

5. Extramural confirmation of this dependence on the reader's response can be found in letters responding to favorable or thoughtful reviews of or responses to his fiction, which, as I read them, are more intense even than good business in an era of puffery would indicate. Some of the most appreciative letters are to third parties, and they strikingly emphasize the reader's contribution to the exchange. His remark on E. P. Whipple is typical: his "notices have done more than please me; for they have helped me see my book." *Letters 2*, 435. See also, for example, 9, 421–22, 459–60, 493; and *Letters 1*, 599.

6. Compare Edgar Dryden's suggestion that Hawthorne's elusiveness "makes it impossible for the reader to enjoy an innocent relation to his text"; the prefaces create a "suspicious, probing," even a "violent" reader, convinced that "the es-

sential . . . may be grasped only after the inessential surface has been violated if not destroyed." *Poetics of Enchantment,* 125–27.

7. "Further Recommendations in the Technique of Psychoanalysis: Recollection, Repetition and Working Through (1914)," trans. Joan Riviere, in *Therapy and Technique,* ed. Philip Rieff (New York: Collier Books, 1963), 157–66. The citation appears on 165, and can be found in vol. 12 of *The Standard Edition of the Complete Psychological Works of Sigmund Freud,* ed. James Strachey (London: Hogarth Press, 1953–74), 154. Since this chapter's first emergence, Peter Brooks has published an extremely interesting and wide-ranging exploration of the kind of analogy between narrative and transference that I have found, locally, in Hawthorne's theory of romance. See chap. 8, "Narrative Transaction and Transference," of *Reading for the Plot.*

8. I am thinking particularly of the work of Karen Halttunen on the way that middle-class anxieties about the new marketplace world find expression in the ideal of sincerity and the cultural practices associated with it *(Confidence Men and Painted Women: A Study of Middle-Class Culture in America* [New Haven: Yale University Press, 1982]); and Mary Ryan's work, already mentioned, on the formation of middle-class character (*Cradle of the Middle Class*). A reading of the letters of other middle-class people at the time, especially courtship letters, suggests that it is hard to exaggerate the cultural force of the longing for intimacy that Hawthorne is dramatizing here (and expressing in his letters to Sophia), and reminds us that men, too, shared in this yearning. See Ellen K. Rothman, *Hands and Hearts: A History of Courtship in America* (New York: Basic Books, 1984) for a thoughtful description of the ways that antebellum couples explored and moved toward intimacy. Some of Rothman's letters contain language quite like Hawthorne's to describe the negotiation of the boundaries of the private self (See chap. 3, esp. 113–14).

CHAPTER FOUR

1. Of the many commentaries on "The Custom-House," I have found most valuable three that focus on the ways in which Hawthorne uses the essay to define his cultural role as a writer. These are James M. Cox, "*The Scarlet Letter:* Through the Old Manse and the Custom-House," in *Virginia Quarterly Review* 51 (Summer 1975): 432–47; Nina Baym, *The Shape of Hawthorne's Career* (Ithaca: Cornell University Press, 1976), 143–51; and Donald E. Pease, *Visionary Compacts: American Renaissance Writings in Cultural Context* (Madison: University of Wisconsin Press, 1987), chap. 2, who reads the essay as an attempt to connect with the Puritan past and thus to reanimate the idea of civic duty. A cynical view of the elaborate self-dramatization I will be describing is taken by Stephen Nissenbaum, who sees "The Custom-House" as a canny defense against the disgrace of Hawthorne's dismissal from his post. See his introduction to *The Scarlet Letter* (New York: New Modern Library, 1984), viii–xix.

2. Baym and Pease also see Surveyor Pue as an "alternative" ancestor. For Baym, Hawthorne's link with Pue dramatizes the shift in "allegiance from his Puritan conscience to his imagination" that animates *The Scarlet Letter* (*Hawthorne's Career,* 146); for Pease, Pue represents the communal ethos of pre-Revo-

lutionary America (*Visionary Compacts*, 67). On the analogy between General Miller's phrasing and Hawthorne's, and the implication that art, too, may be a heroic career, see Cox, *"The Scarlet Letter,"* 443.

3. The essay that most strikingly pursues this question of meaning is Charles Feidelson's "The Scarlet Letter," which remains, it seems to me, the best comprehensive account of the book that we have. Feidelson's construction of the issue of meaning is quite abstract—he sees the book as an exploration of modern, alienated selfhood and builds his essay on the contrast between the "prison worship" of the Puritan authorities and Hester's "affirmative individualism, humanism, and naturalism"—while I find Hawthorne's pursuit of the question remarkable for its cultural and psychological specificity. Still, some of the important moments in my argument (which I will identify) are really expansions or specifications—appreciations, as it were—of Feidelson's valuable formulations. See "The Scarlet Letter," in Roy Harvey Pearce, ed., *Hawthorne Centenary Essays* (Columbus: Ohio State University Press, 1964), 31–77.

4. Though clearly part of the covert life of the community, witchcraft, as represented by Mistress Hibbins, is to be distinguished from the alternative meaning system I have been describing. In its fealty to the "Black Man," it simply inverts the Puritan community, replacing one authority structure with another; this is why Hawthorne is so careful to notate Hester's refusals to join in that particular form of dissent.

5. Zelda Bronstein emphasizes the nineteenth-century characteristics of Hawthorne's Puritan characters on behalf of a quite different argument about the contemporary force of *The Scarlet Letter*. See "The Parabolic Ploys of *The Scarlet Letter*," in *American Quarterly* 39 (1987): 193–210.

6. See Feidelson, "The Scarlet Letter," 48.

7. For an interesting alternative reading of this scene, see Donald Pease, *Visionary Compacts*, 94–95.

8. Crews, *Sins of the Fathers*, 141–42 (his italics).

9. "On Narcissism: An Introduction (1914)," trans. Cecil M. Baines, in *General Psychological Theory*, ed. Philip Rieff, 73–82.

10. Compare the games of revenge against the Puritan community that Pearl devises, 95.

11. Nina Baym notes that Chillingworth might be seen as Dimmesdale's superego (*Hawthorne's Career*, 138). I am not claiming that Chillingworth is *only* the minister's conscience embodied, but that the representation of the physician, like that of Pearl, wavers between realism and a kind of allegorical functionalism that Hawthorne exploits to represent the dynamic nature of the states of mind that interest him. For an illuminating discussion of the degree of reality assigned by Hawthorne to Chillingworth, see Richard H. Brodhead, *Hawthorne, Melville, and the Novel*, 63: "The way in which we are asked to believe in them as characters is a function of the way in which they believe in themselves." Even as a realistic character, Chillingworth is of the narcissistic party, as his description of his love for Hester makes plain: "I drew thee into my heart . . . and sought to warm thee by the warmth which thy presence made there"(74).

12. For a description of these narcissistic strategies, see "Instincts and their Vicissitudes (1915)," trans. Cecil M. Baines, in *General Psychological Theory*,

96. In light of Chillingworth's identification with the diseased superego, it is interesting to note Freud's description of the sexual aspect of "moral masochism" (i.e., the pathological punishment of the self by conscience): "Conscience and morality arose through overcoming, desexualizing the Oedipus-complex; in moral masochism morality becomes sexualized afresh, the Oedipus-complex is reactivated, a regression from morality back to the Oedipus-complex is under way." This regression is expressed in the wish to "have some passive . . . sexual relations with the father." "The Economic Problem in Masochism," trans. Joan Riviere, *General Psychological Theory*, 199–200. The sexual character of Chillingworth's "violation" of Dimmesdale is noted by Leslie Fiedler in *Love and Death in the American Novel*, rev. ed. (New York: Stein and Day, 1966), 234–35.

13. On the cultural significance of the ideals of "intimacy" and "confidence" see Ellen Rothman, *Hands and Hearts*, 107–14, and Karen Halttunen, *Confidence Men and Painted Women*, chap. 2. My own reading in collections of family letters, especially courtship letters, in the Sophia Smith Collection at Smith College has intensified my sense of the central importance of the refuge supplied by intimate connection for middle-class Americans at this time.

14. *Hawthorne, Melville, and the Novel*, 62.

15. On the feminist implications of Hawthorne's portrayal of Hester, see Nina Baym, "Thwarted Nature: Nathaniel Hawthorne as Feminist," in Fritz Fleishmann, ed., *American Novelists Revisited* (Boston: G. K. Hall, 1982), 73–76. But consider also Myra Jehlen's suggestion that the female characters of male novelists tend to represent "the female interior self" of the writer and *his* rebellion against various kinds of social constraint. See "Archimedes and the Paradox of Feminist Criticism," in Elizabeth Abel, ed., *The Signs Reader* (Chicago: University of Chicago Press, 1983), 92–93.

16. See *The Fall of Public Man: On the Social Psychology of Capitalism* (New York: Vintage, 1978), part 3, 123–256.

17. Richard H. Brodhead, "Sparing the Rod: Discipline and Fiction in Antebellum America," in *Representations* 21 (1988): 67–96. His discussion of *The Scarlet Letter*, which also includes an illuminating suggestion about the Chillingworth-Dimmesdale relationship, appears on 77–79.

18. The passage is written in such a way as to suggest that a morally valid justification for his flight—and thus a full participation in Hester's vision—is available to Dimmesdale, that a different version of this scene is latent within it, waiting to be chosen. The narrator offers the minister a list of "extenuations" that culminates in this way: " . . . that, finally, to this poor pilgrim, on his dreary and desert path, faint, sick, miserable, there appeared a glimpse of human affection and sympathy, a new life, and a true one, in exchange for the heavy doom which he was now expiating" (200).

19. For a discussion of Hawthorne's blending of symbolic and dramatic representational modes in this scene, see Brodhead, *Hawthorne, Melville, and the Novel*, 55–56.

20. The Emersonian inflection of Hester's exhortation has been frequently noticed; compare, for instance, "The Divinity School Address." See also Michael J. Colacurcio's persuasive linking of Hester's position here to Anne Hutchinson's antinomianism in "Footsteps of Ann Hutchinson: The Context of *The Scarlet*

Letter," in *ELH* 39 (1972): 459–94. For a valuable discussion of both the Emersonian and antinomian aspects of Hester's speech, see Amy Scrager Lang, *Prophetic Woman: Anne Hutchinson and the Problem of Dissent in the Literature of New England* (Berkeley and Los Angeles: University of California Press, 1987), 182–84.

21. It is difficult to decide fully the relation between the two points I have been making about the failure of Hester's sacrament. The possibility that Dimmesdale's full participation in Hester's vision would, as an act of interchange, have given it the force to found an alternative community in which Pearl might have participated remains open. Pearl is throughout the book a touchstone for Dimmesdale's falseness, and it is the sight of the minister that first makes her pause at the the the edge of the brook. In any case, it is the absence of interchange, in the form of either a communal way of meaning or a meaning-conferring love, that destroys Hester's vision. Charles Feidelson similarly emphasizes Hester's temporary espousal of a "conception of unmitigated freedom" in his account of this scene, and my view of Pearl's insistence on the resumption of the letter is also companionable with his. He sees Pearl as becoming aware of—and claiming a place in—"the concrete world of human sympathy" at this moment. See "The Scarlet Letter," 59 and 75–76.

22. "On Narcissism," 80.

23. Crews, *Sins of the Fathers*, 145–48.

24. Hawthorne's account of his reading is from *English Note-Books*, 14 September 1855, and is quoted by James R. Mellow in *Nathaniel Hawthorne in His Times* (Boston: Houghton Mifflin, 1980), 311. The description of Sophia's response is from Hawthorne's letter to Horatio Bridge (4 February 1850); her comment is cited in a note to that letter (*Letters* 2, 311, 313 n. 3).

25. Sacvan Bercovitch emphasizes these same points—the significance of the problem of Hester's return and Hawthorne's insistence on the reader's interpretive independence—on behalf of a very different argument about the cultural work performed by the book in "The A-Politics of Ambiguity in *The Scarlet Letter*," in *New Literary History* 19 (1988): 629–54, esp. 631, 650–53. I distinguish my view of the book from Bercovitch's more fully presently.

26. See Lang, *Prophetic Woman*, 189–91, and Myra Jehlen, "The Novel and the Middle Class in America," in Sacvan Bercovitch and Myra Jehlen, eds., *Ideology and Classic American Literature* (Cambridge: Cambridge University Press, 1986), 132, 138–39, and, for a somewhat modified argument, *American Incarnation: The Individual, the Nation, and the Continent* (Cambridge: Harvard University Press, 1986), 136–38. Bercovitch's argument is made in two allied essays, "The A-Politics of Ambiguity," already cited, and "Hawthorne's A-Morality of Compromise," in *Representations* 24 (1988): 1–27. Bercovitch is extending an argument made by Jonathan Arac, "The Politics of *The Scarlet Letter*," in Bercovitch and Jehlen, 247–65. For a valuable appreciation of the nature of Hester's radicalism in the context of Puritan Boston, see Michael J. Colacurcio, "The Woman's Own Choice: Sex, Metaphor, and the Puritan Sources of *The Scarlet Letter*," in Michael J. Colacurcio, ed., *New Essays on "The Scarlet Letter*," (Cambridge: Cambridge University Press, 1985), 123–24. For a critical view of Bercovitch's ideological analysis more generally, see Giles Gunn, "Beyond Tran-

scendence or Beyond Ideology: The New Problematics of Cultural Criticism in America," in *American Literary History* 2 (1990): 1–17. Susan L. Mizruchi lucidly disputes Bercovitch and provides a like-minded argument for the ideological unsettling achieved by Hawthorne and other American writers in *The Power of Historical Knowledge*, chap. 1, esp. 6–7.

27. For an alternative reading of this passage, which exemplifies the difference between our accounts of the book's narrative strategy, see David Leverenz, *Manhood and the American Renaissance*, 274–75.

28. "The Custom-House" was written very late in the composition of *The Scarlet Letter*. It was sent to Fields on 15 January 1850 when all but the last three chapters of the manuscript were completed. See *Letters* 2, 305.

CHAPTER FIVE

1. This notion of reparation is characteristic of Hawthorne's response to his own novels and—also characteristically—cuts in two directions: the friendliness of *The House* produces the desire to write something with "an extra touch of the devil" in it, and the bitterness of *The Blithedale Romance* in turn produces the intention to be more "genial" the next time out. See *Letters* 2, 312, 421–22, 462, 604.

2. Michael T. Gilmore, *American Romanticism and the Marketplace* (Chicago: University of Chicago Press, 1986), chap. 5; Walter Benn Michaels, "Romance and Real Estate," in Michaels and Donald E. Pease, eds., *The American Renaissance Reconsidered* (Baltimore: Johns Hopkins University Press, 1985). Other important attempts to place the book ideologically include Kenneth Dauber, *Rediscovering Hawthorne*, and Michael Davitt Bell, *The Development of American Romance*. Two writers on Hawthorne who seem to me to see the scope of his designs upon American culture are Brook Thomas and Donald Pease. See Thomas's argument that Hawthorne's romance demystifies cultural authority, revealing it to be a product of historical—and thus revisable—choices rather than "natural" (*"The House of the Seven Gables*: Reading the Romance of America," in *PMLA* 97 [1982]: 195–211). See also his reworking of that essay, which connects the book to the history of property law, chaps. 2 and 3 of *Cross-Examinations of Law and Literature: Cooper, Hawthorne, Stowe, and Melville* (New York: Cambridge University Press, 1987). Though Pease's chapters on Hawthorne in *Visionary Compacts* (Madison: University of Wisconsin Press, 1987) do not include a reading of *The House*, his sense of Hawthorne as engaged in the rescue and reconstruction of communal connection is congenial to the detailed account of the book that I will be offering. Kenneth Dauber's original and important insight about the book—that it is above all an attempt to achieve intimate connection to a community of readers—has been valuable to me, though he pays the odd and unacceptable price of denying Hawthorne any specific ideas about the culture he is connecting to or any investment in the content of his work. My sense of the specificity and force of Hawthorne's engagement with his readers depends to a great extent upon the description of middle-class culture that has emerged from the work of historians of "woman's sphere," and on the account of

writing by women offered by literary scholars like Nina Baym and Jane P. Tompkins, whose notion of "cultural work" illuminates Hawthorne's work as well as that of the writers whom the traditional canon of American literature has displaced.

3. The legalism of the narrator's language is noticed by Susan L. Mizruchi in *The Power of Historical Knowledge*. Mizruchi's chapter on *The House* offers a valuable account, quite different from my own, of the specific way that Hawthorne's drama of the narrative voice engages antebellum culture. See chap. 3, esp. 103–34.

4. *Novels, Readers, and Reviewers*, esp. chaps. 8–11.

5. Kenneth Dauber interestingly suggests that the preface fixes and contains any hostility Hawthorne feels toward the community, thus preserving the novel proper for the establishment of intimacy between him and his readers. *Rediscovering Hawthorne*, 122–24.

6. "The Narrator as General Consciousness," in *The Form of Victorian Fiction* (Notre Dame: University of Notre Dame Press, 1968), esp. 62–88.

7. *Hawthorne, Melville, and the Novel*, 72.

8. For a valuable account of Hawthorne's insistence on Hepzibah's social representativeness, see Brodhead, *Hawthorne, Melville, and the Novel*, 74–75.

9. The great theorist of this way of thinking about voice within novels is M. M. Bakhtin. In "Discourse in the Novel" he argues that the novel as a genre is defined by its permeability to a culture's different voices and by the competition or "dialogue" between them. The "prose artist" is thus to be regarded as a deployer of these voices. *The Dialogic Imagination*, ed. Michael Holquist (Austin: University of Texas Press, 1981), 259–422. One implication of my argument is that Hawthorne, in composing this version of romance, had to do precisely the kind of theorizing about the novel that Bakhtin has made available to us. Susan Mizruchi notes the "dialogic" quality of *The House*'s narrative in *Historical Knowledge*, 39 n. 49.

10. Let me clarify the way I am using a term that will recur in this essay. I will be using "central" and "centrality" to refer to the place figuratively occupied by the values and understandings that comprise the moral consensus that holds together a particular community. I have chosen that term because of Hawthorne's tendency—in this book, throughout his work, and in describing his own cultural role—to imagine society in terms of the dominant values that hold cultural authority and occupy its central spaces, and the marginal perspectives that define its ethical borders and occupy its spatial outskirts. For an account of the meaning of "ideology," also a crucial term in this chapter, please see the introduction, 9–10.

11. I have borrowed this useful characterization of rural economic life from Jack Larkin, "The Merriams of Brookfield: Printing in the Economy and Culture of Rural Massachusetts in the early Nineteenth Century," in *Proceedings of the American Antiquarian Society* 96 (April 1986): 39–73. Larkin writes that "economic life was concrete, face-to-face, and inextricably entwined with family ties, everyday social interactions, and community relationships." Larkin demonstrates that this rural economy was itself changing in complex ways in response to the emergence of a larger-scale, urban-centered market economy. I was directed to

this essay by Stephen Nissenbaum, to whom I am more generally indebted for an understanding of the ways the material conditions of its making and selling have shaped antebellum literature.

12. Thanks to important work in women's history, the elements of this domestic ideology are now familiar to present-day readers. Classic texts in this historical recovery include Nancy F. Cott, *The Bonds of Womanhood* (New Haven: Yale University Press, 1977); Barbara Welter, "The Cult of True Womanhood," in *A Heritage of Her Own: Toward a New Social History of American Women*, ed. Nancy F. Cott and Elizabeth H. Pleck (New York: Simon and Schuster, 1979); Ann Douglas, *The Feminization of American Culture* (New York: Knopf, 1977); Kathryn Kish Sklar, *Catharine Beecher: a Study in American Domesticity* (New Haven: Yale University Press, 1973); and Mary P. Ryan, *Cradle of the Middle Class* (Cambridge: Cambridge University Press, 1981). It is crucial to remember that the emphasis on sympathy and moral influence as a form of power links "woman's sphere" to a larger, "sentimental" consensus that included men, especially male fiction writers, interested in a model for human connection, social power, and ethical authority that countered the values and methods of the marketplace. I am indebted for this point to the work of Rena Fraden, "The Sentimental Tradition in Dickens and Hawthorne" (Ph.D. dissertation, Yale University, 1983), chap. 1. For a useful account of sentimentality as an intellectual tradition, see Fred Kaplan, *Sacred Tears: Sentimentality in Victorian Literature* (Princeton: Princeton University Press, 1987), introduction and chap. 1.

13. See *Letters 2*, 291, 299, 337, and esp. 494.

14. For a description of this kind of fiction, see Baym, *Novels, Readers, and Reviewers*, 201–7.

15. On the sentimental topos of the inadequacy of language to feeling, see G. A. Starr, "'Only a boy': Notes on Sentimental Novels," in *Genre* 10 (Winter 1977): 501–27, cited in Fraden, "Sentimental Tradition," 14.

16. In his portrait of Clifford as an artist whose claims to special treatment come at the cost of his capacity to wield power, Hawthorne is anticipating later analysts of the social role of the artist in nineteenth-century culture. See Raymond Williams's chapter "The Romantic Artist," in *Culture and Society* (New York: Harper and Row, 1958); and Ann Douglas's account of the perpetual childhood of the antebellum writers of sentimental sketches in *The Feminization of American Culture*, 237–41.

17. Michael Gilmore identifies this "seer" as the marginal, unmarketable Hawthornian artist, *American Romanticism and the Marketplace*, 104.

18. *Confidence Men and Painted Women*, chap. 1.

19. On Holgrave as a figure of fertility, sexuality, and the joyful expenditure of energy, see Nina Baym, *The Shape of Hawthorne's Career*, 158–59.

20. On the cultural force of the rhetoric of "head" and "heart" and the special association of the heart with women and the domestic sphere, see Cott, *The Bonds of Womanhood*, 160–68.

21. The most interesting discussion I have found of the limitations of Holgrave's radicalism and of the contemporary significance of Hawthorne's depiction of his character is George Forgie's in *Patricide in the House Divided*, 115–21. Forgie argues that Holgrave's anxiety-ridden, ultimately self-regarding

politics is typical of the way that private anxiety infiltrated political consciousness in the generation that had to follow the act of the founding fathers. "When domesticity proves such a solvent to radicalism . . . , radicalism is revealed at once as purely personal and emotional in nature. It is not that Holgrave ceases to be a prophet of social revolution. He demonstrates that he never was one."

22. For an illuminating discussion of the explanatory function of the book's romance elements, see Richard Brodhead's discussion of "Alice Pyncheon," in *Hawthorne, Melville, and the Novel*, 84–86.

23. This is the center of my disagreement with Walter Benn Michaels's argument that Hawthorne is engaged in *The House of the Seven Gables* in imagining a safely absolute claim to an inviolable selfhood. I am arguing that Hawthorne is instead demonstrating the impossibility—and the undesirability—of such a form of self-possession, and seeking to discipline the predatory urge to possess others that seems to be a response to the absence of such sovereignty over the self. The conception of selfhood being explored in "Alice Pyncheon" similarly calls into doubt Michael Gilmore's version of Hawthorne's attitudes toward the marketplace, for while he repudiates the urge to own or control others, the notion of self-risking exchange has clear affinities with other kinds of marketplace activities.

24. On the subversiveness of these legends, see Mizruchi, *Historical Knowledge*, 134.

25. Holgrave's actual language is extraordinarily elusive—a stone exterior would give an "*impression* of permanence . . . essential to the happiness of any one moment" (314–15 [my italics])—and in its metaphysical openness hardly amounts to a very solid conservatism. Given the emphasis on transforming the reader in nineteenth-century accounts of the effects and purposes of fiction, it is important not to discount the political force of a character-centered theory of reform. This point is lucidly argued in Fraden, 11–12. For a valuable discussion of the political dimension of Hawthorne's work, see Donald Pease's argument that he is engaged, throughout his writing, in the reconstruction of communal connection through the recovery of a relation to history more complex and sustaining than that provided by the prevailing revolutionary ethos. *Visionary Compacts*, chaps. 2 and 3.

Chapter Six

1. *Marxism and Literature* (Oxford: Oxford University Press, 1977), 131–33. For a lucid account of the social changes that attended this economic transformation and of the anxieties it produced, see Karen Halttunen, *Confidence Men and Painted Women*, chaps. 1 and 2. Another useful account of the effects of the economic and social transformations of the 1830s and 1840s on personality and the culture's characteristic forms of expression is William R. Taylor's *Cavalier and Yankee: The Old South and American National Character* (New York: Harper and Row, 1961), esp. chap. 3.

2. Since my analysis of *The Blithedale Romance* first saw the light—or, shall we say, the scholarly half-light—as a dissertation ("Hawthorne and the Fictions of Conscience" [Ph.D. dissertation, Yale University, 1983]), Gordon Hutner has

published an admirable reading of the novel that also makes two points crucial to my argument: that Coverdale is engaged, through his voyeurism, in an elaborate defense of his individuality; and that his personal psychology is symptomatic of a larger cultural condition. Our specific development of these arguments and the larger view of Hawthorne's enterprise that they advance seem to me significantly different: where Hutner sees Coverdale defending himself against difficult emotions, I see him as protecting himself against an absence of feeling altogether; and his account of cultural psychology is not so specifically linked to the book's picture of economic life as, in my view, it needs to be. I am also interested in the way the book reveals changes or adaptations in Hawthorne's practice of romance. See Gordon Hutner, *Secrets and Sympathy: Forms of Disclosure in Hawthorne's Novels* (Athens: University of Georgia Press, 1988), chap. 3. For an extremely interesting but quite different account of Coverdale's defensiveness and its connection to the marketplace, which emphasizes the fetishistic quality of his strategies of self-preservation, see Gillian Brown, *Domestic Individualism: Imagining Self in Nineteenth-Century America* (Berkeley and Los Angeles: University of California press, 1990), chap. 4.

3. See also the interesting discussion of Coverdale's voyeurism, which connects it to Hawthorne's ambivalence about self-revelation, in Edgar Dryden, *Poetics of Enchantment*, 71–80.

4. On observing as a form of defense against the threats the world poses to a shakily established self, see Helen Block Lewis, "A Case of Watching as a Defense against an Oral Incorporation Fantasy," in *The Psychoanalytic Review* 50 (1963): 68–80.

5. The sexual self-disgust that seems to fuel Coverdale's loathing for Westervelt is confirmed in a later passage. "My dislike for this man was infinite. At that moment, it amounted to nothing less than a creeping of the flesh, as when, feeling about in a dark place, one touches something cold and slimy, and questions what the secret hatefulness may be" (172).

6. I am indebted to the distinction that R. D. Laing makes between true and false guilt in a schizophrenic, in *The Divided Self: An Existential Study in Sanity and Madness* (1959; reprint Harmondsworth, England: Penguin, 1965), 129–33.

7. John Carlos Rowe offers a similar reading of the dream, noting that Priscilla is "a displaced image of Coverdale's own exclusion" and that the dream suggests that both he and Priscilla are "dominated or enchanted by the passion of others." Rowe, however, reads the dream as an important moment in Coverdale's education in the nature of the imagination. *Through the Custom House: Nineteenth-Century American Fiction and Modern Theory* (Baltimore: Johns Hopkins University Press, 1982), 82–83.

8. Various psychoanalytic descriptions of the anxieties of the inadequately established self have been helpful to me in recognizing the logic of Hawthorne's delineation, via the imagery of anxiousness, of endangered identity. R. D. Laing describes schizophrenia as a form of "ontological insecurity," fear for the substantiality, the "being" of the self. Such insecurity manifests itself in ways that a reader of *The Blithedale Romance* will find familiar: as a fear of being "engulfed" by other people that sends its victim into the protection of isolation; as a determination to protect one's inner emptiness from the "implosion" that would attend

its penetration by the world; as a fear of and fascination with "petrification," of the transformation of oneself (terrifyingly) or another (comfortingly) into something rigid and impersonal. It is a condition of mind that induces an intense concern with seeing: with the fear that the self is penetrable, vulnerable to the destroying gaze of another; with maintaining a self-scrutiny that defends against threats to its fragile being; with possession-by-gazing of the presumably authentic selves of others. Hawthorne's Coverdale and Laing's anxious patients inhabit analogous imaginative worlds (*The Divided Self*, parts 1 and 2, esp. chaps. 3 and 7.) Other, more mainstream, psychoanalytic accounts of the characteristic imagery of identity disorders also recall Hawthorne's portrayal of Coverdale. See Stanley R. Palombo and Hilde Bruch, "Falling Apart: The Verbalization of Ego Failure," in *Psychiatry* 27 (1964): 248–58; Helen Block Lewis, "A Case of Watching"; Harold F. Searles, M.D., "Scorn, Disillusionment, and Adoration in the Psychotherapy of Schizophrenia (1962)," in *Collected Papers on Schizophrenia and Related Subjects* (New York: International University Press, 1965), 605–25. I hope it is clear that I am not suggesting that Hawthorne shares the causal theories advanced or implied in these psychoanalytic works.

9. Compare James McIntosh's suggestion that Hawthorne "pictures Coverdale as a key representative of the [cultural] disintegration he reveals, as the self-erasing center of a chaotic world" in an excellent essay on the book, "The Instability of Belief in *The Blithedale Romance*," in *Prospects* 9 (1984): 81.

10. For interesting contemporary instances of the kind of "global" anxiousness that Hawthorne is depicting here, see Joan Burbick's discussion of antebellum medical writing on the causes and treatment of insanity, "'Intervals of Tranquillity': The Language of Health in Antebellum America," in *Prospects* 12 (1987): 175–200.

11. Irving Howe, for example, argues that Hawthorne understood that "the utopian community becomes a competitive unit in a competitive society . . . and must therefore be infected with its mores." *Politics and the Novel* (New York: Horizon Press, 1957), 168. The predatory and exploitative quality of the relations between characters in the novel especially bears out this suggestion.

12. See the interesting discussion of art in the barroom that Coverdale visits in chap. 21 in Joel Porte, *The Romance in America: Studies in Cooper, Poe, Hawthorne, Melville, and James* (Middletown: Wesleyan University Press, 1969), 130–33.

13. For a discussion of the impact of this economic transformation on Hawthorne's work, see Gilmore, chaps. 3, 4, and 5. Gilmore reads "Rappaccini's Daughter," *The Scarlet Letter*, and *The House of the Seven Gables* as allegorizations of Hawthorne's encounters with the literary market. I am arguing here that Hawthorne explores in *The Blithedale Romance* the way that a culture internalizes the marketplace, and that his relation to this issue is analytic, not irresolvably ambivalent or defensive.

14. In a suggestive discussion of the way the market system made value in general seem "fictional," Brook Thomas cites a passage from Gerald T. Dunne's *Justice Story and the Rise of the Supreme Court* ([New York: Simon and Schuster, 1970], 142–43) that helps us see the force of Hawthorne's portrayal of Fauntleroy, particularly his association with financial paper: "The rise of banking cut the

fabric of tradition with an especial sharpness," producing "a revolution in the traditional system of credit, which forced profound changes in outlook and values. Sharply challenged were the old agrarian views under which gold and silver, like fields and flocks, were the true essence of wealth. Rather, wealth was changing in form to the intangible—to paper bank notes, deposit entries on bank ledgers, shares in banks, in turnpikes, in canals, and in insurance companies." *Cross-Examinations of Law and Literature*, 84–85. In her notes to the Penguin edition of *The Blithedale Romance*, Annette Kolodny—relying on work by Charles Swann—suggests the London banker Henry Fauntleroy, whose conviction and hanging for forgery was widely reported in the U.S., as a source for Fauntleroy. One might note, finally, that Hawthorne went to Brook Farm in 1837, the year of the famous financial "Panic," and that he lost, at a time when he could ill afford it, most of his $1,000 investment in the community.

15. Deeply felt anxiety about speculation as an inauthentic, dangerously empty kind of economic activity and the essence of the newly unstable economic world, fueled by the Panic of 1837, is described in Halttunen, *Confidence Men and Painted Women*, 16–20. The fascinating connections suggested in Halttunen's book between the anxieties generated by the development of a market economy and the fears about the integrity and substantiality of the self apparent in the mythology of the Confidence Man (as well as other rituals and practices of middle-class culture) has shaped my view of Old Moodie and helped me recognize the economic aspect of the anxiety that Hawthorne analyzes in *The Blithedale Romance*. Halttunen's account of the figure of the "liminal" young man—culturally dislocated, internally unstable, at sea in the city's slippery world of signs and vulnerable to the manipulation of its erotic and economic predators—derived from the advice literature of the time, is especially helpful in recovering the force of Hawthorne's urban portraiture.

16. For a striking analysis of the way the figure of the Veiled Lady represents important trends in antebellum culture and for an alternative account of the way that Hawthorne in *The Blithedale Romance* is writing the cultural history of his time, see Richard H. Brodhead, "Veiled Ladies: Toward a History of Antebellum Entertainment," in *American Literary History* 1 (Summer, 1989): 273–94.

17. The letter (30 July 1852) can be found in the Hale Family Papers, Sophia Smith Collection, Smith College, and is quoted with permission. Hale often comments on novels in her letters, and might be taken as a particularly intelligent, well-informed but still representative middle-class reader. (This is not the Sarah Hale who edits *Godey's Lady's Book*—though she was involved in the contemporary literary scene through her substantial work on her husband's newspaper, the *Boston Daily Advertiser*.) The most striking and articulate published expression of this readerly anger occurs in an anonymous review of the book in the *Westminster Review* of October 1852, which includes this description of the book's moral stance: "[Hawthorne's] moral faculty is morbid as well as weak; all his characters partake of the same infirmity. . . . The object of art is the development of beauty—not merely sensuous beauty, but moral and spiritual beauty. Its ministry should be one of pleasure, not of pain; but our anatomist, who removes his subjects to Blithedale, that he may cut and hack at them without interference, clears out for himself a new path in art, by developing the beauty of deformity! He would give

you the poetry of the hospital, or the poetry of the dissecting-room; but we would rather not have it. Art has a moral purpose to fulfil; its mission is one of mercy, not of misery." Note the emphasis on the aggressiveness of the book's relation to its characters and its readers. The review appears in J. Donald Crowley, ed., *Hawthorne: The Critical Heritage* (London: Routledge, 1970), 259–64, and is cited by James McIntosh in "Instability of Belief." See also the review from the *American Whig Review* (Crowley, *Hawthorne*, 267–71) for another instance of readerly resentment of the "bitterness" and "want of living tenderness" of the book. For a valuable alternative account of the meaning of *Blithedale* as a social gesture, see the last section (105–11) of McIntosh's essay, which asks "should we admire a book so full of denial?"

CHAPTER SEVEN

1. The most pointed example of the former strategy is Frederick Crews's reading of *The Marble Faun* as a chart of the surfacings of Hawthorne's incestuous desires and of the self-punishments that such desires induce. See *Sins of the Fathers*, chap. 12. The latter strategy at its best is at work in Nina Baym's striking thematic explication of the novel as recording the triumph of patriarchal authority, as it is internalized by Hilda and finally espoused by Kenyon, over the liberating possibility of artistic expression represented by Miriam and Donatello—a reading to which my understanding of the novel is indebted. *The Shape of Hawthorne's Career*, 228–48. There has been a resurgence of interest in the book in recent years, which has produced a number of valuable arguments for its thematic coherence. But these interpretations, too, set aside the sustained experience of interpretive conflict that reading the book provokes, even when they emphasize the readerly response the novel invites or the emergence in the text of tensions characteristic of Hawthornian romance. See Jonathan Auerbach, "Executing the Model," in *ELH* 47 (1980): 103–20; Evan Carton, *The Rhetoric of American Romance*, 252–64; John Michael, "History and Romance, Sympathy and Uncertainty: The Moral of the Stones in Hawthorne's *Marble Faun*," in *PMLA* 103 (1988): 150–61; Gordon Hutner, *Secrets and Sympathy*, chap. 4; and Edgar Dryden, *The Form of American Romance* (Baltimore: Johns Hopkins University Press, 1988), chap. 2. A sophisticated reading of the novel that does begin from its conflicting intramural perspectives on fiction making is offered by Myra Jehlen in *American Incarnation*, chap. 5. Jehlen sees Hawthorne as himself in flight—like Kenyon—from the necessarily "blasphemous" stories his fiction threatens to set in motion, whereas I will be arguing that he is dramatizing his community's response to the perspectives insisted upon by romance—its flight, we might say, from him. Pamela Schirmeister sees the book's intramural conflicts as the result of Hawthorne's purposeful reexamination of his relation to the romance tradition in *The Consolations of Space: The Place of Romance in Hawthorne, Melville, and James* (Stanford: Stanford University Press, 1990), chap. 3.

2. The importance of acts of sympathy within the novel generally and Kenyon's failure of sympathy specifically are usefully discussed by Michael, in "History and Romance," and Hutner, in *Secrets and Sympathy*.

3. Though the causal logic is pretty murky, Hilda's "confession" of the crime

committed by Miriam and Donatello seems to set in motion the punitive apparatus that finally entraps them. I am indebted to Nina Baym's reading of Hilda's trip
to the confessional, which notes both its projective logic and its covert cooperation with the authorities. *The Shape of Hawthorne's Career*, 244.

4. This is Nina Baym's description of Kenyon's psychological trial by carnival:
"The psyche in a state of anarchic turbulence throws up into the light of consciousness a host of horrible fears and fantasies symbolized by a series of grotesque, partly sexual, dream figures"(*Hawthorne's Career*, 246). John Michael
interestingly notes the defensiveness of Kenyon's response to the carnival and
connects Hawthorne's depiction of this site where the complexity of experience
might be grasped to Bakhtin's conception of carnival in *Rabelais and His World*.
"History and Romance," 156–57, n. 13.

5. Richard Brodhead arrives by a different route at a similar account of Hilda's
repudiation of the fortunate fall idea and makes a like-minded argument about
her significance within the novel: Hilda represents generally the emergence of a
steadily more authoritarian and rigid culture, and she devotes herself in particular
to censoring the possibilities of thought and feeling associated with Hawthornian
romance. The great value of Brodhead's essay is its careful connection of Hilda to
the attitudes and institutions that bring about this cultural narrowing. See *The
School of Hawthorne* (New York: Oxford University Press, 1986), 75–79.

6. For an argument that the cultural trend that Hawthorne is pointing to
here—the flight from the erotic as a threat to the stability of the self—is a significant one in antebellum America, see Ben Barker-Benfield, "The Spermatic
Economy: A Nineteenth-Century View of Sexuality," in *Feminist Studies* 1
(1972): 45–74. Like Hawthorne, Barker-Benfield suggests that this anxiety manifests itself in ideas about female sexuality.

7. Baym, *Hawthorne's Career*, 247.

8. Joel Porte identifies Miriam with romance, which he understands as an art
that discloses rather than protects the self. *The Romance in America*, 139–41.

9. Miriam has a notable affinity for the phrasings of the prefaces. Her response
to Donatello is governed by the principle that is to inform our reading of *Twice-
told Tales* and "Rappaccini's Daughter"— the location of "precisely the proper
point of view" (*MOM* 92): "Even for her, however, there was an inexpressible
charm in the simplicity that prompted Donatello's words and deeds; though, unless she caught them in precisely the true light, they seemed but folly, the offspring
of a maimed or imperfectly developed intellect" (80). The description of her momentary playfulness in the Villa Borghese derives from the metaphor in "The Old
Manse" for self-revelation (*MOM* 32): "if her soul was apt to lurk in the darkness
of a cavern, she could sport madly in the sunshine before the cavern's mouth"
(83).

10. Here again, in his account of the later history of Hawthorne's career, Richard Brodhead has valuably specified the historical context for the debate about
the cultural function of art that Hawthorne conducts within *The Marble Faun*.
Brodhead demonstrates that Hawthorne was, thanks to the promotional genius of
his publisher, James T. Fields, at once the beneficiary and the victim of the transformation of literary culture that took place at mid-century and found expression
in the emergence of a canon of literary immortals. As we have seen, the attitudes

that accompany this elevation of art to quasi-sacred, monumental status—and the division of culture into "high" and "low" strata more generally—find their ideal exponent in Hilda. Brodhead argues that these new attitudes toward art are in effect the subject of *The Marble Faun*: the book "reproduces the cultural forms and forces that define its place . . . to the end of exploring what they mean." Hawthorne expresses in the book his sense of the fate of "high art": "removed from the category of general human doing and making," it will be robbed of any cultural function except to "stand for the high as opposed to the low," becoming at last a highly esteemed "bore." *The School of Hawthorne*, 75–80. For a fascinating telling of the story of this cultural stratification as it unfolds while the nineteenth century progresses, see Lawrence Levine, *High Brow, Low Brow* (Cambridge: Harvard University Press, 1988), esp. chap. 1, "Shakespeare in America."

11. For two different views of this connection between the Model and Hawthorne's artistic practice, see Auerbach, "Executing the Model," and Carton, *The Rhetoric of American Romance*, 257–58.

DATE DUE